always up to date

The law changes, but Nolo is always on top of it! We offer several ways to make sure you and your Nolo products are always up to date:

1 **Nolo's Legal Updater**
We'll send you an email whenever a new edition of your book is published! Sign up at **www.nolo.com/legalupdater**.

2 **Updates @ Nolo.com**
Check **www.nolo.com/update** to find recent changes in the law that affect the current edition of your book.

3 **Nolo Customer Service**
To make sure that this edition of the book is the most recent one, call us at **800-728-3555** and ask one of our friendly customer service representatives. Or find out at **www.nolo.com**.

please note

We believe accurate and current legal information should help you solve many of your own legal problems on a cost-efficient basis. But this text is not a substitute for personalized advice from a knowledgeable lawyer. If you want the help of a trained professional, consult an attorney licensed to practice in your state.

2nd edition

Create Your Own Employee Handbook

A Legal and Practical Guide

by Attorneys Lisa Guerin & Amy DelPo

NOLO

SECOND EDITION	MAY 2005
Editor	STEPHANIE BORNSTEIN
Cover Design	SUSAN PUTNEY
Book Design	TERRI HEARSH
Proofreading	JOE SADUSKY
CD ROM Preparation	ANDRÉ ZIVKOVICH
Index	THÉRÈSE SHERE
Printing	DELTA PRINTING SOLUTIONS, INC.

Guerin, Lisa 1964-
    Create your own employee handbook : a legal and practical guide/ by Lisa Guerin &
Amy DelPo.--2nd ed.
        p. cm.
    Accompanied by a CD-ROM
    ISBN 1-4133-0186-X
    1. Employee orientation. 2. Employees--Training of. I. DelPo, Amy, 1967- II. Title.

HF5549.5.I53G84 2005
658.3'01--dc22

                                                                    2005040692

Quantity sales: For information on bulk purchases or corporate premium sales, please contact the
Special Sales Department. For academic sales or textbook adoptions, ask for Academic Sales. Call
800-955-4775 or write to Nolo, 950 Parker Street, Berkeley, CA 94710.

Acknowledgments

The authors would like to thank the following people who helped to make this book possible:

- Our editor on the first edition, Ilona Bray, whose good humor and easy nature made the editing process fun—and whose words and insights never failed to improve upon what we gave her
- Our editor on the second edition, Stephanie Bornstein, whose eye for detail and consistency helped us immeasurably
- Albin Renauer for his wonderful design ideas—and his ability to think "inside the box"!
- Mary Randolph, for helping us mold and formulate our vision of this book
- Nolo jack-of-all-trades Stan Jacobson, who tirelessly haunted libraries throughout the Bay Area to meet our research needs
- Ella Hirst, for her years of hard work on the 50-state charts that appear in this book; and Ray Bernstein, for graciously picking up where Ella left off
- Andre Zivkovich and Jenya Chernoff, who managed to take our printed pages and turn them into a CD-ROM that people could use on their computers
- Terri Hearsh, for working with us on a wonderful book design, and
- Joe Sadusky for his meticulous proofing.

In addition, Amy would like to dedicate her work on this book to her daughter, Sophia, whose early birth delayed the first edition of this book by almost half a year. She is everything and more.

About the Authors

Lisa Guerin worked for Nolo as a research and editorial assistant during her years as a law student at Boalt Hall School of Law. After a stint as a staff attorney at the U.S. Court of Appeals for the Ninth Circuit, Lisa worked primarily in the field of employment law, in both government and private practice. Lisa has litigated on behalf of her clients in all levels of state and federal courts and in agency proceedings. Lisa returned to Nolo in 2000, where she writes and edits books on employment law, civil litigation, and business.

Amy DelPo practiced law for six years before leaving the day-to-day grind of lawsuits to join Nolo's editorial staff in 2000. As an attorney, she specialized in employment law and general civil litigation, representing her clients in all levels of state and federal courts. At Nolo, she continues her work in the field of employment law, authoring and editing a number of books on the subject, including the best-selling *The Employer's Legal Handbook*, by Fred Steingold. She has also added retirement planning to her field of expertise, editing a number of books on the subject.

Together, the authors have written several books published by Nolo, including *Dealing With Problem Employees* and *Federal Employment Laws: A Desk Reference*.

Table of Contents

4 New Employee Information

5 Employee Classifications

6 Hours

7 Pay Policies

8 Employee Benefits

9 Use of Company Property

10 Leave and Time Off

11 Performance

12 Workplace Behavior

13 Health and Safety

21 Ending Employment

Appendixes

A Where to Go for Further Information

B How to Use the CD-ROM

C Forms

Form A: Handbook Acknowledgment Form

Form B: Payroll Deduction Authorization Form

Form C: Expense Reimbursement Form

Form D: Email and Internet Policy Acknowledgment

Index

Introduction

If you're like most supervisors, you (or people who work for you) probably devote a good part of every day to employee relations. If you're in human resources or own a business, you may find yourself making decisions or relaying information about everything from benefits to vacation time to disciplinary problems. Sometimes, you may know the answer right away ("You get ten vacation days"); other times, you may have to think a bit or come up with something new ("What *is* our policy on paternity leave?").

In such situations, a good employee handbook is as essential as any real live manager. It knows all the answers—and it communicates them clearly to employees. Indeed, an employee handbook can do a lot for your company, such as:

- save time by cutting down on the number of questions employees ask every day
- ensure that the company treats employees consistently, and
- provide legal protection when an employment relationship goes sour.

This introduction provides an overview of these benefits (Section A) and explains how this book can help you create an effective handbook (Section B).

A. What an Employee Handbook Can Do for Your Organization

Simply defined, an employee handbook is a written document describing the benefits and responsibilities of the employment relationship. In reality, however, the handbook's role is much more complex and powerful. While it sits quietly on the shelf, the employee handbook can actually help manage and control your company's relationship with its employees.

1. The Purposes of an Employee Handbook

An employee handbook is an indispensable workplace tool, because it can help your company communicate with employees, manage its workers (and managers), stream-line its organization, and protect itself from lawsuits. We cover each of these benefits in detail below.

a. Communication

A handbook tells employees what the company expects from them and what they can expect from the company. "What time do I have to be at work?"; "Does my employer provide health insurance?"; "How do I complain about my supervisor's sexual advances?" A well-drafted handbook will answer all of these questions and many more.

In addition to relaying basic information about benefits, hours, and pay, an employee handbook imparts the company's culture, values, and history. When was the company founded? Why is it successful? What attitude should employees take towards their jobs and customers? This information can help motivate employees to work more effectively and enthusiastically on behalf of the company.

b. Management

Employees are not mind readers. Although you may know what the company's practices and policies are, without a handbook, other employees, managers, and supervisors have no place to turn for this information. This creates an environment ripe for trouble, both legal and practical. Employee morale will drop if employees are treated inconsistently, possibly resulting in a discrimination lawsuit if an employee thinks this different treat-ment is based on race, gender, or some other protected characteristic.

Handbooks promote positive employee relations by ensuring that all employees are treated consistently and fairly. They prevent misunderstandings, confusion, and complaints by giving everyone the same resource for learning company personnel practices. If there is ever any doubt or dispute about a particular policy, you can simply open the book and take a look. You don't need to have long, agonizing discussions or try to reinvent the wheel.

c. Planning

The process of creating a handbook will force your company's management to think about every aspect of its relationship with employees. Rather than doing things just because that's the way they've always been done, you can reflect on how employees have been treated and consider whether any changes are in order. For each policy, your company's decision makers should ask themselves: Do we really want to continue doing things this way? If so, why?

Creating an employee handbook necessarily requires communication with, and feedback from, employees, supervisors, and managers about the company's current personnel practices. This will help determine what works and what doesn't, what is enhancing employee morale, and what is dampening it.

d. Legal Protection

Just having a handbook can help your company comply with the law and reduce its risk of lawsuits. Consider the following:

- Some laws require employers to communicate certain information to their employees. The handbook provides a convenient place to put this information.
- Even when the company isn't required to give information to employees, providing it in a handbook may create important legal protections. For example, no law requires a company to tell employees how to complain about sexual harassment, but a company that has such a policy in place can use the policy as a legal defense should an employee file a harassment lawsuit. (You can find a sexual harassment policy in Chapter 19.)
- Certain policies in a handbook can affirm a company's commitment to equal employment opportunity laws. This is one step toward creating a tolerant and dis-crimination-free workplace—something that most employers are legally obligated to do. (You can find standard equal employment opportunity policies in Chapter 3.)
- In certain situations, a company will be responsible for the actions of its employ-ees and supervisors who violate the law, even if the company did not condone or even know about the illegal conduct. Providing guidance and prohibitions in an employee handbook can cut down the risk of unlawful behavior.

Perhaps the most important reason to have an employee handbook is to protect the company's legal right to terminate employees at will. In theory, employers already have this right. Unless the company has entered into a contract with an employee promising something else, its relationship with that employee is automatically "at will"—meaning the employer can terminate the employment relationship at any time for any reason that is not illegal, and the employee can do the same.

However, just because an employee does not have a written contract does not necessarily guarantee that the employee is working at will. A company can inadvertently destroy its right to terminate at will by creating an implied contract with an employee, promising not to fire the employee without a legitimate business reason. Some employers with badly written handbooks have gotten burned over this issue. Courts have found that certain statements in their handbooks—including that employees will only be fired for certain reasons, that employees won't be fired if they are doing a good job, or that employees are considered "permanent"—created implied contracts that limited the employers' right to fire at will. (For more on at-will employment and implied contracts, see Chapter 2.)

In this book, we help you avoid this trap by providing standard policies that steer clear of any promises of continued employment, as well as disclaimers that specifically state that employment relationships at your company are at will.

2. What an Employee Handbook Is Not

An employee handbook can do a lot, but it can't do everything, nor should it. As we explain more fully in this section, a handbook is just one piece of the employee relations picture. It's up to company managers and supervisors to provide the other pieces.

a. A Handbook Is No Substitute for Personal Interaction

Although a handbook is an important communication tool, it cannot take the place of one-on-one personal interaction between management and employees. An employee handbook can help foster trust, loyalty, and positive employee relations, but it can't do the job on its own. Employees need a human face behind the policies. They need to see, hear, and feel that the company's management is interested in them and the job they are doing.

b. A Handbook Is No Substitute for Good Practices

No matter how many policies you write, they won't do your company any good unless managers follow them. In fact, they might actually do some harm.

From a practical standpoint, personnel practices that are inconsistent with written policies can damage employee relations. Employees who read one thing but experience another won't trust—or feel loyal to—their employer.

From a legal standpoint, a company is courting trouble if it doesn't deliver what it promises in the handbook. Even though the handbook will include disclaimers explaining that the handbook is not a contract (see Chapter 1 for these disclaimers), a judge or jury might think differently and try to hold the company to its words—or at least make it pay for not following them. For these reasons, the handbook should include only those policies that your company is prepared to follow.

c. A Handbook Is Not a Personnel Policy Manual

Employee handbooks are written in general terms, for use by employees. A policy or procedures manual, on the other hand, is a detailed guide that sets out very specifically how supervisors and managers are to do their jobs. Usually, employees are not allowed access to policy or procedures manuals.

You may wonder why you can't just have one book for both audiences. There are a number of reasons, including the following:
- There might be sensitive information (on pay scales, for example) that the company doesn't necessarily want to reveal to employees.
- Employees don't need to be bogged down by every little detail of how things are done in your company. If you throw too much information at employees at once—some of it irrelevant to their day-to-day work—they might feel overwhelmed and not read the handbook at all.
- The details of how policies are implemented are more likely to change than the general policies themselves. If you put these details in the handbook, it will be more difficult for the company to change the way it does things.

B. Who Can Use This Book

This book is for business owners, managers, supervisors, and human resource professionals in any size company, from a small outfit with only a handful of employees to a large corporation. It is also appropriate for virtually every industry, from manufacturing to sales to service provision.

There are two types of workplaces for which this book won't work: public workplaces (that is, workplaces with federal, state, or local government employees) and unionized workplaces.

C. Icons Used in This Book

To aid you in using this book, we include the following icons:

 This icon warns you of potential problems.

 This icon indicates that the information is a useful tip

 This icon refers you to helpful books or other resources.

 This icon indicates when you should consider consulting an attorney or other expert.

■

How to Use This Book

If you're eager to create an employee handbook—or modify an existing handbook—we should warn you that there is a catch. Well, two catches: Handbooks don't write themselves, and there is no such thing as a "one size fits all" handbook. You can't simply purchase a generic handbook, slap your company's name on the cover, and distribute it to employees. If you want an effective handbook, you are going to have to sit down and actually create it, with policies and language that reflect your company's culture, values, and personnel practices.

Don't despair, however. We've designed this book to make the process easy and straightforward, taking you step by step through planning, writing, and distributing a handbook. Using this book, you can create an employee handbook that's tailored to your company's needs, with minimal time and headaches.

In this chapter, we:

- explain what you'll find in the different parts of this book (Section A)
- advise you on what information you'll need to obtain from other sources (Section B), and
- instruct you on each phase of the handbook creation process, from gathering the information you'd like to include in the handbook to picking a distribution method once the handbook is complete (Section C).

⚠ **Don't jump right to the CD-ROM.** The CD-ROM contains all of the policies and modifications discussed in this book. However, you cannot simply print out those policies verbatim and distribute them to employees. If you do that, you will have wasted your money: You will end up with a handbook that doesn't accurately reflect your workplace. Read the discussions that accompany each handbook section in this book first, then cut and paste what you need.

A. What You'll Find in This Book

This book is both a workbook and a guidebook. The heart of the book (Chapters 1 through 21) contains a combination of important material. First, it contains prewritten personnel policies that you'll be able to cut and paste (and modify, if necessary), policy by policy, into the handbook you're creating. Along with prewritten policies, however, these chapters provide valuable explanatory material, including:

- background information
- guidance to help you decide whether you want to include each policy in your handbook
- standard language that you can cut and paste into your handbook (or, if there is no standard way to word a policy, an example of what such policies look like and detailed guidance on writing your own from scratch)
- instructions on completing the standard policy with information specific to your workplace
- when appropriate, alternate modifications that you can use to complete a policy so that it accurately reflects the reality at your company
- when appropriate, additional clauses that you can add to a policy to suit your needs
- information on potential trouble spots, both practical and legal, and
- advice on when to consult an attorney for more assistance.

For each policy, you'll find a box in the margin that provides a quick look at what the policy is, whether there are any alternate modifications or additional clauses you should consider, and whether there are related policies you should review. If you like, you can use these boxes to keep track of your thoughts as you read through the book and to communicate those thoughts to anyone else in your company who may be working with you on the handbook.

When you're ready to start compiling the handbook, you'll find the prewritten portions on the CD-ROM at the back of this book. Instructions for using the CD-ROM are in Appendix B.

Appendix A gives you information on where to go for more assistance.

B. What You Won't Find in This Book

This book is not a treatise on employment law. To keep it trim and to the point, we assume that our readers have personnel practices in place already. This book helps you communicate those practices to your employees; it does not help you choose those practices in the first place. For example, we provide you with a policy that warns employees that they might have to take a drug test, but we don't go into detail on when to conduct drug tests or how to conduct them so that they comply with your state's laws. That's up to your company to figure out through different sources—other books, perhaps, or discussions with an attorney.

Because of this, before you start creating a handbook (or modifying an existing handbook) using this book, you need to understand your company's legal obligations as an employer in your state. If you need information on employment law or your company's legal obligations when dealing with employees, you should refer to other books, such as the following two from Nolo:

- *The Employer's Legal Handbook*, by Fred Steingold.
- *Everyday Employment Law: The Basics*, by Amy DelPo and Lisa Guerin.

You can also find a lot of free information on Nolo's website at www.nolo.com.

C. The Creation Process

By now, you've probably gotten our message that creating a handbook requires more than simply stringing together a bunch of boilerplate paragraphs. It takes planning and research. But don't worry—it doesn't have to be a time-consuming or arduous task. With a little investigation, you can put together a handbook in no time. Let's look at how to start the process (Section 1), your formatting options (Section 2), revising and updating the handbook (Section 3), and distributing the handbook to employees (Section 4).

1. In the Beginning

The very first thing you must do is decide who will be in charge of creating your company's handbook. If you own a small business, that someone will be one or two people—perhaps you, perhaps an office manager. If you work in a larger company, it might make sense to assign this task to a group of people. Whoever is charged with this task should be familiar with your company's employment practices and should have the power to decide what to include in the handbook. When we refer to "you," we are referring to the person or people creating the handbook.

We suggest the following four-step process for creating your handbook:

1. investigate
2. compile and write
3. review and revise, and
4. get final approval from an attorney.

Now let's look at each step in detail.

Step 1: Investigate

Before you can communicate your company's policies to employees, you must know precisely what those policies are. This is often more complex than it sounds. "Policy" is really just a word for how a company treats its employees, and this is something that often happens informally and inconsistently. This is especially true if your company is a small business. Let's say, for example, that you own your own business and your secretary, whom you think the world of, was in a car accident last year. You paid her salary for the two months it took her to rehabilitate. Does this mean that everyone in your company is entitled to two months of paid sick leave? Or only people who are in car accidents? Or only people whom you like?

The situation can be even worse in large companies, where managers or supervisors are in charge of employees' day-to-day work lives. Different managers may do things differently, so a company may have as many variations of a policy as it has managers.

Of course, once you have a handbook in place, these inconsistencies won't be a problem. For now, however, you must put on your Perry Mason hat and figure out how personnel matters are being handled. We suggest the following:

- interview managers and supervisors
- distribute a questionnaire to managers and supervisors
- consult your current personnel policies manual (if you have one)
- consult old handbooks and policy manuals (if they exist)
- obtain handbooks from competitors in your area
- distribute a questionnaire to employees
- talk to people in your human resources and payroll departments
- consult with your benefits administrator and office manager, and
- review bulletin board notices, memos, newsletters, and employee complaints.

The chapters and headings in this book can help you structure your interviews or questionnaires. We recommend scanning them to remind yourself of the various categories that you need to inquire into, from work hours to benefits to complaints procedures.

Step 2: Compile and Write

When you sit down to actually create the policies you want to include in your handbook, start with the standard policies and modifications provided here. By reading the explanatory text, you can decide whether to include that policy in your handbook—and what the policy should address. For the most part, this will be a straightforward cut-and-paste job. However, when you need to modify policies or write them from scratch, keep these rules in mind:

- use simple vocabulary
- use short sentences
- don't use legalese or jargon
- keep paragraphs short
- be clear and concise
- use language that reflects the culture of your company (for example, formal or informal)
- write to the education and sophistication level of your employees
- use terms consistently
- emphasize the positive aspects of any policy, and
- where appropriate, briefly explain the rationale behind the policy.

For many policies, we provide you with ways to modify the policies to fit your workplace. In some cases, you *must* choose one of the possible modifications if you want to complete the policy—we call these "alternate modifications." Other times, you *may* choose whether or not to include a modification to tailor the policy to your workplace—we call these "additional clauses." In other words, if a policy provides "alternate modifications," you must pick one of the alternatives if you want to include that policy in your handbook, whereas if a policy provides "additional clauses," you can choose to modify it or not, but you may include the policy regardless, as it will work with or without the modification.

Step 3: Review and Revise

All managers and supervisors should read the initial draft of the handbook and give feedback. After all, they are the ones on the front lines, dealing with the employees every day—and they are the ones who are going to have to actually enforce the policies you've chosen. They can alert you to inconsistencies or to policies that won't work in the real world. They can also tell you when your writing is unclear or misleading. And they might be able to recommend new or different policies.

Step 4: Get Final Approval From an Attorney

In this book, you will find advice and policies that comply with federal law and the laws of most states. That being said, each state has its own quirks when it comes to employment law. For example, in California, it's illegal to prohibit women from wearing pants. In Kentucky, it's illegal to discriminate against employees for smoking off duty. Although we have tried to anticipate those twists and turns here, there may be requirements in your state—or even your city—that are unique. As a result, we advise having a local attorney spend one or two hours reviewing your final product.

2. Formatting the Handbook

Once you have a final draft of your handbook, the next step is deciding how it should look. We suggest grouping your policies into chapters by topic (for example, your handbook might have a benefits chapter and a payroll chapter). This book presents the standard policies in this way. You can use our organization or come up with your own. Here are some other formatting tips:

- **Include a table of contents at the beginning of your handbook.** Because it is likely that your handbook's most common use will be to answer employees' specific question, a table of contents helps ensure that they'll find the answers.
- **Include an index at the end.** This is also helpful for employees who can't find what they're looking for.
- **Start each policy on a new page.** This enables employees to insert updates and remove old policies without disturbing the surrounding policies.
- **Double space the text of policies.** This makes them easier to read.
- **Give each policy its own bold-faced heading.**
- **Don't use page numbers.** Instead, number your policies by chapter (for example, a policy numbered "1:3" is the third policy in the first chapter). You'll notice that we number our policies in this way as well. This method enables employees to re-move old policies and insert new ones without ruining the handbook's pagination. If you want to insert a policy where there wasn't one before, you can use letters (for example, "1:3a").
- **Put the policies in a three-ring binder.** This allows employees to insert new policies or replace old policies when instructed to do so. Not only does this method make it easy to revise policies, it saves you money, because you invest in the binder only once.

3. Revising and Updating

You have the right to revise and update your handbook at any time. We recommend reviewing it once a year to determine which policies need to be revised or updated. Usually, policies must be revised for one of two reasons: (1) because your personnel practices have changed, or (2) because the law has changed.

If only one or two policies need to be revised, it's easy enough to distribute the new policy to employees, with instructions to remove the old policy and insert the new one in its place. Require employees to return the old policy to you. That way, you know that they actually updated the book and didn't simply drop the new policy in the recycling bin.

Over time, you will see that more and more of the policies in your book are revised policies and not the original ones. You may also notice that the language or tone of the original policies has become outdated or stale. When this happens, it's time to consider revising the entire handbook and handing out a new edition to your employees.

4. Distributing Your Handbook

Once your employee handbook is complete, it's time to distribute it to employees. The best way to do this—particularly if your company has never had a handbook or hasn't had one for a long time—is to hold a meeting.

Call all of your employees together (or, if this is impossible, hold a series of meetings and require each employee to attend one). At the meeting, explain that the company has a new employee handbook to set forth the company's policies. Let employees know that you expect each of them to read the handbook and abide by its contents. And tell everyone that you want them to sign a form acknowledging that they have received the handbook (this important form is contained in Chapter 2).

Once you distribute the handbooks, stick around for a while to answer any employee questions. And make sure to pass out the Handbook Acknowledgment Forms and ask employees to sign them.

When you hire new employees, give them a copy of the handbook—and ask them to sign the acknowledgment form—during their orientation meetings or when they fill out their other first-day paperwork.

■

1

Handbook Introduction

A handbook's introductory statements will be the first policies employees read, so these statements will set the tone for everything else to come. For this reason, they should be friendly and nonthreatening, easing employees into the drier—and sometimes less pleasant—information that will follow. Envision the handbook as a pleasant tour leader, personally guiding employees through the company. Employees will be more receptive to—and pay more attention to—a handbook that they perceive as warm and friendly than a handbook that feels impersonal and cold.

Start by introducing employees to the company, and its history, products, and goals. You'd be surprised how many long-term employees—let alone employees who have just been hired—don't know this basic information. The handbook can be an effective way of indoctrinating employees into a company's culture and values. This knowledge can inform everything the employees do at the company—from choosing how to deal with customers and vendors to deciding what standard of quality to apply to their own work.

Depending on the type of company, some employers might want to make the policies in this chapter more formal, and some might want to make them more casual. Regardless of the level of formality you choose, however, try to make the tone as pleasant and friendly as possible.

<table>
<tr><td>

1:1   Welcome to Our Company!

CD File: 01_Introduction.rtf

Include This Policy?
- ☐ Yes
- ☐ No
- ☐ Use our existing policy
- ☐ Other _____

Alternate Modifications
None

Additional Clauses
Company-Specific Information
Insert?: ☐ Yes   ☐ No

Related Policies
None

Notes

_____
_____
_____
_____
_____
_____
_____
_____
_____
_____
_____
_____
_____
_____
_____
_____
_____
_____

</td></tr>
</table>

1:1   Welcome ing Statement

Though it's not a legal requirement, we recommend you begin the handbook by welcoming employees to the company. After all, the vast majority of employees will only read the handbook from cover to cover at the beginning of their employment. Thereafter, they will only look at it in bits and pieces, finding the information that they need and nothing more.

A hearty welcome can quickly and effectively establish the friendly tone that you want to convey. An effective welcoming statement is positive and upbeat, and it begins the process of selling the company to your employees.

Welcome to Our Company!

It's our pleasure to welcome you to _____

_____

[*Company name*]. We're an energetic and creative bunch, dedicated to high standards of excellence and quality. We value each one of our employees, and we hope that you find your work here rewarding and satisfying.

This section introduces you to our Company's history, purpose, and goals. Please read it carefully so that you can better understand who we are and what we do. We think we are a special place—made all the more so by the hard work and dedication of our employees.

Additional Clause to Insert Company-Specific Information

This welcome will be even more effective if you add some concrete information about the company. Although some of this information will overlap with information you include in your introduction and history sections (see Policies 1.2 and 1.3, below), it doesn't hurt to give employees a preview here. Consider mentioning:

- How long your company has been in existence. For example: "We're an energetic and creative bunch, dedicated to high standards of excellence since 1902 when the Martinez family first opened this company's doors at 311 Main Street."
- The services or products that your company provides. For example: "Our company has dedicated itself to providing superior printing services since 1902."
- A description of your company's culture. For example: "As a family-owned company, we run a casual operation where

people feel free to decorate their workspaces and wear clothes that reflect their personality. Don't let the informality fool you, however. We demand excellence from ourselves and our employees, and we consider ourselves to be the premier printing company in the Tri-State Area."

If you do add company-specific information to this welcome statement, keep it brief. Your employees will be getting more detailed information from the policies that follow.

⚠ Don't make big promises in a handbook. Be careful not to say anything that could create an implied contract with your employees promising to terminate them only for cause. (See Chapter 2 for more about implied contracts and termination for cause.) Avoid statements that promise employees a long future at the company or that describes the company as a "family."

1:2 Introduction to the Company
CD File: 01_Introduction.rtf

Include This Policy?
☐ Yes
☐ No
☐ Use our existing policy
☐ Other _____

Alternate Modifications
None

Additional Clauses
None

Related Policies
None

Notes
_____
_____
_____
_____
_____
_____
_____
_____
_____
_____
_____
_____
_____
_____
_____
_____
_____
_____
_____

1:2   Introduction to the Company

The beginning pages of a handbook are a great place to briefly introduce employees to a company's background, history, and culture. (You will delve into your company's history in more detail later. See Policy 1:3, below.) In the Introduction, speak directly to employees and present the company as you want it presented.

During employees' day-to-day existence at your company, information about your company's values and goals will trickle down to them from supervisors, managers, coworkers, and customers. Unfortunately, this means that sometimes employees will hear things about your company that aren't true or that are distorted by the prejudices and personalities of the people around them. If these are an employee's first impressions of your company, they will be hard to undo. The Introduction is your opportunity to get in the first word about your company—to make a good first impression.

Unfortunately, there is no standard policy language that we can provide to you, because each company is unique. Here is an example of what a typical Introduction looks like.

SAMPLE POLICY LANGUAGE

Juanita Jones founded this company in 1978 on a very basic principle: Customers will pay for exceptional service and knowledge. Using that principle as her beacon, she took a small independent bookstore and created a chain of 300 stores serving customers throughout the Western United States.

Here at J&J Books, we continue to believe that a knowledgeable and courteous staff can sell more books than discount prices can. For this reason, we encourage our employees to read the publishing and literary magazines that you will find in the break room, to use your employee discount to buy and read as many books as possible, and to take advantage of our tuition reimbursement program to take literature and writing classes at local colleges. When our customers come to you with questions, we want you to be able to answer them—with a smile.

We know that only happy and relaxed employees can give the quality and good-natured service that our customers demand. So take all of the breaks you are scheduled for, alert your manager to any problems in your work area, and communicate any ideas you might have for making this a better place to work.

At J&J Books, we want our employees to put the customer first. That's why we, in management, put our employees first. We know that we are only as good as you are.

HANDBOOK INTRODUCTION   1 / 5

Drafting Your Own Policy

All sorts of information can go into your Introduction, from a heart-felt description of your company's values to an inventory of the products you produce. When you write this policy, imagine sitting across from a single employee. What do you want this person to know about your company? What do you think the essence of your company is? What sort of attitude do you want this employee to have toward customers and clients? What information about your company would be useful to this employee in doing the job?

Consider including the following information in this policy:

- The values that are most important to your company's success —for example, customer service, product quality, or high-speed productivity. Be as concrete as possible. Do you always do what the customer wants, no matter how much time and effort it takes? Do you try to fill all orders within one day? Do you always redo orders, no questions asked, if a customer complains?

- An explanation of why each of these values is important to your company's success.

- Any goals your company has—for example, doubling sales in the next decade or lowering operating costs.

- A description of the values and goals that each employee should have—for example, it may be more important to your company that employees develop friendly relationships with customers than that they pressure customers into making purchases they don't really need.

- A description of your company culture.

- A description of the products your company produces or the services it provides.

- An organizational chart for your company.

1:3 History of the Company

CD File: 01_Introduction.rtf

Include This Policy?
- ☐ Yes
- ☐ No
- ☐ Use our existing policy
- ☐ Other _____

Alternate Modifications

None

Additional Clauses

None

Related Policies

None

Notes

_____
_____
_____
_____
_____
_____
_____
_____
_____
_____
_____
_____
_____
_____
_____
_____
_____
_____
_____

1:3　History of the Company

The more pride your employees take in your company as a whole, the more pride they will take in their performance as individual employees. Telling the history of your company is one way to instill this pride. It can make employees feel like they are part of something special.

In addition, knowing this history can make employees more effective in their jobs. Anecdotes about your company's noble beginnings can help your employees sell your company to customers and clients. Funny stories from your company's past can make the company seem more human and friendly.

Although you may have previewed this information in the Welcoming Statement and Introduction to the Company (see Policies 1.1 and 1.2, above), now is the time to go into more detail.

Unfortunately, there is no standard policy language that we can provide to you, because each company is unique. Here is an example of what this kind of policy might look like.

SAMPLE POLICY LANGUAGE

In 1855, Dante DeMarco opened this newspaper's doors at 111 Main Street—right between City Hall and the county courthouse. It was a fitting geographic location for Dante, who always kept both eyes peeled for scandal and corruption among the city's power elite. While he ran this newspaper, he lived and breathed the journalist's creed: "Afflict the comfortable and comfort the afflicted." He often said his proudest moment was the day Mayor Lou Mixon was forced to resign because of the great Black and Tan Scandal of 1925, a scandal uncovered and publicized by "DeMarco's Moles," as the reporters were then called. "I would have gotten away with it if it hadn't been for that meddling paper," Mixon was heard to say on his way up the jailhouse steps.

Here at the Daily Conscience and News, we still believe in the ideals that have won this newspaper three Pulitzer Prizes (the first for the Black and Tan Scandal). As Dante said, we must be the conscience of the city. We want reporters with suspicious and inquisitive minds and editors who won't breath easy until a story is just right. We are committed to hiring the highest-quality staff. We will provide whatever resources our employees need to keep their work at the highest level. We will never bow to pressure from advertisers or civic leaders. In short, we will continue to be the daily conscience of Cedar Falls.

Drafting Your Own Policy

Try to entertain your employees; tell them a good story. Get them hooked on your company—its past and its future. Be as specific as possible. Use concrete details like names, dates, and amounts. If you have pictures from the early days, include them.

In writing your history, don't forget the values and goals that you laid out in the Introduction to the Company section (see Policy 1:2, above). If you can, use the history to illustrate those values and show where they came from.

1:4   The Purpose of This Handbook
CD File: 01_Introduction.rtf

Include This Policy?
☐ Yes
☐ No
☐ Use our existing policy
☐ Other _____

Alternate Modifications
None

Additional Clauses
None

Related Policies
None

Notes
_____
_____
_____
_____
_____
_____
_____
_____
_____
_____
_____
_____
_____
_____
_____
_____
_____
_____

1:4   Handbook Purpose

Every company should include a purpose statement in its employee handbook. From the beginning, you must make it clear to employees that they are expected to read the whole handbook—and to incorporate the information they read into their work. After all, what's the use of a handbook if employees don't read it?

There is also a legal reason to include this policy. As we explained in the Introduction to this book, one of the biggest risks of using an employee handbook is that a judge or jury might view it as a contract and hold the company to what it says. One way to minimize this risk is to plainly state that the handbook is not a contract and to emphasize to employees that the policies can change at any time, for any reason, and without warning.

The Purpose of This Handbook

We think that employees are happier and more valuable if they know what they can expect from our Company and what our Company expects from them. In the preceding sections, we introduced you to our Company's history, values, culture, and goals. We expect you to incorporate that information into your day-to-day job performance, striving to meet our Company's values in everything you do.

The remainder of this Handbook will familiarize you with the privileges, benefits, and responsibilities of being an employee at

_____

[*Company name*]. Please understand that this Handbook can only highlight and summarize our Company's policies and practices. For detailed information, you will have to talk to your supervisor or _____.

In this Company, as in the rest of the world, circumstances are constantly changing. As a result, we may have to revise, rescind, or supplement these policies from time to time. Nothing in this Handbook is a contract or a promise. The policies can change at any time, for any reason, without warning.

We are always looking for ways to improve communications with our employees. If you have suggestions for ways to improve this Handbook in particular or employee relations in general, please feel free to bring them to _____.

How to Complete This Policy

Of course, no handbook can anticipate all of the questions and concerns that your employees might have. For this reason, you must designate people at your company to whom your employees can go for more information. If you have a very small company, there might be only one member of management: you. In larger companies, there might be several levels of management to choose from. Adjust this policy to reflect the situation at your company. If possible, name two people to whom employees can turn (for example, a supervisor and a human resources director). That way, employees have a choice: If they are uncomfortable with one of their options, they can pick the other. Of course, if you have a small company, there may only be one appropriate person. That's fine, too.

<table>
<tr><td>

1:5   Be Sure to Check Out Our
      Bulletin Board

CD File: 01_Introduction.rtf

Include This Policy?
☐ Yes
☐ No
☐ Use our existing policy
☐ Other _____

Alternate Modifications
Specify Who Can Post
  Choose one: ☐ A   ☐ B

Additional Clauses
None

Related Policies
Because it's so important that
employees read the handbook,
we also suggest that you require
them to sign Form A: Handbook
Acknowledgment Form. For this
form and a related discussion, see
Chapter 2.

Notes

_____
_____
_____
_____
_____
_____
_____
_____
_____
_____
_____
_____
_____
_____

</td></tr>
</table>

1:5   Bulletin Board

Many employers use a company bulletin board to communicate with their employees about various events, laws, and rules—and to inform employees about changes to information in the handbook. Typical bulletin board postings include legally required notices (for example, about equal employment opportunity laws, wage and hour laws, and the like), flyers about special company events, and an organizational chart.

   If you have a company bulletin board, include in the introductory section of your handbook a policy that alerts employees to the board's existence, instructs employees to read the board periodically, and identifies who is allowed to put things on the board.

Be Sure to Check Out Our Bulletin Board

You can find important information about this Company and your employment posted on the bulletin board located at

_____ .

This is also the place where we post important information regarding your legal rights, including information about equal employment opportunity laws and wage and hour laws. We expect all employees to read the information on the bulletin board periodically.

Alternate Modifications to Specify Who Can Post

To Prohibit Employees From Posting
Some companies do not want employees posting information on official bulletin boards. If that is the case at your company, add the following paragraph to your policy.

Alternate Modification A

   Because this bulletin board is our way of communicating with employees, we do not allow anyone but managers and Company officials to post information there.

To Allow Employees to Post
Some companies like to allow their employees to post information on company bulletin boards. If you would like to do so, add the following paragraph to your policy.

Alternate Modification B

If you would like to communicate information to your coworkers, consider using the Company bulletin board. To post something, you must first give it to _____

_____

for approval. Employee notices may remain on the bulletin board for 90 days. After that period, they will be removed.

■

2

At-Will Protections

One of the first—and probably the most important—policies to include in the handbook is an at-will statement. This policy confirms that company employees work "at will": that is, they can be fired at any time and for any reason that is not illegal, and they can quit at any time they like. This policy gives employers some very important legal protection against lawsuits. If an employee sues, claiming that the handbook, the company's unwritten personnel practices, or statements by company managers constituted a promise that he or she would not be fired except for good cause, an at-will policy in the handbook will be the employer's best defense.

The law generally presumes that employees work at will unless they can prove otherwise. As evidence, employees will need to show that they entered into an employment contract with their employer that changed the at-will relationship. If an employer enters into a written employment contract that limits its right to fire an employee—such as a contract that the employee will work for the company for a specified period of time, or a contract stating that the employee may only be fired for specified reasons (misconduct, criminal behavior, or good cause are common examples)—that employee no longer works at will. These written contracts won't be affected by the sample at-will policy we provide—and you don't want them to be. In those relatively rare situations when the company really wants an employee to come on board (or stay there) for a set period of time, offering an employment contract that limits the company's right to fire will help you seal the deal.

Montana companies take note. The state of Montana has greatly restricted the doctrine of at-will employment. In Montana, an employee who is fired without good cause after completing the employer's probationary period (or after six months of work, if the employer has no probationary period) has been wrongfully discharged. This means that the employee can sue for lost wages and benefits—and for punitive damages (damages intended to punish the employer for wrongdoing) if the firing was fraudulent or malicious. What's more, an employer that violates its own written policies in firing an employee has also committed a wrongful discharge. Because of these unique rules, Montana employers would be well advised to consult with a lawyer in creating their handbooks.

Even if employees don't have written employment contracts, they can still argue that they were promised, either outright or by implication, that they would not be fired without good cause. These employees might point to conversations with managers ("He said

I would always have a position with the company, as long as my sales numbers were strong"), your company's personnel practices ("The company has never fired someone without a good reason"), or official company statements ("At ABC company, we believe that our employees are our greatest asset—and we treat them accordingly") to argue that they had an unwritten contract of employment that limits the company's right to fire at will. To defeat these types of claims—"oral contract" claims if the employee argues that explicit promises were made limiting the company's right to fire, or "implied contract" claims if the employee argues that statements and actions by company decision makers limited the right to fire—you will need something more than an at-will policy. You'll also need a form for employees to sign agreeing to their at-will status. You'll find both in this chapter.

2:1   At-Will Policy

Your at-will policy should clearly state that the company retains the right to fire employees at will and that nothing in the handbook constitutes a contract or promise to the contrary. You should also designate someone (or more than one person) who is solely authorized to make employment contracts on behalf of the company—this will allow the company to relinquish its at-will rights if necessary for a particular employee.

Employment Is At Will

We are happy to welcome you to _____
_____ [*Company name*].
We sincerely hope that your employment here will be a positive and rewarding experience. However, we cannot make any guarantees about your continued employment at _____
_____
[*Company name*]. Your employment here is at will. This means that you are free to quit at any time, for any reason, just as we are free to terminate your employment at any time, for any reason—with or without notice, with or without cause.

   No employee or company representative, other than _____
_____ ,
has the authority to change the at-will employment relationship or to contract with any employee for different terms of employment. Furthermore, _____
_____
may change the at-will employment relationship only in a written contract, signed by _____
_____ and the employee.
Nothing in this Handbook constitutes a contract or promise of continued employment.

Who Needs This Policy

Some employers—particularly small businesses; "mom and pop" enterprises; and companies with trusted, long-term employees— may wonder if they want an at-will policy. After all, they are not planning to fire employees without a good reason, so why adopt a policy that says they can? The reason is simply to hedge your bets. Even if a company never plans to act without good cause, the safest course of action is to adopt an at-will policy that preserves its right to do so, just in case. If a fired worker decides to challenge the

---

2:1   Employment Is At Will
CD File: 02_Employment.rtf

Include This Policy?
☐ Yes
☐ No
☐ Use our existing policy
☐ Other _____

Alternate Modifications
None

Additional Clauses
None

Related Policies
None

Notes
_____
_____
_____
_____
_____
_____
_____
_____
_____
_____
_____
_____
_____
_____
_____
_____
_____
_____
_____

employer's decision in a lawsuit, the employer won't have to prove that it had good cause to fire the employee—the at-will policy eliminates this requirement. Most judges will be easily convinced to throw out the employee's contract claim very early on in the lawsuit, saving the company from spending a lot of time and money justifying its decisions.

The truth is, companies cannot know ahead of time that they will never have to rely on an at-will policy. Sometimes, an employee just doesn't work out, for reasons that might not conclusively add up to "good cause" to a judge or jury. If the company has a clear at-will policy, it can simply fire that worker and move on. If it does not, the safest course of action from a legal perspective might be to keep the employee on, gathering evidence and documenting problems until management can prove good cause to fire. For as long as it takes, the employee will keep on mucking up the works, while management spends time building a legal case—time that could have been spent running the business.

Despite the benefits of an at-will policy, some companies choose not to adopt one. There are a few advantages to forgoing an at-will policy, with improved employee relations topping the list. Employees are generally not happy to open an employee handbook and read that they can be fired at any time, for any reason. A company that promises to give workers a fair shake might reap some rewards—like improved loyalty and more positive attitudes towards the company.

Every employer has to decide for itself whether to assert its at-will rights in the employee handbook. Given the clear benefits of having such a policy—and the real dangers of leaving one out—we strongly recommend that all employers adopt an at-will policy, whether they plan to rely on it or not. There are plenty of other ways to show employees that the company values their work.

How to Complete This Policy

The sample policy above provides a space where you should name a company officer who can modify the at-will relationship. This provision gives the company discretion to enter into employment contracts that limit its right to fire, while at the same time protecting its at-will rights over the rest of its employees.

Most companies will want to designate the highest company officer—for example, the president, CEO, or owner of the company. Take care to select someone at the highest echelons of company management—the company should have complete control over who gets an employment contract and who doesn't. Also, be sure to designate this person by position (for example, the president of the company) rather than by name. Although you may not anticipate any changes in the company ladder, you never know what the future might bring. By omitting any names from this policy, you ensure that the policy won't require any changes if someone in that position leaves the company.

Some companies designate more than one person who can make contracts. This is fine as long as you authorize only a few people, at most. The more people who have the right to make contracts, the higher the likelihood that someone will enter into a contract that important company decision makers don't know about—and may later come to regret.

Form A: Handbook Acknowledgment Form

Companies that have an at-will policy (see discussion above) should also ask employees to sign a form acknowledging that they understand their employment is at will. (You can find this and all other forms in Appendix C and on the CD-ROM in the back of this book.) To anyone who isn't a lawyer, it probably seems like over-kill to have both a policy and a form that essentially restates that policy. But in the legal world, redundancy is not only encouraged, it is sometimes required. In this case, using both a policy and an acknowledgment form gives the company more protection against future lawsuits.

Using an acknowledgment form offers two important benefits. First, it will prevent employees from arguing that they didn't know about or read the at-will policy in the handbook. While some courts might listen to such an argument—especially if that policy was buried deep in a thousand-page manual—all courts presume that people read a written agreement before signing it. Second, a signed, written agreement legally trumps agreements made in less-reliable forms, such as an oral agreement or an implied contract. While having a written policy helps the employer's side of the argument, it's not a contract: It will weight the scales strongly in the company's favor, but it might not deliver the knockout blow. But a signed written agreement is generally conclusive. Courts are not interested in hearing people argue, "Well yes, I signed it, but I thought it didn't apply to me." If an employee tells a court that the company entered into an oral or implied agreement not to fire him or her without good cause, having an acknowledgment form signed by that employee should put an end to the employee's claim.

The handbook acknowledgment form should explain the importance of the handbook, state that the handbook can be changed at any time and does not constitute a contract of continued employment, and explain the at-will policy again—this time, so employees can sign the form to acknowledge their understanding of the policy.

How to Complete This Form

In the spaces provided, insert the position of the person who has the authority to enter into contracts on behalf of the company. This language should track the language of your at-will policy, above.

Handbook Acknowledgment Form

By signing this form, I acknowledge that I have received a copy of the Company's Employee Handbook. I understand that it contains important information about the Company's policies, that I am expected to read the Handbook and familiarize myself with its contents, and that the policies in the Handbook apply to me. I understand that nothing in the Handbook constitutes a contract or promise of continued employment and that the Company may change the policies in the Handbook at any time.

By signing this form, I acknowledge that my employment is at will. I understand that I have the right to end the employment relationship at any time and for any reason, with or without notice, with or without cause, and that the Company has the same right. I acknowledge that neither the Company nor I have entered into an employment agreement for a specified period of time, that only _____ _____ may make any agreement contrary to the at-will policy, and that any such agreement must be in writing, signed by myself and _____ .

_____   _____
Employee's Signature   Date

_____
Employee's Name (Print)

Reality Check: Don't Ask Employees to Acknowledge That They've Read the Whole Handbook

Many companies ask employees to agree, in the acknowledgment form, that they have already read the handbook. This is not realistic—nor is it sensible. You want employees to sign the at-will acknowledgment right away, preferably as part of the first-day paperwork. This lets employees know where they stand right from the start, so they don't feel like you waited to spring an unpleasant surprise on them. It also gives employees less time to have the kinds of conversations and interactions with others that can lead to implied or oral contract claims. In short, the sooner this form is signed, the better.

On the other hand, most employees are not going to take an hour or more out of their first day of work to read the employee handbook from cover to cover. While we hope the sample policies we provide in this book are down to earth and easy to understand, let's face it—an employee handbook just isn't thrilling reading material. Employees are more likely to skim through the handbook early on in their employment, then read particular policies in detail as the need arises. By asking the employee to acknowledge only that the handbook is important and that the company expects them to read it, you create a form that employees can sign honestly on their first day of work.

For more information on at-will employment and employment contracts, see *Dealing With Problem Employees*, by Amy DelPo and Lisa Guerin (Nolo), which explains both in detail. It also contains a sample at-will offer letter than you can modify for use in your own company.

Hiring

You may wonder why you should discuss hiring in an employee handbook. After all, by the time people read the handbook, they've already been hired, right? Although this is true, your company's current employees do need to know a few things about hiring practices, both for themselves if they choose to apply for another job within the company and for friends and colleagues whom they might try to recruit to join the company. In addition, communicating how a company hires is yet another way to inform employees about company culture and values.

3:1   Equal Opportunity

CD File: 03_Hiring.rtf

Include This Policy?
☐ Yes
☐ No
☐ Use our existing policy
☐ Other _____

Alternate Modifications
Specify Protected Characteristics
Choose one: ☐ A   ☐ B

Additional Clauses
None

Related Policies
None

Notes
_____
_____
_____
_____
_____
_____
_____
_____
_____
_____
_____
_____
_____
_____
_____
_____
_____
_____

3:1   Equal Opportunity

It's nice to start the handbook's hiring section with an Equal Opportunity Policy that acknowledges the existence of anti-discrimination laws and affirms your company's commitment to them, especially in the hiring process. (For more information about antidiscrimination laws, see Chapter 19.)

Commitment to Equal Opportunity

[*Company name*] believes that all people are entitled to equal employment opportunity.

Who Needs This Policy

Although neither state nor federal law requires it, all employers who are covered by any combination of state or federal antidiscrimination laws should begin the hiring section of their handbook with a statement acknowledging these laws. The statement should also include a promise to follow the laws throughout the hiring process. Not only will employees appreciate hearing this, the handbook language can be a handy piece of evidence should a disgruntled applicant ever file a lawsuit against your company alleging discriminatory hiring practices.

If you don't know which antidiscrimination laws apply to your company, then you should find out—and fast. These laws cover every aspect of your company's relationship with its employees, and ignorance of them leaves your company vulnerable to costly and embarrassing accusations and lawsuits. See Chapter 19 for help in finding out which laws cover your workplace.

Alternate Modifications to Specify Protected Characteristics

If You Follow State and Federal Laws

If your company is big enough to be covered by state and federal antidiscrimination laws, but you do not want to list specific protected characteristics in your policy, add the following language to your policy.

Alternate Modification A

> We follow state and federal laws prohibiting discrimination
> in hiring and employment. We do not discriminate against
> employees or applicants in violation of those laws.

To List Specific Characteristics

If you know which state and federal laws cover your workplace, and
if you know which characteristics these laws protect (for example,
race, color, religion, national origin, gender, age, disability, and
veteran status, among others), you can be more specific in this
policy and actually list for your employees the characteristics that
are protected. To do so, add the following language to your policy.

Alternate Modification B

> We do not discriminate against employees or applicants on the
> basis of _____
>
> _____
>
> _____
>
> _____
>
> _____
>
> _____
>
> _____
>
> [*list characteristics protected by the state and federal laws
> covering your workplace*], or any other characteristic protected
> by state or federal law.

3:2 Recruitment
CD File: 03_Hiring.rtf

Include This Policy?
☐ Yes
☐ No
☐ Use our existing policy
☐ Other _____

Alternate Modifications
None

Additional Clauses
Encourage Current Employees to Apply
  Insert?: ☐ Yes ☐ No

Referral Bonus Program
  Insert?: ☐ Yes ☐ No

Related Policies
None

Notes

_____
_____
_____
_____
_____
_____
_____
_____
_____
_____
_____
_____
_____
_____
_____
_____
_____
_____
_____

3:2   Recruitment

If you want current employees to help in recruitment efforts, then ask for their help in the hiring section of the handbook. The following policy explains where and how your company will look for new employees. It also encourages current employees to help generate ideas about how to find talented people who will fit into the workplace.

Recruitment

We know that we are only as good as our employees, so we search as widely as possible for talented and motivated individuals to fill vacant positions in our Company. Our recruitment methods include _____

_____

_____

[*list the methods you use—for example, advertising, employment agencies, and referrals*].

Although these methods have served us well in the past, we know that the marketplace is ever changing and that finding high-quality people is an evolving process. We encourage our employees to share with us their ideas about what more we can do to find and recruit talented and motivated individuals.

We conduct all recruiting in a fair and nondiscriminatory manner.

Additional Clause to Encourage Current Employees to Apply

If you would like to encourage current employees to apply for transfer or promotion to vacant positions (see Policy 3:3, below, for more on this), make the following paragraph the second-to-the-last paragraph of the policy.

Additional Clause

> In addition to looking outside the Company for new hires, we also look within. After all, we already know the value and quality of our current employees. We post all internal job openings on
>
> _____
>
> _____
>
> [_give the location where you will post job openings_]. If you see a posting for a job that interests you, we encourage you to apply for it by following our Internal Application Procedures (see below).

Although some commentators suggest that employers promise to give priority for vacant positions to current employees, we recommend against limiting your options in this way. Sometimes, you'll want to look outside your workplace for a new hire, even if there is someone currently on staff who would be perfect for the position.

Additional Clause If You Have a Referral Bonus Program

If you give bonuses to employees who refer new hires to you (see Policy 3:4, below, for more on this), make the following paragraph the second-to-the-last paragraph of the policy.

Additional Clause

> We also encourage employees to recruit and refer external applicants for open positions. If you refer someone whom we eventually hire, we will thank you for your efforts with a referral bonus. See Refer a New Hire; Get a Bonus!, below, for details.

3:3   Internal Application Process

If you'd like to encourage current employees to apply for open positions, a good place to start is in the handbook. Allowing good employees to change jobs within your company (as opposed to looking for better jobs outside your company) is a win-win situation: It means that your company gets to retain good employees, while the employees get to keep fresh and motivated by taking jobs that interest them rather than staying in a job that has grown stale.

The following policy gives employees permission to apply for vacancies and tells them how to do so. Again, it's a good idea to list the position of the person to whom employees should apply rather than a particular name so that you do not have to change the policy if the person holding that position should change.

3:3   Internal Application Procedures

CD File: 03_Hiring.rtf

Include This Policy?
- ☐ Yes
- ☐ No
- ☐ Use our existing policy
- ☐ Other _____

Alternate Modifications
None

Additional Clauses
None

Related Policies
None

Notes

_____
_____
_____
_____
_____
_____
_____
_____
_____
_____
_____
_____
_____
_____
_____
_____
_____
_____
_____
_____
_____

Internal Application Procedures

Sometimes, the best person for a job is right under our Company's nose. As a result, we encourage current employees to apply for vacant positions that interest them.

We post all internal job openings on _____ _____ [*give location*]. To apply for a position, give a cover letter, current resumé, and copy of the job posting to _____ _____ .

3:4   Employee Referral Bonus Program

Sometimes, a company's employees are the ones best situated to find and recruit new talent on its behalf. Although some employees will do this out of dedication to the company (and their job-seeking friends), others need a little more motivation. Many employers like to sweeten the pot by promising bonuses to employees who find successful applicants for open positions.

The following policy promises a bonus to employees who successfully refer a potential employee to fill a vacant position.

Refer a New Hire; Get a Bonus!

Our employees know our needs and Company culture better than anyone else and are often the best situated to find and recruit new employees to fill open positions within our ranks.

Alternate Modifications to Specify Bonus Details

To Give One Bonus for All Positions

You will have to decide what kind of bonus to give to employees. In part, this will depend upon your company's culture and finances, and in part it will depend upon the standards in your industry. For example:

- Many nonprofits give one or two paid days off as a bonus.
- Small businesses give anything from $500 to $1,000.
- Corporate law firms give as much as $10,000.

To specify one bonus in your policy, add the following language:

Alternate Modification A

To encourage employees to act as recruiters on our behalf, and to reward employees who help make a successful match, we operate an Employee Referral Bonus Program. We will give
_____ [*specify the bonus that you are offering*] to any employee who refers an individual whom we hire.

To find out more about the program, or to refer a potential applicant for an open position, contact _____
_____ .

3:4   Refer a New Hire; Get a Bonus!

CD File: 03_Hiring.rtf

Include This Policy?
- ☐ Yes
- ☐ No
- ☐ Use our existing policy
- ☐ Other _____

Alternate Modifications
Specify Bonus Details
Choose one: ☐ A   ☐ B

Additional Clauses
Exclude Some From the Policy
Insert?: ☐ Yes   ☐ No

Related Policies
None

Notes
_____
_____
_____
_____
_____
_____
_____
_____
_____
_____
_____
_____
_____
_____
_____
_____
_____
_____
_____

To Offer Different Bonuses for Different Positions

Some companies would pay a king's ransom to find a top-notch professional, such as a design engineer or a chief financial officer, but wouldn't pay peanuts to locate a rank-and-file employee, such as an assembly line worker or a sales clerk.

If there are positions that your company values more highly than others, you can create a policy that pays a different bonus depending on the position. For example, if you operate a law firm, you might offer a bonus of $5,000 for lawyers, $2,500 for paralegals, $1,000 for secretaries, and $500 for file clerks.

You can either name the positions (as in the previous example) or you can give a category of positions (for example, professional, support staff, and so on).

If you would like to create a tiered bonus system, simply add the following language to your policy.

Alternate Modification B

> To encourage employees to act as recruiters on our behalf, and to reward employees who help make a successful match, we operate an Employee Referral Bonus Program. The amount of the bonus depends on the position that you have helped to fill:
>
> - Position: _____ Bonus: _____
> - Position: _____ Bonus: _____
> - Position: _____ Bonus: _____
> - Position: _____ Bonus: _____

Additional Clause to Exclude Some From the Policy

If you have people in your company whose job it is to find new employees for you, their paycheck is reward enough for accomplishing the task—you don't need to add a bonus on top of that. These people usually include officers in the company (the president, the chief executive officer, and the chief financial officer), members of the human resources department, and on-staff recruiters.

If you would like to exclude people in certain positions from the bonus program, add the following paragraph to your policy.

Additional Clause

> People holding the following positions may not participate in the Employee Referral Bonus Program: _____
>
> _____.

3:5   Nepotism

Many employers like to think of their company as a family. However, when actual family members of employees start filling a company's ranks, complications can arise. How does your company feel about a husband supervising a group of employees that includes his wife? What about the CEO's son taking a part-time job in the mailroom? Or siblings working side by side on the assembly line?

Even if your company doesn't have any concerns about these things, employees might. For example, it could be a little awkward for the mailroom manager to supervise and discipline his boss's son. Or downright impossible for an employee to complain to a supervisor about the behavior of the supervisor's spouse. Not to mention the troubles that can arise for coworkers when family members don't get along.

Many employers choose to allow family members to work for the same company, so long as they don't work together—or at least don't supervise each other. Other employers have a strict policy against nepotism, preferring to play it safe and keep clear of any potential conflicts or favoritism that could crop up.

Policy A, below, allows employment of relatives. Policy B, below, prohibits employment of relatives.

If your company operates in a state that prohibits discrimination based on marriage or family status, check with a lawyer for assistance in creating and administering the nepotism policy. Some of these states (for example, Montana) view it as discriminatory to transfer, terminate, or refuse to hire someone because he or she is married or related to a coworker—and these states allow lawsuits against employers who do it. Other states view a nepotism policy as an acceptable exception to the antidiscrimination law. You'll need a lawyer's assistance to find out where your state stands on these issues. To find out if you live in a state that prohibits discrimination based on marriage or family status, see the chart at the end of Chapter 19.

3:5   Employment of Relatives

CD File: 03_Hiring.rtf

Include This Policy?
☐ Yes
   Choose one: ☐ A   ☐ B
☐ No
☐ Use our existing policy
☐ Other _____

Alternate Modifications
None. (Entire policy has two alternate versions from which you must choose.)

Additional Clauses
Policy B only: Current Employees Who Become Related
   Insert?: ☐ Yes   ☐ No

Related Policies
None

Notes
_____
_____
_____
_____
_____
_____
_____
_____
_____
_____
_____
_____
_____
_____
_____
_____

Policy A

Employment of Relatives

Usually, this Company will not refuse to hire someone simply because he or she is related to one of our current employees. If you have a relative who might be perfect to fill an open position in our Company, please don't hesitate to refer this person to us.

There are times, however, when employing relatives is inappropriate and has the potential to affect the morale of other employees and to create conflicts of interest for the relatives involved.

Therefore, we will not hire relatives of current employees where one relative will have to supervise the other.

If two employees become related while working for this Company, and if one of them is in a position of supervision over the other, only one of the employees will be allowed to keep his or her current position. The other will either have to transfer to another position or leave the Company.

Under this policy, the term "relatives" encompasses husbands, wives, live-in partners, parents, children, siblings, in-laws, cousins, aunts, and uncles. This policy covers biological relationships, marriage relationships, and step relationships.

Policy B

Employment of Relatives

Although we value all of our employees and, by extension, their families, we do not allow family members of current employees to take jobs with our Company. We believe the risk of morale problems, security problems, and conflict of interest problems is too great.

Under this policy, the term "relatives" encompasses husbands, wives, live-in partners, parents, children, siblings, in-laws, cousins, aunts, and uncles. This policy covers biological relationships, marriage relationships, and step relationships.

Additional Clause for Current Employees Who Become Related

Sometimes, current employees become related through marriage. In such a situation, an employer with a strict antinepotism policy will have to decide whether it will make an exception for those employees or whether it will force one of the employees to quit.

Doing the latter is certainly the most consistent approach, but it has a few significant drawbacks:

- It punishes employees for marrying each other rather than just dating.
- It forces an otherwise valuable employee to leave your ranks.
- It could pose a problem if your state prohibits discrimination based on marital status. (See "If your company operates in a state that prohibits discrimination based on marriage or family status...," above.)

Only you can decide the way you want to go on this issue. If you would like to allow current employees to marry, add the following paragraph to the policy.

Additional Clause

If two employees become related while working for this Company, they will both be allowed to remain with the Company. However, if one of them supervises the other, only one of the employees will be allowed to keep his or her current position. The other will either have to transfer to another position or leave the Company.

■

CHAPTER

4

New Employee Information

Although the entire handbook will include information for both new and long-term employees, there are a few policies to include exclusively for new employees. In this section of your handbook, you can tell new employees what to expect during their initial weeks of employment. You can also advise them about information the company will collect for the government regarding their immigration status and any outstanding child support obligations.

<table>
<tr><td>

4:1   New Employee Orientation

CD File: 04_New Employee Info.rtf

Include This Policy?
☐ Yes
☐ No
☐ Use our existing policy
☐ Other _____

Alternate Modifications
None

Additional Clauses
None

Related Policies
Form A: Handbook Acknowledg-
ment Form should be part of every
employee's first-day paperwork.
For this form and a related discus-
sion, see Chapter 2.

Notes
_____
_____
_____
_____
_____
_____
_____
_____
_____
_____
_____
_____
_____
_____
_____
_____
_____

</td></tr>
</table>

4:1   New Employee Orientation

Some employers schedule an orientation meeting or program for new employees. This meeting can take many forms. Large employers who routinely hire many employees at a time might schedule a group gathering in a conference room, while smaller employers might simply set up a time for a new hire to get together with a benefits administrator or human resources employee. No matter what type of orientation your company uses, it serves three purposes: (1) to explain company procedures to new employees (for example, about payroll, scheduling vacations, and signing up for health insurance benefits); (2) to take care of all of that pesky first-day paperwork; and (3) to answer any questions new employees might have.

New Employee Orientation

Within a day or two of starting work, you will be scheduled for a new employee orientation meeting. During this meeting, you will receive important information about our Company's policies and procedures. You will also be asked to complete paperwork and forms relating to your employment, such as tax withholding forms, emergency contact forms, and benefits paperwork.

　　Please feel free to ask any questions you might have about the Company during the orientation meeting. If additional questions come up after the meeting, you can ask your supervisor or _____
_____.

How to Complete This Policy

In the blank, insert the title or position of the person who conducts the new employee orientation meetings (for example, human resources manager, benefits administrator, or office manager).

4:2   Orientation Period

Many employers use an orientation period for their new employees. During this time, the employee can learn how to do the job and what the company expects, and the company can offer the employee extra supervision and make sure that the employee is going to make the grade. As sensible as such policies may be, they can also create a legal risk for employers. Orientation policies must be carefully drafted with an eye towards preserving the at-will employment relationship. (For more on at-will employment, see Chapter 2.)

Employers get into trouble with orientation policies that state or imply that completion of the orientation period guarantees the worker a job, makes the worker a "permanent employee," or otherwise limits the employer's right to fire the worker at will. The orientation period is a trial run of sorts: It gives both employer and employee a chance to make sure that there's a good fit between the worker and the job. But emphasizing this too strongly in an orientation policy can lead workers to expect that completing their orientation means they've "made the cut" and, thereafter, will be fired only for good cause. To avoid this potential legal pitfall, the sample policy we provide clearly states that employment is at will both during and after the orientation period.

⚠ **Montana employers must follow different rules.** The state of Montana has greatly limited the doctrine of at-will employment. Montana law provides that an employee who has completed the employer's probationary period—or who has worked for the employer for at least six months, if the employer has not adopted a probationary period—may be fired only for good cause. Because of this requirement, Montana employers probably won't want to adopt a probationary or orientation period of less than six months. If your company does business in Montana, get some legal advice on how best to preserve your rights while staying within the law.

Who Needs This Policy

Employers are not required to have an orientation policy or to make any special arrangements to train new employees. If your company treats new employees like everyone else, you don't need this policy.

However, many employers do use a probationary, orientation, or "new employee" period. If your company is one of them, using this policy will help you avoid jeopardizing the company's right to fire employees at will.

This orientation policy offers other benefits as well. It lets new workers know where to go with questions or concerns, and it allows the company to create a waiting period before employee benefits go into effect. (See "How to Complete This Policy," below.)

4:2   Orientation Period

CD File: 04_New Employee Info.rtf

Include This Policy?
☐ Yes
☐ No
☐ Use our existing policy
☐ Other _____

Alternate Modifications
None

Additional Clauses
Extend Orientation Period
   Insert?:   ☐ Yes   ☐ No

Related Policies
None

Notes

_____

_____

_____

_____

_____

_____

_____

_____

_____

_____

_____

_____

_____

_____

_____

_____

_____

_____

_____

_____

Orientation Period

The first _____ days of your employment are an orientation period. During this time, your supervisor will work with you to help you learn how to do your job successfully and what the Company expects of you. This period also provides both you and the Company with an opportunity to decide whether you are suited for the position for which you were hired.

When your employment begins, you will meet with _____ _____ , who will explain our benefits and payroll procedures and assist you in completing your employment paperwork. (For our Company's benefits policies, see Section _____ of this Handbook.) You will also meet with your supervisor to go over your job goals and performance requirements. During the orientation period, your supervisor will give you feedback on your performance and will be available to answer any questions you might have.

Employees are not eligible for the following benefits unless and until they complete the orientation period: _____ _____ .

Although we hope that you will be successful here, the Company may terminate your employment at any time, either during the orientation period or afterwards, with or without cause and with or without notice. You are also free to quit at any time and for any reason, either during the orientation period or afterwards, with or without notice. Successful completion of your orientation period does not guarantee you a job for any period of time or in any way change the at-will employment relationship. (For an explanation of at-will employment, see Section _____ of this Handbook.)

New employees have legal rights, too. Although employers are allowed to require new employees to work for a certain period of time before they are eligible for fringe benefits—benefits of the job that employers are not legally required to provide, such as insurance coverage or a company car—employers must follow the law in dealing with new employees. Wage and hour laws, anti-discrimination laws, occupational safety laws, and many other workplace protections apply to workers from their very first day on the job. While employers can condition discretionary benefits on tenure at the company legally, they cannot place their new employees' legal rights on hold until they complete an orientation period.

How to Complete This Policy

Our sample policy leaves you a space to indicate how long the orientation period will be. Ninety days is a fairly standard length for an orientation period. It's long enough to give employees a chance to learn the ropes and show what they can do, but not so long that you'll be stuck mentoring new workers forever. However, some employers use a 60-day period or some other time frame that better fits their business model. For example, if workers have quarterly sales goals or change assignments every two months, you might want to use these time periods instead.

We also leave you space to list the benefits that won't be available to new employees during the orientation period. For example, many employers impose a waiting period for health insurance coverage or employer contributions to a retirement fund. Some employers do not allow their employees to use sick or vacation time during the orientation period. If you plan to impose such a waiting period, list the benefits that will not be available to new employees here.

We also leave you space to designate the person who will explain benefits, payroll procedures, and other administrative matters to new employees. If you have a human resources function, you can insert someone from the human resources department here. If not, designate the position that handles these matters (for example, the payroll administrator or benefits coordinator).

Additional Clause to Extend Orientation Period

Some orientation policies provide that the orientation period can be extended at the employer's discretion. The purpose of such an addition is to provide some extra time to evaluate a worker, if necessary. For example, if the worker doesn't seem to be getting the hang of things, or if unusual circumstances during the orientation period prevented the worker from receiving sufficient training and feedback, the option of a longer period might be helpful. If you wish to include this provision, add this language to the end of the first paragraph.

Additional Clause

Your orientation period may be extended if the Company decides that such an extension is appropriate.

4:3   Proof of Work Eligibility

CD File: 04_New Employee Info.rtf

Include This Policy?
- ☐ Yes
- ☐ No
- ☐ Use our existing policy
- ☐ Other _____

Alternate Modifications
New Employee Orientation Procedures
Choose one: ☐ A   ☐ B

Additional Clauses
None

Related Policies
Your policy on personnel files should explain where employees' I-9 Forms will be kept. For this policy and a related discussion, see Chapter 16.

Notes
_____
_____
_____
_____
_____
_____
_____
_____
_____
_____
_____
_____
_____
_____

4:3   Work Eligibility

A federal law called the Immigration Reform and Control Act (IRCA) requires all employers to verify, within the first three days of employment, that a new hire is legally eligible to work in the United States. The employer must require each new employee to complete an I-9 form, show identification, and present proof of employment eligibility.

The work eligibility policy should tell employees that they will have to present certain documents and complete the I-9 Form and where they can go for more information.

Proof of Work Eligibility

Within three business days of your first day of work, you must complete federal Form I-9 and show us documentation proving your identity and your eligibility to work in the United States. The federal government requires us to do this.

If you have worked for this Company previously, you need only provide this information if it has been more than three years since you last completed an I-9 Form for us or if your current I-9 Form is no longer valid.

Alternate Modifications for New Employee Orientation Procedures

For Companies That Do Not Hold Orientation Meetings

If your company does not provide forms to new employees at a new hire interview or orientation meeting, you should add language to the policy explaining who will provide the I-9 Form and examine the employee's documentation. Simply add the language below as the last paragraph of the policy. In the blank space, designate someone to be responsible for completing and answering questions about the I-9 Form. Typically, that person is the human resources manager or office manager. The same person who deals with new employees' tax and insurance forms can also handle this form.

Alternate Modification A

_____
will give you an I-9 Form and tell you what documentation you must present to us.

For Companies That Hold New Employee Orientation Meetings

If you adopt the first policy in this chapter, your company will hold new hire interviews or orientation meetings at which a designated person will give new employees all the forms they'll need to complete as part of joining the company. This stack of forms often includes a Handbook Acknowledgment Form (see Chapter 2), an IRS W-4 Form, and a Form I-9. If your company uses this type of process for new employees, add the following language as the last paragraph of the policy. In the first blank, insert whatever you call this initial meeting—"new hire interview" or "orientation meeting," for example. In the second blank, identify the person who is responsible for completing and answering questions about the I-9 Form. Typically, that person is the human resources manager or office manager. The same person who deals with new employees' tax forms and insurance forms can also handle this form.

Alternate Modification B

At your _____
_____ [*title of meeting—for example, "new hire interview" or "orientation"*], you should have received a blank Form I-9 and instructions on completing it. If you did not, contact _____
_____
immediately.

Reality Check: Citizenship and Employment Eligibility Are Two Different Things

Asking for proof of employment eligibility is not the same thing as asking whether an employee is a citizen of the United States. Employers are legally required to verify that an employee is authorized to work in the U.S. but are legally prohibited from asking whether an employee or applicant for employment is a citizen of this country. Discrimination on the basis of citizenship status is illegal.

Noncitizens are eligible to work in this county as long as they have proper authorization from the government. For example, lawful permanent resident aliens, aliens granted asylum in the U.S., and aliens allowed into the U.S. as refugees are all entitled to work here, as long as they have documents proving their identity and eligibility to do so.

<table>
<tr><td>

4:4   Child Support Reporting
       Requirements

CD File: 04_New Employee Info.rtf

Include This Policy?
☐ Yes
☐ No
☐ Use our existing policy
☐ Other _____

Alternate Modifications
None

Additional Clauses
None

Related Policies
None

Notes

_____
_____
_____
_____
_____
_____
_____
_____
_____
_____
_____
_____
_____
_____
_____
_____
_____
_____

</td></tr>
</table>

4:4   Child Support Reporting Requirements

All employers are required to report information on new employees to a government agency in their state: the State Directory of New Hires. Once the state receives this information, it checks to see whether any of these new employees appear on its list of parents who owe child support. If the government finds a match, it will send the employer a withholding order requiring that a certain amount of that employee's income be withheld and paid to the other parent.

Every state requires employers to provide at least the employee's name, address, and Social Security number, as well as the employer's name, address, and employer identification number, to this agency. Some states require additional information, such as the employee's birth date or the date of the employee's first day of work. Some states allow you to simply submit a copy of the employee's W-4 form; others require you to use a different format.

Child Support Reporting Requirements

Federal and state laws require us to report basic information about new employees, including your name, address, and Social Security number, to a state agency called the State Directory of New Hires. The state collects this information to enforce child support orders. If the state determines that you owe child support, it will send us an order requiring us to withhold money from your paycheck to pay your child support obligations.

Who Needs This Policy

You don't have to tell employees about this requirement; many employers simply gather the information and send it off, without ever mentioning it to their employees. However, an explicit policy explaining the requirement to employees can prevent hassles down the road. If a new hire owes child support and the company has to withhold money from his or her paycheck, you will have to explain the situation—including how the state found the employee in the first place. By explaining up front that the company is legally required to provide this information and obey withholding orders, you let employees know that the company isn't singling anyone out or going out of its way to cause problems for anyone. You also pave the way for easier conversations about any withholding orders that must be followed in the future.

We recommend that employers include a brief policy in their handbook explaining this requirement. You can also include a form for employees to fill out, giving the information your state requires.

For more information on I-9 Forms and employer responsibilities under the Immigration Reform and Control Act, see *Federal Employment Laws: A Desk Reference*, by Amy DelPo and Lisa Guerin (Nolo). You can also get free information about the law from Citizenship and Immigration Services, a bureau of the federal Department of Homeland Security, at http://uscis.gov.

For more information on child support reporting requirements, see *Federal Employment Laws: A Desk Reference*, by Amy DelPo and Lisa Guerin (Nolo). You'll also find several helpful resources on these requirements at the website of the Administration for Children and Families, a subdivision of the federal government's Department of Health and Human Services, at www.acf.hhs.gov/programs/cse. The website includes a list of each state's requirements and agency information; access it by going to www.acf.hhs.gov/programs/cse/newhire/employer/contacts/contacts.htm and clicking on "State New Hire Reporting Information."

■

5

Employee Classifications

In any given workplace, there might be five, ten, 30, or more classifications of employees—including such categories as "regular," "temporary," "on call," "per diem," and so on. The list is as endless as the employer's imagination.

Employers like to group workers into classifications for a wide variety of reasons, most having to do with identifying which employees are entitled to which wages, benefits, and privileges. For example, an employer who does not want to provide benefits to employees who are scheduled to work fewer than 40 hours per week will likely classify employees as part time or full time and will have a policy that allows only full-time employees to receive benefits.

For the most part, the law does not dictate how you classify employees. For example, you can decide how many hours per week employees have to work to be considered full-time employees.

The more complicated your workplace, the more employee classifications you might have. We cannot cover all of the various categories into which different employers group their employees. Instead, we tackle the most common ones. The classifications covered by policies in this chapter will meet the needs of the vast majority of small- to mid-sized businesses.

It is important to understand that these categories are not mutually exclusive. They divide employees up according to different criteria, so you could use all (or none) of these classifications depending on your needs. For example, an employee easily could be both full time and exempt. This would mean that the employee is scheduled to work at least 40 hours per week (full time) and is not entitled to receive overtime under state or federal law (exempt). We discuss these possibilities further in the descriptions of the various employee classifications throughout this chapter.

5:1   Temporary Employees

Most companies experience times when they need a little extra help. Perhaps you run a toy shop and tend to hire more salespeople during the holiday season, or maybe you operate an accounting firm and must hire additional clerical help during tax season.

Regardless, you must distinguish temporary employees from permanent ones. Most companies choose not to extend optional benefits (such as health insurance and life insurance) or the ability to accrue leave to temporary employees, and they reserve their right to terminate the employees once the need for their services ends.

Depending on your state law, you might have to extend some legally mandated benefits—such as workers' compensation and state disability insurance—to your temporary employees. Contact your state labor department for details. (See Appendix A for contact information.)

The following Temporary Employees policy distinguishes those employees who are working for you on a temporary basis from those whose jobs with you are more long-term. It also explains that temporary employees are not entitled to the same benefits and privileges as are regular employees.

5:1   Temporary Employees
CD File: 05_Employee Class.rtf

Include This Policy?
☐ Yes
☐ No
☐ Use our existing policy
☐ Other _____

Alternate Modifications
None

Additional Clauses
None

Related Policies
For information and policies about at-will employment, see Chapter 2. For information and policies on which benefits part-time employees are and are not entitled to, see Chapters 8 and 10.

Notes

Temporary Employees

Periodically, it becomes necessary for us to hire individuals to perform a job or to work on a project that has a limited duration. Typically, this happens in the event of a special project, special time of year, abnormal workload, or emergency.

Individuals whom we hire for such work are temporary employees. They are not eligible to participate in any of our Company benefit programs, nor can they earn or accrue any leave, such as vacation leave or sick leave.

Of course, we will provide to temporary employees any and all benefits mandated by law.

Temporary employees cannot change from temporary status to any other employment status by such informal means as remaining in our employ for a long period of time or through oral promises made to them by coworkers, members of management, or supervisors. The only way a temporary employee's status can change is through a written notification signed by

_____.

Like all employees who work for this Company, temporary employees work on an at-will basis. This means that both they and this Company are free to terminate their employment at any time for any reason that is not illegal—even if they have not completed the temporary project for which they have been hired.

How to Complete This Policy

Sometimes, temporary employees will begin to feel that they are regular employees simply by virtue of the length of time that they have spent with a company. And sometimes, they will think that their status has changed because of something you or a manager or supervisor has said to them.

It is important that you don't allow the status of temporary employees to change through these informal methods. Otherwise, you may find yourself obligated to provide benefits and leave to individuals whom you never wanted to hire in the first place.

Of course, you may on occasion find that you do want to hire temporary employees on a more regular basis, so you'll need some method by which you can change the status of temporary employees.

The fourth paragraph of the sample policy, above, warns temporary employees that their status cannot change informally or by implication. It does, however, give you the ability to change their status through a written notification signed by someone within your company. Choose a person who is likely to be involved in all of the hiring decisions at your company or who oversees employee benefit or leave programs. A human resources manager or an office manager is often a good choice.

Are Those Temporary Employees Really Independent Contractors?

An individual who works for you on a temporary basis may really be an independent contractor, not a temporary employee. If possible, it will usually be to your advantage to classify a worker as an independent contractor, because independent contractors tend to be less expensive than temporary employees. For example, you don't have to provide workers' compensation insurance for them, nor do you have to withhold any taxes from their compensation. To learn more about independent contractors, see *Working With Independent Contractors*, by Stephen Fishman (Nolo).

5:2   Part-Time and Full-Time
        Employees

CD File: 05_Employee Class.rtf

Include This Policy?
- ☐ Yes
- ☐ No
- ☐ Use our existing policy
- ☐ Other _____

Alternate Modifications
None

Additional Clauses
None

Related Policies
None

Notes
_____
_____
_____
_____
_____
_____
_____
_____
_____
_____
_____
_____
_____
_____
_____
_____
_____

5:2   Part-Time and Full-Time Employees

If you have any employees who work fewer than 40 hours per week, you may want to treat them differently from your other employees in terms of benefits and other perks. To do this, it's helpful to classify employees as either part time or full time, depending on how many hours they work each week.

Be aware that under some circumstances, state or federal law will govern whether you can deny certain benefits to part-time workers. Understanding these benefits laws can be difficult, and determining which workers must be allowed to participate can require complex calculations. Talk to your benefits administrator, accountant, or financial adviser before denying benefits to part-time employees.

Part-Time and Full-Time Employees

Depending on the number of hours per week you are regularly scheduled to work, you are either a part-time or a full-time employee. It is necessary that you understand which of these classifications you fit into, because it will be important in determining whether you are entitled to benefits and leave. (See Section _____ of this Handbook for information about who is entitled to benefits and leave.)

Part-time employees: Employees who are regularly scheduled to work fewer than _____ hours per week are part-time employees.

Full-time employees: Employees who are regularly scheduled to work at least _____ hours per week are full-time employees.

How to Complete This Policy

Your company must decide how many hours per week it requires of employees to entitle them to benefits and leave. Many employers require 40 hours; others require 32 or only 24. Regardless, you have the option of prorating benefits and leave. For example, you may call an employee who works 32 hours per week a full-time employee, thereby guaranteeing the employee some benefits and leave, but still prorate the amount of vacation that person is entitled to based on a 40-hour work week. Under such a system, if an employee who works 40 hours per week would earn five vacation days per year, then an employee who works 32 hours per week (4/5 time) would only earn four (4/5 of full-time vacation benefits).

5:3 Exempt and Nonexempt Employees

Depending on the type of work employees do, they may be entitled to overtime pay for any hours they work in excess of 40 hours in a week (or, in some states, in excess of eight hours in a day). Classifying workers as exempt or nonexempt is not a matter of choice for you; it is a matter of state and federal law. Most likely, you have already determined for payroll purposes which workers fall into which category.

This policy explains to employees that their right to overtime compensation depends on whether they are classified as exempt or nonexempt—and it explains to them the difference between the two classifications.

Exempt and Nonexempt Employees

Your entitlement to earn overtime pay depends on whether you are classified as an exempt or a nonexempt employee.

Exempt employees are those who do not earn overtime because they are exempt from the overtime provisions of the federal Fair Labor Standards Act and applicable state laws.

Nonexempt employees are those who meet the criteria for being covered by the overtime provisions of the federal Fair Labor Standards Act and applicable state laws.

If you are uncertain about which category you fall into, speak to _____ .

5:3   Exempt and Nonexempt Employees

CD File: 05_Employee Class.rtf

Include This Policy?
☐ Yes
☐ No
☐ Use our existing policy
☐ Other _____

Alternate Modifications
None

Additional Clauses
None

Related Policies
None

Notes

_____
_____
_____
_____
_____
_____
_____
_____
_____
_____
_____
_____
_____
_____
_____
_____
_____
_____
_____
_____
_____
_____

6

Hours

Employers generally want to be able to dictate when their employees will work: what time they will start and finish, when they will take breaks, and how much—if any—overtime they will work. The policies in this chapter will help your company set these standards. Although some state and federal laws impose restrictions on work hours—for example, requiring employers to pay certain employees an overtime premium if they work more than a prescribed number of hours in a day or week, or mandating that employees receive certain breaks during their shifts—employers are generally free to tell their employees when they must work.

CD File: 06_Hours.rtf

Include This Policy?
☐ Yes
☐ No
☐ Use our existing policy
☐ Other _____

Alternate Modifications
Include Schedule Information
Choose one: ☐ A ☐ B ☐ C

Additional Clauses
None

Related Policies
None

Notes

_____
_____
_____
_____
_____
_____
_____
_____
_____
_____
_____
_____
_____
_____
_____
_____
_____
_____
_____

6:1   Hours of Work

Your policy on work hours should tell employees when the company is open for business and when they are expected to be at work. This policy will set the stage for company policies on absenteeism and punctuality. (See Chapter 12.)

Hours of Work

Our Company's regular hours of business are from _____ [*start time*] to _____ [*end time*], _____ _____ [*days of operation— for example, "Monday through Friday" or "seven days a week"*] .

Alternate Modifications to Include Schedule Information

To Have Supervisors Provide Schedule

Some employers want company supervisors to set employee work hours, particularly if employees work a variety of schedules or if employee schedules are subject to change. This allows supervisors to make staffing decisions as they see fit. To use this modification, simply add the following language to your policy.

Alternate Modification A

Your supervisor will let you know your work schedule, including what time you will be expected to start and finish work each day.

To Specify Hours for All Employees

In some companies, all employees work the same hours. For example, if an employer has limited hours (such as a convenience store that caters to office workers or an after-hours nightclub), it may need all employees to start work at the same time and stop work at the same time. You can use this modification to set the schedule for all workers. Simply add the following language to the end of your policy.

Alternate Modification B

> All employees are expected to be here, ready to start work, when we open. Unless you make other arrangements with your supervisor, you are expected to work until closing time.

To Include Shift Schedules

A variety of businesses, from restaurants and stores to manufacturers and hospitals, operate in shifts. If your company assigns workers to shifts with set schedules, you should modify the work hours policy to let employees know when each shift starts and ends. This will not only tell workers when they are expected to work, but will also let them know what other shifts might be available, if they need or want to change their work schedules.

This modification also advises that any shift changes, whether temporary or permanent, must be approved by a supervisor. This will put employees on notice that they may not simply swap shifts with a coworker whenever they wish, which will give the company more control over work schedules.

If you want to include a shift schedule in your policy, add the following modification to the end of your policy. In the blanks, fill in the number of shifts your company uses and the start and end time of each shift. Our modification includes space for three shifts; if your company has more or fewer shifts, you will have to modify this accordingly.

Alternate Modification C

> Our Company operates in _____ shifts: from _____ to _____, from _____ to _____, and from _____ to _____ . Your supervisor will let you know your shift assignment.
>
> If you wish to change shifts permanently, talk to your supervisor. Although the Company will consider all requests to change shifts, we cannot guarantee that any particular request will be granted.
>
> You may exchange shifts with another employee (that is, switch shifts on a one-time basis) only with the prior approval of your supervisor.

<table>
<tr><td>

6:2   Flexible Scheduling
      ("Flextime")

CD File: 06_Hours.rtf

Include This Policy?
☐ Yes
☐ No
☐ Use our existing policy
☐ Other _____

Alternate Modifications
None

Additional Clauses
None

Related Policies
None

Notes
_____
_____
_____
_____
_____
_____
_____
_____
_____
_____
_____
_____
_____
_____
_____
_____
_____
_____
_____
_____

</td></tr>
</table>

6:2   Flexible Scheduling ("Flextime")

Many companies offer their employees some form of flexible scheduling, often to accommodate the busy lives of working parents, employees who are attending school, or those who have other pressing needs off the job.

Companies can reap many benefits from allowing their employees to work a flexible schedule. Employees who have sufficient time off work to deal with their outside concerns, be they family commitments, health problems, volunteer work, or school responsibilities, will be better able to concentrate and perform well when they are on the job. Showing concern about employees' lives outside the workplace also goes a long way towards instilling respect and commitment to the company. And some workers simply do a better job—they are more efficient or productive—during certain times of the day. If there are a lot of "morning people" on the payroll, for example, allowing them to start work earlier could boost the bottom line.

If you adopt a flexible scheduling policy, it should tell workers how to request a flexible schedule and what kinds of schedules might be allowed.

Flexible Scheduling

We understand that many employees have to balance the demands of their job with the needs of their families and other outside commitments. Therefore, we offer our employees the opportunity to work a flexible schedule.

If you would like to change your work schedule—for example, to come in and leave a couple of hours earlier or to work more hours on some days and fewer on others—please talk to your supervisor. The Company will try to accommodate your request, to the extent practical. Because not all jobs are suitable to flexible scheduling, and because we must ensure that our staffing needs are met, we cannot guarantee that the Company will grant your request.

Reality Check: Deciding Who Gets to Flex

Flexible scheduling can be a tremendous boon to employer and employee alike. However, employers who choose to offer this opportunity must make sure that they dole out the benefits fairly.

An employer that offers a discretionary benefit—that is, a benefit that may be granted for some employees but not for others—must be very careful to have solid business reasons for these decisions. Otherwise, the employer may face legal claims of discrimination. For example, if working mothers are routinely allowed to alter their schedules to meet child care needs but the same benefit isn't always extended to working fathers, an employer could get into trouble. Decision makers must consider each claim for flexible scheduling on its own merits: Can the company accommodate the request without substantial disruption? Does the employee's job lend itself to flexibility? Has the employee demonstrated the responsibility and self-motivation to work outside usual work hours?

6:3   Meals

CD File: 06_Hours.rtf

Include This Policy?
- ☐ Yes
- ☐ No
- ☐ Use our existing policy
- ☐ Other _____

Alternate Modifications

None

Additional Clauses

None

Related Policies

None

Notes

_____
_____
_____
_____
_____
_____
_____
_____
_____
_____
_____
_____
_____
_____
_____
_____
_____
_____
_____

6:3   Meal and Rest Breaks

Most companies offer their employees some breaks during the day. The laws in seven states require employers to provide paid breaks; other states require breaks but don't insist that employers pay employees for this time. You can find out what your state requires by consulting "State Meal and Rest Break Laws" at the end of this chapter.

Even if your state doesn't require any breaks, you should adopt a break policy if your company generally allows employees to take breaks. Having a written policy will reduce confusion over how much time can be taken and whether it will be paid or unpaid.

Your policy on meal and rest breaks should let employees know when they get breaks, how long they can take, and whether those breaks are paid. If employees must schedule their breaks or take them at a particular time, your policy should include this information as well.

Meal and Rest Breaks

Employees are allowed a _____-minute break every _____ hours. These breaks will be _____ [*paid or unpaid*]. In addition, all employees who work at least _____ hours in a day are entitled to take a _____-minute meal break. Meal breaks are generally unpaid. However, employees who are required to work or remain at their stations during the meal break will be paid for that time.

How to Complete This Policy

Federal law doesn't require employers to offer employees breaks of any length during the workday. However, federal law does require employers to pay employees for any breaks of 20 minutes or less that they choose to provide. A handful of states—including California and Washington—currently require employers to provide paid breaks during the workday. State laws are summarized in "State Meal and Rest Break Laws", at the end of this chapter.

To complete this policy, fill in the blanks with the length and frequency of the break your state requires—or the length of the break your company offers, as long as it meets or exceeds your state's legal requirements. Also, indicate whether rest breaks will be paid or unpaid. Because no state explicitly requires paid meal breaks, our policy provides that such breaks will be unpaid.

6:4   Overtime

If you anticipate that any company employees will be asked to work overtime, you should adopt an overtime policy. An overtime policy offers a number of benefits. For starters, it lets workers know, up front, that they will be expected to work overtime when necessary. This will go a long way towards eliminating later complaints when managers actually have to ask employees to stay beyond their scheduled shifts. An overtime policy also protects the company from having to pay workers for unnecessary overtime—or overtime work made necessary only by the employee's poor planning or faulty time management. Our sample policy requires workers to get advance authorization before working any overtime hours, which should prevent these abuses. The policy also explains how overtime is calculated, including which hours count towards the overtime threshold. Placing this information in the policy will save you the time it would otherwise take to explain the system to each worker who puts in extra time on the job.

Overtime

On occasion, we may ask employees to work beyond their regular scheduled hours. We expect employees to work a reasonable amount of overtime—this is a job requirement.

We will try to give employees advance notice when overtime work is necessary; however, it will not always be possible to notify workers in advance.

Exempt employees will not be paid for working beyond their regular scheduled hours. Nonexempt employees are entitled to payment for overtime, according to the rules set forth below. (For information on which employees are exempt and which are nonexempt, see Section _____ of this Handbook.)

- All overtime work must be approved in writing, in advance, by the employee's supervisor. Working overtime without permission violates Company policy and may result in disciplinary action.

- For purposes of calculating how many hours an employee has worked in a day or week, our workweek begins at 12:01 a.m. on Monday and ends at midnight on Sunday. Our workday begins at 12:01 a.m. and ends at midnight each day.

- Nonexempt employees will be paid 1½ times their regular hourly rate of pay for every hour worked in excess of _____ .

6:4   Overtime

CD File: 06_Hours.rtf

Include This Policy?
☐ Yes
☐ No
☐ Use our existing policy
☐ Other _____

Alternate Modifications
Calculate Time Worked
Choose one: ☐ A   ☐ B

Additional Clauses
Pay a Premium for Holiday Work
Insert?:   ☐ Yes   ☐ No

Choose Employees for Overtime
Insert?:   ☐ Yes   ☐ No

Related Policies
None

Notes

_____
_____
_____
_____
_____
_____
_____
_____
_____
_____
_____
_____
_____
_____
_____
_____
_____

**Reality Check:
Calculating a Worker's Regular Rate of Pay**

Federal law requires employers to pay overtime based on the employee's regular rate of pay—the total amount the employee generally earns per hour. However, this may add up to more than just the employee's hourly rate. Other compensation the employee regularly receives must also be included in the regular rate of pay, unless that compensation is discretionary. For example, say an employee regularly receives $10 per hour but works one eight-hour swing shift per week, for which he receives an additional shift differential of $2 per hour. That employee's regular rate of pay would not be $10 per hour but would instead be his total pay for a 40-hour week divided by 40 hours ($10 x 32 hours = $320, plus $12 x 8 hours =$96, for a total of $416, divided by 40 hours), or $10.40.

Any nondiscretionary pay—such as regular bonuses or shift differentials—must be included in the employee's regular rate of pay, but discretionary pay may be excluded. For example, if excellent performers sometimes receive a bonus, you don't have to include that money in a worker's regular rate of pay.

How to Complete This Policy

In the blank, insert the overtime standard—state or federal—that your company has to follow. Federal law requires employers to pay overtime to any nonexempt worker who works more than 40 hours in a seven-day week. However, a few states (including California) have a daily overtime standard, which requires employers to pay overtime to covered workers who put in more than a specified number of hours in a single workday. Check "State Overtime Rules" at the end of this chapter for information on your state's rules. Then complete the policy as follows: If federal law is more protective, or as protective, of workers as your state's law, insert "40 hours in a workweek" in the blank. If your state has a daily overtime standard, insert that standard in the blank. For example, California employers should insert "eight hours in a workday or 40 hours in a workweek."

California employers take note. California offers employees more extensive wage and hour protections than most other states. In California, not only are workers entitled to time-and-a-half for any hours worked beyond eight in a day or 40 in a week, but they are also entitled to double time—that is, twice their regular hourly wage—for hours worked beyond 12 in a day or for working more than eight hours on a seventh consecutive workday. (See "State Overtime Rules" at the end of this chapter for details.) And California law defines the categories of workers who are entitled to overtime more broadly than federal law. If your company does business in California, you should consult with an employment lawyer to make sure that your policies don't violate these rules.

Alternate Modifications to Calculate Time Worked

To Count Only Hours Spent Working as Time Worked

Most employers will want to pay overtime only when they are legally required to do so. Under federal law, paid hours that are not worked—such as vacation days, sick time, or holidays—do not count towards the overtime threshold of 40 hours per week. If your company will follow this federal standard, add the following bullet to the end of your policy.

Alternate Modification A

- Only time actually spent working counts as hours worked. Vacation time, sick days, holidays, or any other paid time during which an employee did not actually work will not count as hours worked.

To Count Paid Time Off as Time Worked

Although federal law does not require it, employers are free to count paid hours as hours worked, and some choose to do so. An employer might adopt this more generous policy to recognize the value of paid time off—which, after all, is supposed to be a true break from the job. The therapeutic value of paid days off diminishes if an employee has to work extra hours as a result.

If your company will treat some or all paid time off as hours worked, simply add the following bullet to the end of your policy In the blank, insert the types of paid time off that will count as hours worked, for example, paid vacation days or paid sick days. If all paid time off will count as hours worked, insert "all days off for which the employee is paid."

Alternate Modification B

- Hours worked means all time spent actually working, plus _____ .

Additional Clause to Pay a Premium for Holiday Work

Federal law does not require employers to pay extra for hours worked on a holiday, unless those hours push the employee's weekly total above 40 hours. Nonetheless, some employers want to reward their employees for working unpopular shifts. Any employer who has tried to staff shifts on Thanksgiving or New Year's Day knows that a little incentive helps fill the ranks.

If your company wants to pay employees more to work on holidays, add the following clause to the overtime policy. In the first blank, list the holidays for which employees will receive a premium (for example, New Year's Eve and New Year's Day). In the second blank, insert the premium that will be paid (such as two times the employee's regularly hourly wage).

Additional Clause

The Company will pay employees a premium for working on the following holidays: _____
_____
_____ .

Employees who agree to work on these days will receive _____
_____ .

Additional Clause to Choose Employees for Overtime

In certain industries and businesses, employees jump at the chance to earn the extra money that overtime work provides. Other companies might find that no one ever wants to work overtime. In either situation, you may want to adopt a policy that explains how employees are chosen for overtime work. Such a policy will assure employees in companies where overtime is popular that the company is doling out the opportunity to work overtime fairly. And, in companies where no one wants to work overtime, it will let workers know that they will have to put in their time when their turns come.

Additional Clause

Please let your supervisor know if you want to work overtime. Your supervisor will add your name to the overtime list. When overtime is available, it will be offered first to employees on the list, in the order in which their names appear.

If overtime work is necessary and no employees on the list are available, employees who are eligible to perform the work—that is, employees who do the same type of work during their regular work hours—will be asked to work overtime, in alphabetical order. Once an employee, on the list or off, has worked overtime, the next employee on the list or in alphabetical order will be asked to work overtime when it next becomes available, and so on.

State Meal and Rest Breaks

Note: The states of Alabama, Alaska, Arizona, Arkansas, District of Columbia, Florida, Idaho, Indiana, Iowa, Louisiana, Maryland, Michigan, Mississippi, Missouri, Montana, New Jersey, New Mexico, North Carolina, Ohio, Oklahoma, Pennsylvania, South Carolina, South Dakota, Texas, Utah, Virginia, and Wyoming are not listed in this chart because they do not have laws or regulations on rest and meal breaks for adults employed in the private sector. Many states also exclude professional, administrative, and executive employees from these rules.

Other exceptions may apply. Check the statute or check with your state department of labor if you need more information. (See Appendix A for contact list.)

California
Cal. Code Regs. tit. 8, §§ 11010, 11160; Cal. Lab. Code §§ 512, 1030

Applies to: Employers in most industries.

Exceptions: Motion picture, agricultural, wholesale baking, and household occupations.

Meal Break: 30 minutes, unpaid, after 5 hours, except when workday will be completed in 6 hours or less and employer and employee consent to waive meal break. Employee cannot work more than 10 hours a day without a second 30-minute break, except, if workday is no more than 12 hours, second meal break may be waived if first meal break was not waived.

On-duty paid meal period permitted when nature of work prevents relief from all duties and parties agree in writing.

Rest Break: Paid 10-minute rest period for each 4 hours worked or major fraction thereof; as practicable, in the middle of the work period. Not required for employees whose total daily work time is less than 3½ hours.

Breastfeeding: Reasonable time to breastfeed infant or to express breast milk; paid if taken concurrent with other break time; otherwise, unpaid.

Colorado
Colo. Code Regs. § 1103-1

Applies to: Retail and service, food and beverage, commercial support service, and health and medical industries.

Exceptions: Employees in administrative and professional occupations.

Meal Break: 30 minutes, unpaid, after 5 hours of work. On-duty paid meal period permitted when nature of work prevents break from all duties.

Rest Break: Paid 10-minute rest period for each 4 hours or major fraction worked; if practical, in the middle of the work period.

Connecticut
Conn. Gen. Stat. Ann. §§ 31-51ii, 31-40w

Applies to: All employers, except as noted.

Exceptions: Employers who pay for rest breaks as described below, those with a written agreement providing other break rules, and those granted an exemption for reasons listed in statute.

Meal Break: 30 minutes, unpaid, after first 2 hours of work and before last 2 hours for employees who work 7½ or more consecutive hours.

Rest Break: As alternative to meal break, a total of 30 minutes paid in each 7½ hour work period.

Breastfeeding: Employee may use meal or rest break for breastfeeding or expressing breast milk.

Delaware
Del. Code Ann. tit. 19, § 707

Applies to: All employers, except as noted.

Exceptions: Employers with alternative written agreement and those granted exemptions specified in statute.

Meal Break: 30 minutes, unpaid, after first 2 hours and before the last 2 hours, for employees who work 7½ consecutive hours or more.

Georgia
Ga. Code Ann. § 34-1-6

Applies to: All employers.

Breastfeeding: Reasonable unpaid break time to breastfeed infant or to express breast milk.

Hawaii
Haw. Rev. Stat. § 378-2

Applies to: All employers.

Breastfeeding: Allowed during any break required by law or collective bargaining agreement.

Illinois
820 Ill. Comp. Stat. § 140/3, § 260/10

Applies to: All employers.

Exceptions: Employees whose meal periods are established by collective bargaining agreement.

Employees who monitor individuals with developmental disabilities or mental illness, or both, and who are required to be on-call during an entire 8-hour work period; these employees must be allowed to eat a meal while working.

State Meal and Rest Breaks (continued)

Meal Break: 20 minutes, no later than 5 hours after the beginning of the shift, for employees who work 7½ or more continuous hours.

Breastfeeding: Reasonable unpaid break time to breastfeed infant or express breast milk.

Kansas

Kan. Admin. Reg. 49-30-3(b)(2)(A)

Applies to: Employees not covered under FLSA.

Meal Break: Not required, but if less than 30 minutes is given, break must be paid.

Kentucky

Ky. Rev. Stat. Ann. §§ 337.355, 337.365

Applies to: All employers, except as noted.

Exceptions: Written agreement providing different meal period; employers subject to Federal Railway Labor Act.

Meal Break: Reasonable off-duty period close to the middle of the shift; can't be required to take it before the third or after the fifth hour of work.

Rest Break: Paid 10-minute rest period for each 4-hour work period.

Rest period must be in addition to regularly scheduled meal period.

Maine

Me. Rev. Stat. Ann. tit. 26, § 601

Applies to: Most employers.

Exceptions: Small businesses with fewer than 3 employees on duty who are able to take frequent breaks during the workday. Collective bargaining or other written agreement between employer and employee may provide for different breaks.

Meal or Rest Break: 30 minutes, unpaid, after 6 consecutive hours of work, except in cases of emergency.

Massachusetts

Mass. Gen. Laws ch. 149, §§ 100, 101

Applies to: All employers, except as noted.

Exceptions: Excludes iron works, glass works, paper mills, letterpresses, print works, and bleaching or dyeing works. Attorney general may exempt businesses that require continuous operation if it won't affect worker safety. Collective bargaining agreement may also provide for different breaks.

Meal Break: 30 minutes, if work is for more than 6 hours.

Minnesota

Minn. Stat. Ann. §§ 177.253, 177.254, 181.939

Applies to: All employers.

Exceptions: Excludes certain agricultural and seasonal employees.

A collective bargaining agreement may provide for different rest and meal breaks.

Meal Break: Sufficient unpaid time for employees who work 8 consecutive hours or more.

Rest Break: Paid adequate rest period within each 4 consecutive hours of work, to utilize nearest convenient restroom.

Breastfeeding: Reasonable unpaid break time to breastfeed infant or express milk.

Nebraska

Neb. Rev. Stat. § 48-212

Applies to: Assembly plant, workshop, or mechanical establishment.

Exceptions: Other written agreement between employer and employees.

Meal Break: 30 minutes off premises.

Nevada

Nev. Rev. Stat. Ann. § 608.019

Applies to: Employers of two or more employees.

Exceptions: Employees covered by collective bargaining agreement; exemptions for business necessity.

Meal Break: 30 minutes for 8 continuous hours of work.

Rest Break: Paid 10-minute rest period for each 4 hours or major fraction worked; as practicable, in middle of the work period. Not required for employees whose total daily work time is less than 3½ hours.

New Hampshire

N.H. Rev. Stat. Ann. § 275:30-a

Applies to: All employers.

Meal Break: 30 minutes after 5 consecutive hours, unless the employer allows the employee to eat while working and it is feasible for the employee to do so.

New York

N.Y. Lab. Law § 162

Applies to: Factories, workshops, manufacturing facilities, mercantile (retail and wholesale) establishments.

Meal Break: Factory employees, 60 minutes between 11 a.m. and 2 p.m.; mercantile employees, 30 minutes between 11 a.m. and 2 p.m. If a shift starts before 11

State Meal and Rest Breaks (continued)

a.m. and ends after 7 p.m., every employee gets an additional 20 minutes between 5 and 7 p.m. If a shift starts between 1 p.m. and 6 a.m., a factory employee gets 60 minutes, and a mercantile employee gets 45 minutes, in the middle of the shift. Labor commissioner may permit a shorter meal break; the permit must be in writing and posted conspicuously in the main entrance of the workplace.

North Dakota
N.D. Admin. Code § 46-02-07-02(5)

Applies to: Applicable when two or more employees are on duty.

Exceptions: Waiver by employee, or other provision in collective bargaining agreement.

Meal Break: 30 minutes for each shift over 5 hours. Unpaid if employee is completely relieved of duties.

Oregon
Or. Admin. R. § 839-020-0050

Applies to: All employers except as noted.

Exceptions: Agricultural workers and employees covered by a collective bargaining agreement.

Meal Break: 30 minutes, unpaid if relieved of all duties; paid time to eat if employee cannot be relieved of duty; a 20-minute paid break, if employer can show that it is industry practice or custom.

Rest Break: Paid 10-minute rest period for each 4 hours or major fraction worked; if practical, in the middle of the work period.

Rest period must be in addition to usual meal break and taken separately; can't be added to meal period or deducted from beginning or end of shift to reduce length of total work period.

Rest period is not required for certain solo adult employees serving the public, although they must be allowed to use rest room.

Rhode Island
R.I. Gen. Laws § 28-3-14, 23-13-2.1

Applies to: Factory, workshop, and mechanical or mercantile establishments.

Exceptions: Nighttime switchboard operators who can sleep during shift.

Meal: 20 minutes after 6 hours of work.

Employees are not entitled to a break if shift lasts for 6½ hours or less and ends by 1 p.m.; or if shift lasts for 7½ hours or less and ends by 2 p.m., and employee has enough time to eat during work.

Breastfeeding: Reasonable unpaid break time to breastfeed infant or express breast milk.

Tennessee
Tenn. Code Ann. §§ 50-2-103(d), 50-1-305

Applies to: Employers with 5 or more employees.

Meal or Rest Break: 30 minutes unpaid for employees scheduled to work 6 consecutive hours or more unless work is such that there is ample time for breaks throughout the day.

Breastfeeding: Reasonable unpaid break time to breastfeed infant or express breast milk.

Vermont
Vt. Stat. Ann. tit. 21, § 304

Applies to: All employers.

Meal Break: Employees must be given reasonable opportunities to eat and use toilet facilities during work periods.

Washington
Wash. Admin. Code 296-126-092, 286-131-020

Applies to: All employers except as noted.

Exceptions: Newspaper vendor or carrier, domestic or casual labor around private residence, sheltered workshop. Separate provisions for agricultural labor.

Meal Break: 30-minute break, if work period is more than 5 consecutive hours, not less than 2 hours nor more than 5 hours from beginning of shift. This time is paid if employee is on duty or is required to be at a site for employer's benefit. Employees who work 3 or more hours longer than regular workday are entitled to an additional ½ hour, before or during overtime.

Agricultural employees: 30 minutes if working more than 5 hours; additional 30 minutes if working 11 or more hours in a day.

Rest Break: Paid 10-minute rest break for each 4-hour work period, scheduled as near as possible to midpoint of each work period. Employee cannot be required to work more than 3 hours without a rest break.

Scheduled rest breaks not required where nature of work allows employee to take intermittent rest breaks equivalent to required standard.

Agricultural employees: 10-minute paid rest break for each 4 hours worked.

West Virginia
W.Va. Code § 21-3-10a; W.Va. Code St. R. § 42-5-2(2.6)

Applies to: All employers.

State Meal and Rest Breaks (continued)

Meal Break: At least 20-minute break for each 6 consecutive hours worked, unless employees are allowed to take breaks as needed or to eat lunch while working.

Rest Break: Rest breaks of 20 minutes or less must be counted as paid work time.

Wisconsin
Wis. Admin. Code § DWD 274.02

Applies to: All employers.

Meal Break: Recommended but not required: 30 minutes close to usual meal time or near middle of shift. Shifts of more than 6 hours without a meal break should be avoided. If employee is not free to leave the workplace, meal period is considered paid time.

Current as of February 2005

State Overtime Rules

This chart covers private sector employment only. The overtime rules summarized are not applicable to all employers or all employees. Occupations that generally are not subject to overtime laws include health care and attendant care, emergency medical personnel, seasonal workers, agricultural labor, camp counselors, nonprofits exempt under FLSA, salespeople working on a commission, transit drivers, baby sitters and other household workers, and many others. For more information contact your state's department of labor and be sure to check its website, where most states have posted their overtime rules. (See Appendix A for contact details.)

Alabama

No overtime provisions.

Alaska

Alaska Stat. §§ 23.10.055 and following

Time and a half after x hours per DAY: 8

Time and a half after x hours per WEEK: 40

Employment overtime laws apply to: Employers of 4 or more employees; commerce or manufacturing businesses.

Notes: Voluntary flexible work hour plan of 10-hour day, 40-hour week, with premium pay after 10 hours is permitted.

Arizona

No overtime limits for private sector employers.

Arkansas

Ark. Code Ann. §§ 11-4-211, 11-4-203

Time and a half after x hours per WEEK: 40

Employment overtime laws apply to: Employers of 4 or more employees.

Employment excluded from overtime laws: Employment that is subject to the FLSA.

Notes: Employees in retail and service establishments who spend up to 40% of their time on nonexempt work must be paid at least twice the state's minimum wage ($572 per week).

California

Cal. Lab. Code §§ 510 and following; Cal. Code Regs. tit. 8, §§ 11010 and following

Time and a half after x hours per DAY: 8; after 12 hours, double time.

Time and a half after x hours per WEEK: 40. On 7th day: Time and a half for the first 8 hours; after 8 hours, double time.

Employment excluded from overtime laws: Computer software employees who design, develop, create, analyze, test, or modify programs using independent judgment, or who are paid at least $45.84/hour.

Notes: Alternative four 10-hour day work week is permitted, if established prior to 7/1/99. 7th day premium pay not required when employee works no more than 30 hours per week or 6 hours per day.

Colorado

Colo. Rev. Stat. § 8-13-102; 7 Colo. Code Regs. § 1103-1(4)

Time and a half after x hours per DAY: 12

Time and a half after x hours per WEEK: 40

Employment overtime laws apply to: Employees in retail and service, commercial support service, food and beverage, health and medical industries.

Connecticut

Conn. Gen. Stat. Ann. § 31-76b; Conn. Agencies Regs. § 31-62-E1(c)

Time and a half after x hours per WEEK: 40; premium pay on weekends, holidays, or 6th or 7th consecutive day.

Notes: In restaurants and hotels, time-and-a-half pay required for the 7th consecutive day of work or for hours that exceed 48 per week.

Delaware

No overtime provisions.

District of Columbia

D.C. Code Ann. § 32-1003(c); D.C. Mun. Regs. tit. 7, § 906

Time and a half after x hours per WEEK: 40

Florida

No overtime provisions.

Georgia

No overtime provisions.

Hawaii

Haw. Rev. Stat. §§ 387-1; 387-3

Time and a half after x hours per WEEK: 40. Dairy, sugar cane, and seasonal agricultural work: 48 hours per week.

Employment excluded from overtime laws: Employees earning guaranteed compensation of $2,000 or more per month.

Idaho

No state overtime rules that differ from FLSA.

State Overtime Rules (continued)

Illinois
820 Ill. Comp. Stat. §§ 105/3(d), 105/4a
Time and a half after x hours per WEEK: 40
Employment overtime laws apply to: Employers of 4 or more employees.

Indiana
Ind. Code Ann. § 22-2-2-4(j)
Time and a half after x hours per WEEK: 40
Employment excluded from overtime laws: Employment that is subject to the FLSA, movie theaters, seasonal camps and amusement parks, FLSA-exempt nonprofits.
Notes: Collective bargaining agreements ratified by the NLRB may have different overtime provisions. Domestic service work is not excluded from overtime laws.

Iowa
No state overtime limits.

Kansas
Kan. Stat. Ann. § 44-1204
Time and a half after x hours per WEEK: 46
Employment excluded from overtime laws: Employment that is subject to the FLSA.

Kentucky
Ky. Rev. Stat. Ann. §§ 337.050, 337.285
Time and a half after x hours per WEEK: 40
Employment excluded from overtime laws: Retail, hotel, and restaurant businesses.
Notes: 7th day, time and a half.

Louisiana
No overtime provisions.

Maine
Me. Rev. Stat. Ann. tit. 26, § 664(3)
Time and a half after x hours per WEEK: 40
Employment excluded from overtime laws: Auto mechanics, parts clerks, and salespersons; hotels, motels, and restaurants; canning, freezing, packing, and shipping produce and perishable foods.
Notes: Employee cannot be required to work more than 80 hours of overtime in any 2-week period.

Maryland
Md. Code Ann., [Lab. & Empl.] § 3-420
Time and a half after x hours per WEEK: 40; 48 hours for bowling alleys and residential employees caring for the sick, aged, or mentally ill in institutions other than hospitals; 60 hours for agricultural work.

Massachusetts
Mass. Gen. Laws ch. 151, § 1A
Time and a half after x hours per WEEK: 40
Employment excluded from overtime laws: Agriculture, farming, fishing; hotel, motel, or restaurant; seasonal workers less than 5 months; hospital, nursing home, or rest home; public transit.
Notes: Sunday or holiday: Time and a half as overtime unless already paid that rate as part of regular compensation.

Michigan
Mich. Comp. Laws §§ 408.382 and following
Time and a half after x hours per WEEK: 40
Employment overtime laws apply to: Employers of 2 or more employees.
Employment excluded from overtime laws: Employees not subject to state minimum wage laws.

Minnesota
Minn. Stat. Ann. § 177.25
Time and a half after x hours per WEEK: 48

Mississippi
No overtime provisions.

Missouri
Mo. Rev. Stat. §§ 290.500 and following
Time and a half after x hours per WEEK: 40; 52 hours for seasonal amusement or recreation businesses.
Employment excluded from overtime laws: Employment that is subject to the FLSA; retail or service business with gross annual sales or contracts of less than $500,000.

Montana
Mont. Code Ann. §§ 39-3-405 and following
Time and a half after x hours per WEEK: 40; 48 hours for students working seasonal jobs at amusement or recreational areas.

Nebraska
No overtime provisions.

Nevada
Nev. Rev. Stat. Ann. § 608.018
Time and a half after x hours per DAY: 8
Time and a half after x hours per WEEK: 40
Employment excluded from overtime laws: Businesses with a gross annual sales volume of less than $250,000.
Notes: Employer and employee may agree to flextime schedule of four 10-hour days.

State Overtime Rules (continued)

New Hampshire

N.H. Rev. Stat. Ann. § 279:21(VIII)

Time and a half after x hours per WEEK: 40

Employment excluded from overtime laws: Employees covered by the FLSA; employees in amusement, seasonal, or recreational business open 7 months or less a year.

New Jersey

N.J. Stat. Ann. §§ 34:11-56a(4) and following

Time and a half after x hours per WEEK: 40

Employment excluded from overtime laws: June to September: Summer camps, conferences, and retreats operated by nonprofit or religious groups.

New Mexico

N.M. Stat. Ann. § 50-4-22(C)

Time and a half after x hours per WEEK: 40

New York

N.Y. Lab. Law §§ 160(3), 161; N.Y. Comp. Codes R. & Regs. tit. 12, § 142-2.2

Time and a half after x hours per WEEK: 40 for nonresidential workers; 44 for residential workers.

Employment excluded from overtime laws: Same exemptions as FLSA.

North Carolina

N.C. Gen. Stat. §§ 95-25.14, 95-25.4

Time and a half after x hours per WEEK: 40; 45 hours a week in seasonal amusement or recreational establishments.

Employment excluded from overtime laws: Employment that is subject to the FLSA.

North Dakota

N.D. Admin. Code § 46-02-07-02(4)

Time and a half after x hours per WEEK: 40; 50 hours per week, cab drivers.

Employment excluded from overtime laws: Computer professionals who design, develop, create, analyze, test, or modify programs using independent judgment or who are paid at least $27.63/hour.

Ohio

Ohio Rev. Code Ann. § 4111.03

Time and a half after x hours per WEEK: 40

Employment overtime laws apply to: Employers who gross more than $150,000 a year.

Oklahoma

No state overtime provisions.

Oregon

Or. Rev. Stat. §§ 653.261, 653.265

Time and a half after x hours per WEEK: 40

Notes: Time and a half required after 10 hours a day in canneries, driers, packing plants, mills, factories, and manufacturing facilities.

Pennsylvania

43 Pa. Cons. Stat. Ann. § 333.104(c); 34 Pa. Code § 231.41

Time and a half after x hours per WEEK: 40

Rhode Island

R.I. Gen. Laws §§ 28-12-4.1 and following, 5-23-2(h)

Time and a half after x hours per WEEK: 40

Notes: Time and a half for Sunday and holiday work is required for most retail businesses (these hours are not included in calculating weekly overtime).

South Carolina

No overtime provisions.

South Dakota

No overtime provisions.

Tennessee

No overtime provisions.

Texas

No overtime provisions.

Utah

No overtime provisions.

Vermont

Vt. Stat. Ann. tit. 21, §§ 382, 384(b); Vt. Code R. 24 090 001

Time and a half after x hours per WEEK: 40

Employment overtime laws apply to: Employers of 2 or more employees

Employment excluded from overtime laws: Retail and service businesses if 75% of annual sales not for resale; hotels, motels, restaurants; transportation workers exempt under FLSA.

Virginia

No overtime provisions.

Washington

Wash. Rev. Code Ann. § 49.46.130

Time and a half after x hours per WEEK: 40

State Overtime Rules (continued)

West Virginia

W. Va. Code §§ 21-5c-1(e), 21-5c-3

Time and a half after x hours per WEEK: 40

Employment overtime laws apply to: Employers of 6 or more employees at one location

Employment excluded from overtime laws: Employees that are subject to the FLSA.

Wisconsin

Wis. Stat. Ann. §§ 103.01, 103.03; Wis. Admin. Code DWD 274.01 and following

Time and a half after x hours per WEEK: 40

Employment overtime laws apply to: Manufacturing, mechanical, or retail businesses; beauty parlors, laundries, restaurants, hotels; telephone, express, shipping, and transportation companies.

Wyoming

No overtime provisions.

Current as of February 2005

Pay Policies

Let's face it—no matter how wonderful your company is to work for and no matter how much management encourages camaraderie, creativity, and teamwork on the job, employees don't show up every day for the fun of it. They work to get paid.

The basic exchange of the work relationship—labor for money—is easy enough to understand. But the laws regulating when, how, and how much employers must pay workers can get pretty complicated. One of the reasons for this complexity is that every level of government gets involved in legislating pay. The federal government has one set of rules, state governments have another, and sometimes even local or municipal governments get involved. Employers have to follow whichever law gives workers the most rights in any particular situation—which means they have to piece together a complex quilt of laws from a variety of sources.

In this chapter, we'll show you how to put together compensation policies that tell workers what they need to know: when they will get paid, what kinds of work might entitle them to extra pay, and the reasons why money might have to be withheld from their paychecks.

7:1   Payday

The title pretty much says it all: Your payday policy should tell employees when they will get paid. It should also let employees know when they will get their paychecks if a payday falls on a holiday.

How often employers must pay employees is governed by state law (federal law doesn't require employers to follow any particular pay schedule). You can get information on your state's wage laws by contacting your state labor department. (See Appendix A for contact information.) For information on payday requirements, you can also check the U.S. Department of Labor's website, which provides a chart of state payday laws at www.dol.gov/esa/programs/whd/state/payday.htm.

Payday

Employees are paid _____ . You will receive your paycheck on _____ .
If payday falls on a holiday, you will receive your paycheck on the last workday immediately before payday.

How to Complete This Policy

To complete this policy, you will need to determine how often and on what day of the week or month employees will be paid. Many states require employers to pay workers no less frequently than a certain interval—for example, weekly, biweekly, twice a month, or once a month. An employer may pay workers more often but may not make them wait longer to receive their paychecks than the law allows.

Some states, including Connecticut and New York, require employers to pay workers on a weekly basis. Some of these laws apply to only certain kinds of workers—for example, manual laborers. If your company does business in one of these states, it might adopt a two-part payday policy, one part for the workers who must be paid every week and the other for everyone else.

Other than the handful of states that require at least some workers to be paid weekly, state law usually allows employers to pay workers every other week. However, some states allow employers to pay workers less frequently—for example, twice a month or even monthly.

Once you figure out how often employees must be paid—and how often the company wants to pay them, if you are considering more frequent paychecks—you can fill in the blanks in our sample policy. If your company does business in a state that requires week-

---

7:1 Payday
CD File: 07_Pay Policies.rtf

Include This Policy?
☐ Yes
☐ No
☐ Use our existing policy
☐ Other _____

Alternate Modifications
None

Additional Clauses
Require Submission of Time Cards
Insert?: ☐ Yes ☐ No

Related Policies
None

Notes

ly paychecks, insert "every week" in the first blank and insert the day of the week on which employees will be paid (usually Friday) in the second blank. For biweekly paychecks, insert "every other week" in the first blank and, again, insert the day of the week on which employees will be paid in the second blank. For paydays that fall twice a month, insert "twice a month" in the first blank and the dates of the month on which employees will be paid in the second blank (often the 1st and the 15th of each month). Finally, for monthly paychecks, insert "monthly" in the first blank and the date of the month on which employees will be paid in the second blank (usually the 1st of the month or the last day of the month).

Who Needs This Policy

Your state's law may require employers to give employees written notice of when they will be paid in certain circumstances. For example, Vermont requires workers to be paid weekly but allows employers to pay workers less frequently if they give their workers written notice of the pay schedule. If your company does business in one of these states, adopting a written payday policy may not only be a good idea but may also be a legal requirement.

Even if state law doesn't require employers to put their pay schedule in writing, doing so is generally a good idea. Workers take an active interest in when they will be paid, for understandable reasons. Adopting a written policy can help you avoid having to answer a lot of anxious questions about when paychecks will arrive.

Reality Check: Pay Employees Before a Holiday

Our sample policy provides that paychecks will be distributed on the last working day before a payday, if the designated payday falls on a holiday. The purpose of this language is to make sure that your company meets your state's time limits: If your state requires workers to be paid every week or two, or provides (as a few do) that no more than a specified number of days may elapse between paychecks, your company has to hit that mark, no matter what the calendar says. If workers are paid late because the designated payday came on a holiday or weekend, your company will be in violation of the law.

For more information on state payday requirements, go to the Department of Labor's website, which provides a chart of state payday laws at www.dol.gov/esa/programs/whd/state/payday.htm.

Additional Clause to Require Submission of Time Cards

If your company requires workers to turn in a written record of hours worked each pay period, specify that in your payday policy. For example, some employers require workers to hand in time cards, time sheets, or other records. Below is an optional clause you can add to our sample policy if your company requires such records. Note that you may have to tinker with our wording if you use some other form of time keeping. The blank space allows you to tell employees how many days in advance they must submit their time records. Most employers require workers to turn in their hours at least two or three days before payday.

Additional Clause

Employees must submit their time cards or time sheets to their supervisor _____ [*number of days*] before payday.

7:2   Advances

Advances (loans made against an employee's coming paycheck) can be the bane of a payroll administrator's existence. They create additional record-keeping hassles and exceptions to the usual procedures. And there are some employees who are happy to take advantage of an employer's liberal policy by requesting frequent advances rather than spending the time (and using the willpower) to balance their personal budgets more carefully.

Because of these potential problems, many employers choose not to offer advances at all or to offer advances on a discretionary basis only, for situations that legitimately qualify as emergencies. Employers who allow advances often limit how often an employee can request them and how much money the employee can receive in advance of a paycheck. To allow you to choose the policy that best meets your company's needs, we offer alternative sample policies. Policy A prohibits advances; Policy B allows advances only at the company's discretion.

No law requires an employer to provide advances—or even to notify its employees of its policy on advances one way or the other. However, regardless of how your company decides to handle pay advances, adopting a policy setting out the rules will save time and help prevent misunderstandings. Some employees may assume that they can take an advance; if advance requests are routinely denied, these employees will be in for an unpleasant surprise. If your company does offer advances, you should let employees know how and when advances must be paid back—and that the company reserves the right not to grant an advance request.

Policy A

No Advances

Our Company does not allow employees to receive pay advances for any reason.

Policy B

Advance Policy

Please submit requests for pay advances to _____
_____; requests will be granted or denied at the sole discretion of the Company.

If we grant your request for an advance, you may receive no more than _____ .

7:2 Advance Policy

CD File: 07_Pay Policies.rtf

Include This Policy?
- ☐ Yes
  - *Choose one:* ☐ A   ☐ B
- ☐ No
- ☐ Use our existing policy
- ☐ Other _____

Alternate Modifications
Policy B only: Repayment of Advances
Choose one: ☐ A   ☐ B

Additional Clauses
Allow Advances for Vacations
Insert?: ☐ Yes   ☐ No

Related Policies
None

Notes

_____
_____
_____
_____
_____
_____
_____
_____
_____
_____
_____
_____
_____
_____
_____
_____
_____
_____

How to Complete This Policy

Sample Policy B includes two blanks for you to fill in: the person to whom advance requests must be submitted and the amount of money an employee can receive in advance of a paycheck.

- **Who receives advance requests.** In this blank, designate someone with a substantial amount of authority, such as the Chief Financial Officer, President, or Director of Human Resources. You should designate the person who will ultimately decide whether advances will be granted, to minimize the paper shuffling needed to resolve the request. It doesn't hurt to choose someone whose gravitas will cut back on the number of frivolous advance requests.
- **How much money can be advanced.** In this blank, you can use either a dollar figure (such as $200, $500, or $1,000) or a percentage of the employee's pay (25% or 50% of the employee's regular earnings, for example). Make sure to set a reasonable limit, based on what workers generally earn—otherwise, it could prove hard for the employee to pay back the advance.

Alternate Modifications for Repayment of Advances (Policy B Only)

To Set Time Limits for Repayment

Use this modification to let employees know when advances must be paid back, if they will be expected to repay the company on their own. (To require employees to repay advances through payroll deductions, use Alternate Modification B, below). Add the language below to the end of Policy B. In the blank space, insert the time limit for repayment. The time limit should be based, in part, on how large an advance the company allows. If employees may take only limited advances, 30 days should be sufficient. If the advance is substantial, it might take workers more than a month to repay it—perhaps 60 days.

Alternate Modification A

All advances must be repaid within _____ days. Your request for an additional advance will be denied automatically if you have not yet repaid a previous advance.

To Allow Payroll Deductions to Pay Back Advances

Some employers adopt advance policies that allow them to deduct money from an employee's paycheck to repay an advance. These policies are eminently sensible—after all, it's much easier to get the money back if the employee never lays a hand on it. However, state laws may restrict an employer's right to withhold money to repay an advance—and federal law puts some limits on how much an employer can deduct.

Under federal law, an employer is allowed to deduct money from an employee's paycheck to repay an advance, but only if the money the employee actually receives, after the deduction, is at least equal to the minimum wage (currently $5.15 an hour, under federal law). Many states are more restrictive: Some do not allow employers to deduct money from an employee's paycheck to repay an advance or other employer loan, while others allow such deductions only if the employee agrees to them in writing.

Contact your state labor department to find out your state's requirements. (You can find contact information in Appendix A.) If your company is allowed to take these deductions, with or without written consent, add the paragraph below to the end of Policy B. Fill in the blank with the number of days employees will have to repay advances. If written consent is required, use Form B (below) to obtain the employee's authorization for the deduction.

Alternate Modification B

All advances must be paid back, through payroll deductions, within _____ days. Your request for an additional advance will be denied automatically if you have not yet repaid a previous advance.

Additional Clause to Allow Advances for Vacations

Even employers who don't allow any advances may be willing to give early paychecks to employees who will be on vacation or on other paid leave when payday comes around. Although this is an advance of sorts, it's much easier for the employer to manage because the employee is simply getting paid a bit early, rather than borrowing money that will have to be paid back later. Your payroll administrator won't have to change the size of the employee's paychecks, just the timing.

If your company wants to allow these advances, you can add the following language to the end of either Policy A or Policy B, above.

Additional Clause

An employee who will be on vacation or other paid leave on payday may request an early paycheck. Please submit these requests to the payroll administrator. Although we cannot guarantee that every request will be granted, we will do our best to accommodate your request.

Form B: Payroll Deduction Authorization Form

If employees will be required to repay an advance through payroll deductions, ask them to sign the Payroll Deduction Authorization Form before they receive their money. (You can find this and all other forms in Appendix C and on the CD-ROM that accompanies this book.) The amount of the advance, what the employee earns, and your state's law on payroll deductions will dictate how you fill in the blanks. Once you figure out how much the company is legally entitled to withhold from each paycheck, calculate how many paychecks it will take for the employee to repay the advance. Do this by dividing the total amount of the advance by the amount you can withhold from each paycheck. Then fill in the blanks accordingly.

Payroll Deduction Authorization Form

I have requested an advance from the Company. This advance is a loan, which I am fully obligated to repay. In consideration of the Company's decision to grant this request, I agree to repay the Company through payroll deductions. I hereby authorize the Company to withhold _____ from my paycheck in _____ equal installments to repay the advance. The total amount deducted from my pay shall be equal to the amount of the advance.

If my employment is terminated or I quit before this advance is repaid, I hereby authorize the Company to deduct the full amount I still owe the Company from my final paycheck, if allowed by law.

_____   _____
Employee's Signature   Date

_____
Employee's Name (Print)

7:3   Tip Credits

If employees earn tips from customers, their employer may be entitled to pay them a salary that is less than the minimum wage, as long as that salary plus the tips they actually earn adds up to at least the minimum wage per hour worked. If your company follows this procedure (referred to as a "tip credit"), it is legally required to adopt a policy explaining the process to employees. Adopting a written policy also lets workers know what to expect, so they won't be surprised when they get that first paycheck.

Not all states allow employers to take a tip credit. Consult "State Minimum Wage Laws for Tipped and Regular Employees" at the end of this chapter to find out whether your state allows tip credits —and how large the credit can be. The chart also indicates each state's minimum wage, how much employers must pay workers per hour if they take a tip credit, and which workers qualify for a tip credit.

Tip Credit

Employees who hold certain positions in our Company receive some of their compensation in the form of tips from customers. If you receive tips, the Company will pay you an hourly wage of at least _____. However, if that wage plus the tips you actually earn during any pay period does not add up to at least the minimum wage for every hour you work, the Company will pay you the difference.

Who Needs This Policy

Only companies that employ workers who receive tips and pay those workers less than the minimum wage need this policy. In other words, an employer doesn't necessarily need this policy just because its workers receive tips: If a company pays its workers an hourly wage (before tips) that meets or exceeds the minimum wage, this policy is inapplicable.

7:3 Tip Credit
CD File: 07_Pay Policies.rtf

Include This Policy?
☐ Yes
☐ No
☐ Use our existing policy
☐ Other _____

Alternate Modifications
None

Additional Clauses
None

Related Policies
None

Notes

_____
_____
_____
_____
_____
_____
_____
_____
_____
_____
_____
_____
_____
_____
_____
_____
_____
_____
_____
_____
_____

7:4 Tip Pooling

CD File: 07_Pay Policies.rtf

Include This Policy?
☐ Yes
☐ No
☐ Use our existing policy
☐ Other _____

Alternate Modifications
None

Additional Clauses
None

Related Policies
None

Notes

_____
_____
_____
_____
_____
_____
_____
_____
_____
_____
_____
_____
_____
_____
_____
_____
_____
_____
_____
_____

7:4 Tip Pooling

Tip pooling (also known as "tipping out") is a source of much anxiety and frustration in the tipped workforce. Some employees—particularly those who have to deal most with the customers, such as wait staff or bell persons—deeply resent having to share their tips with employees who have less customer contact. Adopting a policy that explains exactly who is required to share how much of their tips can help ease this problem. If everyone knows ahead of time how the tip pool will work, there is less likelihood of confusion and resentment.

Tip Pooling

Employees in the following positions are required to pool tips: _____. If you hold one of these positions, you must contribute _____% of your tips to the pool at the end of each workday. The pool will be divided equally among all employees who worked that day and hold one of the positions listed above.

How to Complete This Policy

A tip pooling policy must meet certain legal requirements. First, an employer can only require tip pooling among employees who customarily receive tips, such as wait staff, bussers, bartenders, bellhops, and counter clerks. Workers who do not receive tips of their own—such as dishwashers, cooks, chefs, and janitors—cannot be included in the pool. Keeping these rules in mind, fill in the first blank, above, with the titles of all the positions that will be required to contribute to the tip pool.

The law also limits how much workers can be required to contribute to a pool. Only tips in excess of tips used for the tip credit may be taken for a pool—in other words, employees must be allowed to keep enough of their own tips to earn the minimum wage, when those tips are combined with the employees' hourly wage. In addition, tipped employees cannot be required to contribute a greater percentage of their tips than is customary and reasonable. This amount varies depending on your industry and location—check with a local trade organization to find out what percentage is usual. Once you do, insert that percentage in the second blank.

⚠️ **Don't take a dip in the tip pool.** All of the money in the tip pool must be shared among the workers who contribute to it—and only those workers. Employers cannot take any portion of the pooled tips for themselves under any circumstances. If an employer violates this basic rule, the Department of Labor will find its tip pooling arrangement invalid, disallow any tip credit it takes, and require the employer to pay back the money it took from workers, plus interest and penalties.

Who Needs This Policy

Only companies that employ workers who receive tips and require those employees to share their tips with other workers need this policy.

7:5 Shift Premiums

CD File: 07_Pay Policies.rtf

Include This Policy?
- ☐ Yes
- ☐ No
- ☐ Use our existing policy
- ☐ Other _____

Alternate Modifications
None

Additional Clauses
None

Related Policies
For information and a policy on overtime, see Chapter 6. If employees will be allowed—or required—to put in overtime hours, use this policy to explain the rules.

Notes

_____
_____
_____
_____
_____
_____
_____
_____
_____
_____
_____
_____
_____
_____
_____
_____

7:5   Shift Premiums

A shift premium policy should tell employees whether they'll be paid extra for working certain shifts, if applicable.

Employers in industries that work in shifts often find it difficult to staff shifts that fall outside of the regular 9 a.m. to 5 p.m. workday. Some employers find that offering workers higher pay to work night shifts, swing shifts, or split shifts solves this problem. If your company offers a shift premium, you should adopt a policy explaining the premium in your handbook. After all, the incentive only works if employees know about it.

> **Shift Premiums**
>
> Employees who work the _____ shift will be paid a premium for each shift. This premium will be _____ .

How to Complete This Policy

In the first blank, insert the shifts for which your company pays a premium (for example, night shift, graveyard shift, or 3 p.m. to 11 p.m. shift). In the second blank, insert the premium amount. If all workers make the same wage, you can simply insert the dollar amount these shift workers will receive per hour. If workers earn varying rates, you can insert the dollar amount or percentage by which their pay will be increased for agreeing to work the tough-to-fill shift (for example, two dollars more per hour in addition to their regular hourly pay or an additional 20% of their regular hourly pay).

Some states, including California, require employers to pay their workers a certain premium for working a split shift—that is, for working one shift then coming back to work another shift after a relatively short break. Contact your state labor department (you can find contact details in Appendix A) to find out if your state imposes this type of requirement. If so, your company must pay split shift workers this premium—and you should set the premium in your policy to at least meet the minimum amount required by law.

7:6   Payroll Deductions

Your payroll deduction policy should explain the mandatory deductions that will be taken from employees' paychecks, as well as the deductions an employee can request. Although all the information is usually right there on the pay stub, a policy can help clarify the reasons why deductions are taken (and why that paycheck is always so much smaller than the worker thinks it will be).

Payroll Deductions

Your paycheck reflects your total earnings for the pay period, as well as any mandatory or voluntary deductions from your paycheck. Mandatory deductions are deductions that we are legally required to take. Such deductions include federal income tax, Social Security tax (FICA), and any applicable state taxes. Voluntary deductions are deductions that you have authorized. Such deductions might include _____

_____ .

If you have any questions about your deductions, or wish to change your federal withholding form (Form W-4), contact

_____ .

How to Complete This Policy

In the space for voluntary deductions, list any contributions employees are allowed to make through payroll withholding, such as:

- insurance premiums
- flexible spending accounts
- contributions to pensions, 401(k)s, or other retirement accounts
- union dues
- charitable contributions, or
- contributions to credit unions or savings accounts.

In the second blank, insert the name of the person or position that handles payroll matters. This might be the payroll administrator, human resources department, benefits coordinator, or whoever makes sure that paychecks go out on time or reports employee compensation to the IRS.

7:6 Payroll Deductions
CD File: 07_Pay Policies.rtf

Include This Policy?
- ☐ Yes
- ☐ No
- ☐ Use our existing policy
- ☐ Other _____

Alternate Modifications
None

Additional Clauses
None

Related Policies
None

Notes

_____
_____
_____
_____
_____
_____
_____
_____
_____
_____
_____
_____
_____
_____
_____
_____
_____
_____
_____
_____

7:7   Wage Garnishments

Any employer can be required—by a court order, the IRS, or another government agency—to garnish an employee's wages. Most employers dislike these orders, because wage garnishments are a payroll hassle. An employer who receives one will have to deduct the prescribed amount from the employee's wages, either for a limited amount of time (for example, when the employee owes a specified amount of money in unpaid taxes or student loans) or indefinitely (for example, for garnishments relating to child or spousal support), depending on the order.

No matter how much an employer dislikes having to deal with a wage garnishment order, the employee whose wages will be garnished is even more put out by the order. Adopting a policy lets employees know that the company has no choice but to comply with these orders—and that it intends to do so. Employees will know that there's not much point asking the employer to reduce, forgive, or postpone the garnishment—it's out of the company's hands. And, hopefully, employees who are upset about a garnishment will take their complaints to the responsible person or agency, rather than to you—who can't change the situation.

Your wage garnishment policy should explain what a wage garnishment is and why an employee's wages might be garnished—and let employees know that the company must comply with orders to garnish wages.

7:7 Wage Garnishments
CD File: 07_Pay Policies.rtf

Include This Policy?
☐ Yes
☐ No
☐ Use our existing policy
☐ Other _____

Alternate Modifications
None

Additional Clauses
None

Related Policies
None

Notes

Wage Garnishments

A wage garnishment is an order from a court or a government agency directing us to withhold a certain amount of money from an employee's paycheck and send it to a person or agency. Wages can be garnished to pay child support, spousal support or alimony, tax debts, outstanding student loans, or money owed as a result of a judgment in a civil lawsuit.

If we are instructed by a court or agency to garnish an employee's wages, the employee will be notified of the garnishment at once. Please note that we are legally required to comply with these orders. If you dispute or have concerns about the amount of a garnishment, you must contact the court or agency that issued the order.

For more information on wage garnishments, the Department of Labor's website offers a helpful fact sheet on related federal law, including how much of an employee's wages can be garnished. You can download it at www.dol.gov/asp/programs/guide/garnish.htm.

7:8 Expense Reimbursement

Expenses often become a source of conflict between workers and management. Workers don't want to incur work-related expenses that the company refuses to pay. They want to know ahead of time what they will be reimbursed for, what they need to do to get reimbursed, and when they can expect repayment. Just as understandably, employers don't want to get hit with requests for reimbursement for extravagant, fraudulent, or unnecessary expenses—and they want some proof that the worker actually incurred the expenses claimed. An expense reimbursement policy can help you set things straight before your employees incur any expenses on behalf of the company.

Your expense reimbursement policy should tell employees which expenses will be reimbursed, how to get authorization to incur expenses, and the procedures for requesting reimbursement.

Expense Reimbursement

From time to time, employees may incur expenses on behalf of

_____

[*Company name*]. We will reimburse you for the actual work-related expenses you incur, as long as those expenses are reasonable. You must follow these procedures to get reimbursed:

- Get permission from your supervisor before incurring an expense.
- Spend the Company's money wisely—make an effort to save money and use approved vendors if possible.
- Keep a receipt or some other proof of payment for every expense.
- Submit your receipts, along with an expense report, to your supervisor for approval within 30 days of incurring an expense.
- Your supervisor is responsible for submitting your expense report to _____

_____ .

If your report is approved, you will receive your reimbursement _____ .

Remember that you are spending the Company's money when you pay for business-related expenses. We expect you to save money wherever possible. Your supervisor can assist you in deciding whether an expense is appropriate.

7:8 Expense Reimbursement

CD File: 07_Pay Policies.rtf

Include This Policy?
- ☐ Yes
- ☐ No
- ☐ Use our existing policy
- ☐ Other _____

Alternate Modifications
None

Additional Clauses
Require Employees to Use Particular Vendors
Insert?: ☐ Yes ☐ No

Include More Detail on Travel Expenses
Insert?: ☐ Yes ☐ No

Allow Mileage Reimbursement
Insert?: ☐ Yes ☐ No

Related Policies
None

Notes

_____

_____

_____

_____

_____

_____

_____

_____

_____

_____

_____

_____

_____

_____

Reality Check: An Expense by Any Other Name

Sometimes, state law dictates whether the employer or employee has to pay for a particular expense. For example, some states require employers to pay the cost of everything an employee needs in order to do the job—including uniforms and tools. Other states don't have such strict requirements; they allow employers to pass these costs on to their employees (or to refuse to reimburse these expenses, as the case may be). Contact your state labor department (you can find contact information in Appendix A) to find out what your state requires.

How to Complete This Policy

In the first blank, insert the position or department responsible for payroll matters (for example, the payroll department, the accounting department, or human resources). In the second blank, indicate when and how employees will receive their reimbursements (for example, with your next paycheck or within fourteen days).

Additional Clause to Require Employees to Use Particular Vendors

If your company has business accounts with particular vendors, such as messengers, caterers, or suppliers, you may want to modify our standard policy to require employees to do business with those vendors, if possible. This will save time and money: The company will know it's getting a good deal, and workers won't have to shop around. If you want to make this addition, insert the additional clause at the end of our sample policy. Fill in the blank with the name of the position or department that handles payroll.

Additional Clause

> • The Company maintains a list of preferred vendors for various work-related items and services. You must use these vendors, if possible. You can get a current copy of the list from _____
> _____ .

Additional Clause to Include More Detail on Travel Expenses

The sample policy above is sufficient to handle very occasional employee travel. However, if the nature of your company's business requires employees to travel frequently, you may need a more-detailed travel expense policy. Employees need to know what expenses will be reimbursed: Are they allowed to fly first class? To stay in a four-star hotel? You can modify the basic expense reimbursement policy above by simply adding this language at the end.

In the blank, insert the total amount employees will be paid per day for meals and other incidentals. To get an idea of how much other employers in the same field are offering as a per diem, contact a local industry organization or professional association—or ask at your local Chamber of Commerce.

Additional Clause

Procedures for Travel Expenses

If employees are required to travel for work, the Company will reimburse you for your travel expenses, including:

- the cost of travel to and from the airport or train station, including parking expenses and tolls
- the cost of airline or train tickets—such tickets must be coach class if possible
- the cost of an economy class rental car, if necessary
- a mileage reimbursement, for those employees who prefer to use their own cars for company travel
- the cost of lodging—employees should select moderately priced lodging if possible, and
- the cost of meals and other incidental expenses, up to a per diem of _____ per day.

You must request advance approval of all travel expenses from your supervisor and follow the procedures above to have your expenses reimbursed.

Additional Clause to Allow Mileage Reimbursement

If employees use their own cars for company business, you should modify our standard policy to include mileage reimbursement. Employees should also be required to have a valid driver's license and adequate auto insurance coverage.

To complete the additional clause, insert the rate of reimbursement in the first blank. Most employers pay a per-mile rate based on IRS standards (currently 40.5 cents per mile). In the second blank, include the name of the department or position that handles payroll—which should be identical to what you inserted in the main Expense Reimbursement policy, above.

Additional Clause

Mileage Reimbursement

Employees who use their own vehicle for Company business will be reimbursed at the rate of _____. Employees are not entitled to separate reimbursement for gas, maintenance, insurance, or other vehicle-related expenses—the reimbursement rate above is intended to encompass all of these expenses.

Before using a personal vehicle for work-related purposes, employees must demonstrate that they have a valid driver's license and adequate insurance coverage.

The Company does not reimburse employees for their commute to and from the workplace.

To claim mileage reimbursement, you must follow these procedures:

- Keep a written record of your business-related travel, including the total mileage of each business trip, the date of travel, the location to which you traveled, and the purpose of your trip.
- If you anticipate having to travel an unusually long distance, get your supervisor's approval before making the trip.
- Submit your record to your supervisor for approval on the last day of the month.
- Your supervisor is responsible for submitting your record to _____ .

If your record is approved, you will receive your reimbursement payment with your next paycheck.

Form C: Expense Reimbursement Form

If employees will incur expenses, you should provide them with an expense form. A preprinted form will remind employees of what they have to submit along with their expense request—and stream-line your paperwork. (You can find this and all other forms in Appendix C and on the CD-ROM that accompanies this book.)

Expense Reimbursement Form

Date of Expense	Item or Service Purchased	Reason for Expense	Cost	Receipt Attached
_____	_____	_____	_____	☐ Yes ☐ No
_____	_____	_____	_____	☐ Yes ☐ No
_____	_____	_____	_____	☐ Yes ☐ No
_____	_____	_____	_____	☐ Yes ☐ No
_____	_____	_____	_____	☐ Yes ☐ No
_____	_____	_____	_____	☐ Yes ☐ No
_____	_____	_____	_____	☐ Yes ☐ No
_____	_____	_____	_____	☐ Yes ☐ No
_____	_____	_____	_____	☐ Yes ☐ No
_____	_____	_____	_____	☐ Yes ☐ No
_____	_____	_____	_____	☐ Yes ☐ No
_____	_____	_____	_____	☐ Yes ☐ No
_____	_____	_____	_____	☐ Yes ☐ No
_____	_____	_____	_____	☐ Yes ☐ No
_____	_____	_____	_____	☐ Yes ☐ No
_____	_____	_____	_____	☐ Yes ☐ No
_____	_____	_____	_____	☐ Yes ☐ No
_____	_____	_____	_____	☐ Yes ☐ No
_____	_____	_____	_____	☐ Yes ☐ No

_____   _____
Employee's Signature   Date Submitted

_____
Employee's Name (Print)

_____   _____
Supervisor's Signature   Date Approved

_____
Supervisor's Name (Print)

State Minimum Wage Laws for Tipped and Regular Employees

The chart below gives the basic state minimum wage laws. Depending on the occupation, the size of the employer's business, or the conditions of employment, the minimum wage may vary from the one listed here. Minimum wage rates in a number of states change from year to year; to be sure of your state's current minimum, contact your state department of labor or check its website, where most states have posted the minimum wage requirements. (See Appendix A for contact information.) Also, some local governments have enacted ordinances that set a higher minimum wage—contact your city or county government for more information.

"Maximum Tip Credit" is the highest amount of tips that an employer can subtract from the employee's hourly wage. The employee's total wages minus the tip credit cannot be less than the state minimum wage. If an employee's tips exceed the maximum tip credit, the employee gets to keep the extra amount.

"Minimum Cash Wage" is the lowest hourly wage that an employer can pay a tipped employee

State and Statute	Notes	Basic Minimum Hourly Rate (*=tied to federal rate)	Maximum Tip Credit	Minimum Cash Wage for Tipped Employee	Minimum Tips to Qualify as a Tipped Employee (monthly unless noted otherwise)
United States 29 U.S.C. § 206	This is the current federal minimum wage.	$5.15	$3.02	$2.13	More than $30
Alabama	No minimum wage law				
Alaska Alaska Stat. § 23.10.065; Alaska Admin. Code Tit. 8, § 15.120		$7.15	No tip credit	$7.15	N/A
Arizona	No minimum wage law				
Arkansas Ark. Code Ann. §§ 11-4-210 to -213	Applies to employers with 4 or more employees	$5.15	50%	$2.575	Not specified
California Cal. Code Regs. tit. 8, § 11000		$6.75	No tip credit	$6.75	N/A
Colorado Colo. Rev. Stat. § 8-6-109; 7 Colo. Code Regs. § 1103-1	Minimum wage applies to these industries: retail and service, commercial support service, food and beverage, and health and medical	$5.15	$3.02	$2.13	More than $30
Connecticut Conn. Gen. Stat. Ann. § 31-58(j)		$7.10 or 0.05% more than FLSA minimum, if it is higher	29.3% waiters; 8.2% bartenders; $0.35 others	$5.02 waiters; $6.52 bartenders; $6.75 others	Not specified
Delaware Del. Code Ann. tit. 19, § 902(a)		$6.15 or FLSA rate if higher	$3.92	$2.23	More than $30
District of Columbia D.C. Code Ann. §§ 32-1003 to -1004		$6.60 $7 starting 1/1/06	$4.33	$2.27	Not specified
Florida Fla. Const., Art X		$6.15 effective May 05	$3.02	$3.13	More than $30
Georgia Ga. Code Ann. § 34-4-3	Applies to employers with 6 or more employees and more than $40,000 per year in sales	$5.15	Minimum wage does not apply to tipped employees	N/A	N/A

State Minimum Wage Laws for Tipped and Regular Employees (continued)					
State and Statute	**Notes**	**Basic Minimum Hourly Rate** (*=tied to federal rate)	**Maximum Tip Credit**	**Minimum Cash Wage for Tipped Employee**	**Minimum Tips to Qualify as a Tipped Employee** (monthly unless noted otherwise)
Hawaii *Haw. Rev. Stat. §§ 387-1 to 387-2*		$6.25	$0.25	$6.00	More than $20; employee's cash wage plus tips must be at least $.50 higher than the minimum wage
Idaho *Idaho Code § 44-1502*		$5.15	35%	$3.35	More than $30
Illinois *820 Ill. Comp. Stat. § 105/4; Ill. Admin. Code tit. 56, § 210.110*	Applies to employers with 4 or more employees	$6.50 $6 for employees under 18	$2.60	$3.90 $3.60 if under 18	At least $20
Indiana *Ind. Code Ann. § 22-2-2-4*	Applies to employers with 2 or more employees	$5.15	$3.02	$2.13	Not specified
Iowa *Iowa Code § 91D.1*	Minimum wage does not apply to first 90 calendar days of employment	$5.15*	40%	$3.09	At least $30
Kansas *Kan. Stat. Ann. § 44-1203*	Applies to employers not covered by the FLSA	$2.65	40%	$1.59	More than $20
Kentucky *Ky. Rev. Stat. Ann. § 337.275*		$5.15*	$3.02	$2.13	More than $30
Louisiana	No minimum wage law				
Maine *Me. Rev. Stat. Ann. tit. 26, §§ 663(8), 664*		$6.35 $6.50 starting 10/01/05	50%	$3.18 $3.25 starting 10/01/05	More than $20
Maryland *Md. Code Ann., [Lab. & Empl.] §§ 3-413, 3-419*		$5.15*	$2.77	$2.38	More than $30
Massachusetts *Mass. Gen. Laws ch. 151, § 1; Mass. Regs. Code tit. 455, §§ 2.02 & following*		$6.75, or $0.10 above FLSA rate if it is higher	$4.12	$2.63	More than $20
Michigan *Mich. Comp. Laws §§ 408.382 to 408.387a*	Applies to employers with 2 or more employees. Excludes all employers subject to the FLSA, unless state minimum wage is higher than federal	$5.15	$2.50	$2.65	Not specified
Minnesota *Minn. Stat. Ann. § 177.24*	$4.90 for small employer (business with annual receipts of less than $500,000)	$5.15	No tip credit	$5.15	N/A
Mississippi	No minimum wage law				
Missouri *Mo. Rev. Stat. §§ 290.502, 290.512*	Doesn't apply to retail or service business with gross annual sales of less than $500,000	$5.15*	Up to 50%	$2.575	Not specified

State Minimum Wage Laws for Tipped and Regular Employees (continued)

State and Statute	Notes	Basic Minimum Hourly Rate (*=tied to federal rate)	Maximum Tip Credit	Minimum Cash Wage for Tipped Employee	Minimum Tips to Qualify as a Tipped Employee (monthly unless noted otherwise)
Montana *Mont. Code Ann. §§ 39-3-404, 39-3-409; Mont. Admin. R. 24.16.1508 & following*	$4.00 for businesses with gross annual sales of $110,000 or less	$5.15*	No tip credit	$5.15*	N/A
Nebraska *Neb. Rev. Stat. § 48-1203*	Applies to employers with 4 or more employees	$5.15	$3.02	$2.13	Not specified
Nevada *Nev. Rev. Stat. Ann. §§ 608.160, 608.250*	Voters approved $1 increase in 2004; will require another vote in 2006 to go into effect	$5.15*	No tip credit	$5.15	N/A
New Hampshire *N.H. Rev. Stat. Ann. § 279:21*		$5.15*	$2.57	$2.38 or 45% of minimum wage, if higher	More than $20
New Jersey *N.J. Stat. Ann. § 34:11-56a4; N.J. Admin. Code tit. 12, §§ 56-3.1 & following, 56-14.4*		$5.15*	Depends on occupation	Depends on occupation	Not specified
New Mexico *N.M. Stat. Ann. § 50-4-22*		$5.15*	50% minimum wage	$2.575	More than $30
New York *N.Y. Lab. Law § 652; N.Y. Comp. Codes R. & Regs. tit. 12, § 137-1.4*		$6 $6.75 starting 1/1/06 $7.15 starting 1/1/07	Depends on occupation	Depends on occupation	Depends on occupation
North Carolina *N.C. Gen. Stat. §§ 95-25.2(14), 95-25.3*		$5.15*	$3.02	$2.13	More than $20
North Dakota *N.D. Cent. Code § 34-06-03; N.D. Admin. Code R. 46-02-07-201(17) to -03*		$5.15	33%	$3.45	More than $30
Ohio *Ohio Rev. Code Ann. § 4111.02*	$3.35 for employers with gross annual sales of $150,000 to $500,000; $2.80 for employers with gross annual sales of less than $150,000	$5.15	50%	$3.075; $2.01 for employers with sales under $500,000	More than $30
Oklahoma *Okla. Stat. Ann. tit. 40, §§ 197.2, 197.4, 197.16*	Applies to employers with 10 or more full-time employees OR gross annual sales over $100,000; $2.00 for all other employers who are not subject to the FLSA	$5.15*	50% for tips, food, and lodging combined	$2.58	Not specified

		State Minimum Wage Laws for Tipped and Regular Employees (continued)			
State and Statute	**Notes**	**Basic Minimum Hourly Rate** (*=tied to federal rate)	**Maximum Tip Credit**	**Minimum Cash Wage for Tipped Employee**	**Minimum Tips to Qualify as a Tipped Employee** (monthly unless noted otherwise)
Oregon Or. Rev. Stat. §§ 653.025, 653.035(3)	Adjusted annually for inflation; posted at www.boli.state.or.us	$7.25	No tip credit	$7.25	N/A
Pennsylvania 43 Pa. Cons. Stat. Ann. §§ 333.104 & following; 34 Pa. Code § 231.1		$5.15*	$2.32	$2.83	More than $30
Rhode Island R.I. Gen. Laws §§ 28-12-3 & following		$6.75	$3.86	$2.89	Not specified
South Carolina	No minimum wage law				
South Dakota S.D. Codified Laws Ann. §§ 60-11-3 to -3.1		$5.15	$3.02	$2.13	More than $35
Tennessee	No minimum wage law				
Texas Tex. Lab. Code Ann. §§ 62.051 & following	Applies to employers not covered by the FLSA	$5.15*	$3.02	$2.13	More than $20
Utah Utah Code Ann. §§ 34-40-102 to -103; Utah Admin. R. 610-1	Applies to employers not covered by the FLSA	$5.15*	$3.02	$2.13	More than $30
Vermont Vt. Stat. Ann. tit. 21, § 384(a); Vt. Code R. 24 090 001 & following	Applies to employers with 2 or more employees	$7.00	$3.35 for employees of hotels, motels, restaurants, and tourist places; no tip credit otherwise	$3.65	More than $30
Virginia Va. Code Ann. §§ 40.1-28.9(D) to 28.10	Applies to employers with 4 or more employees	$5.15*	Tips actually received	Minimum wage less tips actually received	Not specified
Washington Wash. Rev. Code Ann. § 49.46.020; Wash. Admin. Code 296-126-022	Adjusted annually for inflation; posted at www.lni.wa.gov	$7.35	No tip credit	$7.35	N/A
West Virginia W.Va. Code §§ 21-5C-2, 21-5C-4	Applies to employers with 6 or more employees at one location who are not covered by the FLSA	$5.15	20%	$4.12	Not specified
Wisconsin Wis. Admin. Code DWD 272.03		$5.15	$2.42	$2.33	Not specified
Wyoming Wyo. Stat. § 27-4-202		$5.15	$3.02	$2.13	More than $30

Current as of February 2005

8

Employee Benefits

Most companies spend a significant amount of their workforce budget on benefits for their employees. Indeed, about 40% of an average employee's compensation package goes toward benefits. Employers do this with good reason: Generous employee benefits can help entice high-quality workers, retain valuable employees, and improve labor relations. In addition, good benefits can actually help employees be more productive and effective in their jobs. For example, an employee with health insurance is less likely to miss work due to an untreated illness than an employee who's worried about racking up doctor bills.

Of course, your company can only reap these rewards if employees actually know about—and take advantage of—these benefit programs. Too often, employers pay for benefit programs that their employees don't even use, because the employees either don't know about the program or don't understand it. The employee handbook is the ideal place to acquaint employees with their benefits.

The handbook is not, however, the ideal place to educate employees about every last detail of each benefit program. This is because benefit programs, unlike employee handbooks, tend to change, even if only slightly, every year. If you put too much information in the handbook, you'll have to rewrite it every time your company needs to change and adjust the benefit programs. Or, if you leave out-of-date information in your handbook, you risk having employees rely on that information, unaware that the benefit no longer exists or may have changed significantly. This could damage labor relations (the opposite of what you want) and even leave your company vulnerable to a claim from the employee that it breached a contract (in the form of handbook language) over benefits.

As a result, most companies choose to describe their benefits quite generally in their employee handbooks and leave the details to separate handouts and brochures that they can distribute to employees whenever the need arises. The policies in this chapter follow that model. They allow you to toot your company's own horn and announce how wonderful the benefits are without binding your company to the details.

The benefits that employers provide usually fall into one of two groups: those that the employer provides voluntarily and those that are mandated by law. Voluntary benefit programs include health insurance, dental insurance, on-site child care, life insurance, and retirement coverage (for example, a pension plan or a 401(k) plan). Legally mandated benefit programs include workers' compensation coverage and unemployment insurance. To find out what sorts of benefits are mandated by law in your state, contact your state labor department. (See Appendix A for contact information.)

Your handbook should contain policies for every kind of benefit program you offer, regardless of whether the program is voluntary or legally mandated.

8:1   Employee Benefits: Introductory Statement

As explained above, you don't want to pack too many details into your benefits section, because you want to maintain flexibility. You should be able to change the benefits you provide at any time, and you want to avoid making promises in your handbook that you won't be able to keep.

This standard language maintains your company's flexibility to change benefits, explains the significance of official plan documents, and tells employees where to go for more information.

Employee Benefit Plans

As part of our commitment to our employees and their well-being, _____
[*Company Name*] provides employees with a variety of benefit plans: _____
_____
_____
_____
_____

[*List all of the voluntary and legally mandated benefit plans that you provide—for example, health insurance, retirement benefits, stock options, unemployment compensation, workers' compensation, and so on*].

Although we introduce you to those plans in this section, we cannot provide the details of each plan here. You should receive official plan documents for each of the benefit plans that we offer. Those documents (along with any updates that we give to you) should be your primary resource for information about your benefit plans. If you see any conflict between those documents and the information in this Handbook, the official plan documents are what you should rely upon.

The benefits we provide are meant to help employees maintain a high quality of life—both professionally and personally. We sincerely hope that each employee will take full advantage of these benefits. If you don't understand information in the plan documents or if you have any questions about the benefits we offer, please talk to _____
_____ .

8:1   Employee Benefit Plans

CD File: 08_Employee Benefits.rtf

Include This Policy?
- ☐ Yes
- ☐ No
- ☐ Use our existing policy
- ☐ Other _____

Alternate Modifications
None

Additional Clauses
None

Related Policies
None

Notes

How to Complete This Policy

In addition to listing all of the benefits that your company offers, you will have to choose someone to whom employees can go for more information about the various benefit plans. Try to pick someone in your company who is willing and able to get up to speed on these matters—for example, an office manager or a human resources worker. Don't simply instruct employees to call the customer service numbers at the various providers of your benefits plans. If employees are to make the most of the benefits that you offer—and if you are to get your money's worth in terms of improved labor relations—you need to have someone on site who can help employees wade through the often confusing maze of benefits rules.

Reality Check: Be Aware of ERISA

The word ERISA often strikes fear into the hearts of employers, because it is the acronym for one of the most dense and confusing federal laws on the books: The Employee Retirement Income Security Act.

Although it has the word "retirement" in its title, ERISA does not limit itself to retirement plans alone. In fact, the law governs the operation of virtually all employee benefit plans and most likely covers every benefit plan that you offer to your employees.

Among ERISA's many rules are those governing the information that employees must receive about their benefit plans. This information includes a summary plan description, notification of any changes to the plan, and information about how to appeal any adverse decisions made by the plan.

If you pay someone to administer a plan for you (for example, if a health insurance company provides the health care coverage for your employees), that plan administrator will usually take care of complying with ERISA's requirements. Talk to your plan administrator and make sure that ERISA is being followed to the letter.

If you administer your own plan, however, that burden will fall on you. Unless you are incredibly sophisticated and experienced in ERISA matters, complying with ERISA is not something you can do on your own. Seek out professional help. To learn more about ERISA and other federal employment laws, see *Federal Employment Laws: A Desk Reference*, by Amy DelPo and Lisa Guerin (Nolo).

8:2   Domestic Partner Coverage

In the past few decades, our concept of family has changed dramatically. In 1998, only 25% of U.S. households were living in "traditional" family units consisting of a husband, wife, and children. What was everyone else doing? Well, 5.9 million people were living with a domestic partner, and 28% of those partnerships were same-sex partnerships.

Just as our concept of family is evolving, so too is our concept of who should be covered by an employee's benefits. Everyone expects an employee's spouse or child to be eligible for coverage, but what about an employee who is in a committed relationship who either chooses not to marry or is legally prohibited from getting married?

To keep up with this evolving set of norms, employers are increasingly providing coverage for domestic partners. Deciding whether to include domestic partner coverage is a very complicated task, one that involves research into your state and local laws. Some localities require domestic partners to be covered; others prohibit it. Therefore, this is not something you can decide to do—or not to do—based solely on your gut instinct or sense of morality. Make this decision only after consulting with your company's benefits administrator and/or lawyer.

The wording of your domestic partner policy will depend on many things, including state and local laws and the wording choices of your benefits administrator. The following is just an example of what such a policy might look like.

For a comprehensive guide to domestic partner coverage, including information on state and local laws and advice on how to decide whether to offer such coverage in your own workplace, see *Domestic Partner Benefits: An Employer's Guide*, by Joseph Adams and Todd Solomon (Thompson Publishing Group).

SAMPLE POLICY LANGUAGE

At J&J Books, we recognize that some of our employees are members of families that do not meet the traditional definition of the word—that is, a husband, wife, and, perhaps, children. For those employees who are not married but who are in a committed relationship with another adult, we provide domestic partnership coverage.

To be eligible for benefits, the employee and the employee's partner must meet *all* of the following criteria:

- They must have lived together in an exclusive committed relationship for at least 12 months.
- They must be at least 18 years of age.
- They must live together in the same residence.

8:2   Domestic Partner Coverage

CD File: 08_Employee Benefits.rtf

Include This Policy?
- ☐ Yes
- ☐ No
- ☐ Use our existing policy
- ☐ Other _____

Alternate Modifications
None

Additional Clauses
None

Related Policies
None

Notes

_____

_____

_____

_____

_____

_____

_____

_____

_____

_____

_____

_____

_____

_____

_____

_____

_____

_____

_____

_____

_____

_____

- They cannot be legally married to—or in a registered domestic partnership with—anyone else.
- They must not be related by blood more closely than would be allowed under the marriage laws of this state.
- They must complete and sign a Domestic Partnership Affidavit.

8:3   Health Care Benefits

The health care coverage that you offer to your employees is the flagship of your employee benefits program. No matter what other benefits you offer (tuition reimbursement, employee assistance programs, and the like) the most important one to your employees will be your health care program. Health care benefits include more than simply medical coverage. They also include any vision, dental, or similar benefits that you provide.

Because health care benefits have so many permutations and options, we cannot provide you with a standard policy to place in your handbook. We do, however, provide an example of a health care policy, followed by detailed guidance on how to write one of your own.

SAMPLE POLICY LANGUAGE

Because your health is of great importance to us, we provide you with the following health care benefits: medical, dental, vision, and alternative care (including acupuncture and massage). If you have not already received detailed plan documents about each of these benefits, contact Myrtle Means in the Human Resources Department. She can provide you with all the information you need to start enjoying your health care benefits package right away. Even if you have received plan documents, Myrtle can answer any questions you might have.

Eligibility to receive health care benefits depends on your employee classification. (See Section D of this Handbook for information about employee classifications.) If you are a regular full-time or regular part-time employee, you are eligible to receive full health care benefits, and we will pay 100% of the cost of health care insurance premiums for you. We will also pay 100% of the cost of health care insurance premiums for your eligible dependents (including domestic partners).

You and your dependents become eligible for benefits 30 days after the day you start work.

As with all of the policies in this Handbook, our health care coverage may change at any time. For the most up-to-date information about your health care benefits, refer to the plan documents or contact Myrtle.

What to Include in This Policy

When writing your health care benefits policy, it's important to keep in mind both pieces of advice we gave at the beginning of this chapter:

8:3   Health Care Benefits

CD File: 08_Employee Benefits.rtf

Include This Policy?
☐ Yes
☐ No
☐ Use our existing policy
☐ Other _____

Alternate Modifications
None

Additional Clauses
None

Related Policies
None

Notes

_____
_____
_____
_____
_____
_____
_____
_____
_____
_____
_____
_____
_____
_____
_____
_____
_____
_____
_____
_____

- keep the information in the handbook general and non-specific, and
- refer employees to official plan documents for details.

That being said, there are some details that you should include in your policy language. These details are not about the benefit itself but are about who is eligible for the benefit and who will pay for it. Include the following information in your medical benefits policy:

- the classification(s) of employees who are eligible for the benefit—for example, regular full-time employees (see Chapter 5 for policy language about employee classifications)
- the classification(s) of employees who are not eligible for the benefit—for example, temporary employees
- the amount of the premium that you will pay
- the amount of the premium that the employee must pay, and
- whether dependents and/or domestic partners will be covered.

8:4   State Disability Insurance

Some states require employers to withhold a portion of an employee's paycheck to pay for disability insurance. When employees suffer nonwork injuries that prevent them from doing their jobs, they can receive disability benefits.

Even though money is taken out of their paychecks to pay for this benefit, many employees do not know about or understand it. This policy explains in general terms who is eligible for state disability benefits and alerts employees to the difference between disability coverage and workers' compensation.

State Disability Insurance

Sometimes, an employee suffers an illness or injury outside of the workplace that prevents the employee from working and earning income. If this happens to you, state disability insurance may provide you with a percentage of your salary while you are unable to work. All employees are eligible for this coverage and pay for it through deductions from their paychecks.

To find out more about state disability insurance, contact _____ .

If you suffer from an illness or injury that is work-related, then you may be eligible for workers' compensation insurance instead of state disability insurance. See the Workers' Compensation policy, below, or contact _____ _____ for more information.

Who Needs This Policy

If your state requires you to withhold a percentage of your employees' wages to fund a state disability insurance program, you should have this policy in your handbook. Your payroll department should know whether you are withholding disability money—or you can contact your state department of labor. (See Appendix A for contact information.)

8:4   State Disability Insurance

CD File: 08_Employee Benefits.rtf

Include This Policy?
☐ Yes
☐ No
☐ Use our existing policy
☐ Other _____

Alternate Modifications
None

Additional Clauses
None

Related Policies
None

Notes

_____

_____

_____

_____

_____

_____

_____

_____

_____

_____

_____

_____

_____

_____

_____

_____

_____

_____

_____

_____

_____

8:5   Workers' Compensation
       Insurance

CD File: 08_Employee Benefits.rtf

Include This Policy?
☐ Yes
☐ No
☐ Use our existing policy
☐ Other _____

Alternate Modifications
None

Additional Clauses
Refer to State Disability Insurance
Insert?: ☐ Yes ☐ No

Related Policies
8:4 State Disability Insurance (See
Policy 8:4, above, for this policy
and related discussion.

Notes

_____
_____
_____
_____
_____
_____
_____
_____
_____
_____
_____
_____
_____
_____
_____
_____
_____
_____
_____

8:5   Workers' Compensation

Most employers must carry workers' compensation insurance to cover them when an employee suffers a work-related injury. This policy explains what workers' compensation insurance is, and it instructs employees to notify the company immediately if they are injured or become ill. This is a very important requirement, because it will encourage employees to address a work-related illness or injury as soon as it occurs rather than waiting until the injury or illness worsens. It can also help prevent harm to other employees.

Workers' Compensation Insurance

If you suffer from an illness or injury that is related to your work, you may be eligible for workers' compensation benefits. Workers' compensation will pay for medical care and lost wages resulting from job-related illnesses or injuries.

If you are injured or become ill through work, please inform your supervisor immediately regardless of how minor the injury or illness might be.

To find out more about workers' compensation coverage, contact _____ .

Who Needs This Policy

All employers who are required by state law to provide workers' compensation coverage must have this policy in their handbooks. Contact your state labor department to find out about workers' compensation requirements in your state. (See Appendix A for contact information.)

Additional Clause to Refer to State Disability Insurance

If your state has a state disability insurance program (as discussed in Policy 8:4, above), you may want to add a sentence to your workers' compensation policy that refers to when an employee may be eligible for state disability insurance instead of workers' compensation. While workers' compensation covers work-related injuries and illnesses (for example, a construction worker who falls off a scaffolding while at work, breaks a leg, and is temporarily unable to work), it does not cover illnesses or injuries that are not related to an employee's work but that require the employee to miss work (for example, a construction worker who breaks a leg while on vacation skiing and is temporarily unable to work). Below is an optional clause you can add to the end of our sample workers' compensation policy if your state has a state disability insurance program.

Additional Clause

If you are unable to work because of an illness or injury that is not related to work, then you might be eligible for state disability insurance instead of workers' compensation. See the State Disability Insurance policy, above, or contact _____

_____

for more information.

<table>
<tr><td>

8:6   Unemployment Insurance

CD File: 08_Employee Benefits.rtf

Include This Policy?
- ☐ Yes
- ☐ No
- ☐ Use our existing policy
- ☐ Other _____

Alternate Modifications
None

Additional Clauses
None

Related Policies
None

Notes

_____

_____

_____

_____

_____

_____

_____

_____

_____

_____

_____

_____

_____

_____

_____

_____

_____

_____

</td>
<td>

8:6   Unemployment Insurance

Unemployment insurance is another state-mandated benefit. Depending on your state, unemployment insurance is funded through employer contributions, withholdings from employees' paychecks, or some combination of the two. Unemployment insurance pays benefits to employees who suddenly find themselves out of work.

The ins and outs of who is eligible for unemployment insurance can be rather complicated. As a result, this policy simply notifies employees that this benefit exists, and it instructs them on whom to contact for more information.

Unemployment Insurance

If your employment with our Company ends, you may be eligible for unemployment benefits. These benefits provide you with a percentage of your wages while you are unemployed and looking for work. To find out more, contact _____
_____ .

Who Needs This Policy

All employers who are required by state law to provide unemployment coverage must have this policy in their handbooks. Contact your state labor department to find out about requirements in your state. (See Appendix A for contact information.)

■

</td>
</tr>
</table>

9

Use of Company Property

In virtually every workplace, employees must use company equipment and property to do their jobs. This includes everything from the $2 stapler to the $2,000 computer. Because you invest so much money in your equipment, it makes sense to say something about it in your handbook. There are a lot of issues to address, from personal use to proper maintenance and safety.

9:1   Company Property

CD File: 09_Company Property.rtf

Include This Policy?
- ☐ Yes
- ☐ No
- ☐ Use our existing policy
- ☐ Other _____

Alternate Modifications

None

Additional Clauses

None

Related Policies

For policies on personal use of the telephone and voicemail systems, see Chapter 14.

For policies on personal use of computers, software, and the Internet, see Chapter 15.

For policies on confidentiality and intellectual property, see Chapter 18.

Notes

_____

_____

_____

_____

_____

_____

_____

_____

_____

_____

_____

_____

_____

9:1   General Use of Company Property

Regardless of the type of company property or equipment your employees use, you probably want them to take good care and limit their use to company business. Anything less would affect your company's bottom line, as replacement and repair costs could pile up.

The following general use policy explains to employees what constitutes proper use of company equipment, what you expect of them when using company property, and why this matters in the first place.

Company Property

We have invested a great deal of money in the property and equipment that you use to perform your job. It is a senseless and avoidable drain on this Company's bottom line when people abuse Company property, misuse it, or wear it out prematurely by using it for personal business.

We ask all employees to take care of Company property and to report any problems to _____ _____ . If a piece of equipment or property is unsafe for use, please report it immediately.

Please use property only in the manner intended and as instructed.

We do not allow personal use of Company property unless specifically authorized in this Handbook.

Failure to use Company property appropriately, and failure to report problems or unsafe conditions, may result in disciplinary action, up to and including termination.

For information on use of the voicemail system, see Section _____ of this Handbook.

For information on use of computers, the Internet, and software, see Section _____ of this Handbook.

How to Complete This Policy

Choose an individual to whom employees can report problems. At some companies, this will simply be the employee's supervisor. Other companies designate one person to track and maintain company equipment.

9:2   Company Cars

If you provide cars for employees to drive, then you should explain the rules for their use in your handbook. This policy will need to address a variety of issues, from maintenance to personal use.

Company Cars

We have invested in Company vehicles so that our employees can use them on Company business in place of their own vehicles. This saves wear and tear on personal vehicles and eliminates the need for keeping track of mileage.

We need your help in keeping Company cars in the best condition possible. Please keep them clean, and please remove any trash or personal items when you are finished using the vehicles.

Please immediately report any accidents, mechanical problems, or other problems to _____ _____ . We will try to have Company vehicles repaired or serviced as soon as possible.

Only authorized employees may use Company cars, and they may do so only on Company business.

You may not use Company vehicles while under the influence of drugs or alcohol or while otherwise impaired.

You must have a valid driver's license to use Company cars, and we expect that you will drive in a safe and courteous manner. If you receive any tickets for parking violations or moving violations, you are responsible for taking care of them.

Violating this policy in any way may result in disciplinary action, up to and including termination.

Additional Clause for Employees With Assigned Cars

At some workplaces, the company car is not simply a vehicle that the employee checks out for a few hours while attending some event off site. In these workplaces (often in places where employees are salespeople who are almost constantly on the road), employees are assigned a company car on a more or less permanent basis. For as long as the employee works for the company, the employee is in possession of the car and uses it for all business.

In such a situation, employers often place on the employee's shoulders the responsibility for maintaining the car. If you are in such a workplace, add the following paragraph to your policy.

9:2   Company Cars

CD File: 09_Company Property.rtf

Include This Policy?
- ☐ Yes
- ☐ No
- ☐ Use our existing policy
- ☐ Other _____

Alternate Modifications

None

Additional Clauses

Employees With Assigned Cars
    Insert?:   ☐ Yes   ☐ No

Related Policies

None

Notes

Additional Clause

If you have been assigned a Company car, it is your responsibility to keep the car in good condition and repair. At a minimum, this means keeping the car clean, bringing it in for scheduled maintenance by an authorized service department, and checking and changing the oil on schedule. Periodically, we may inform you of other ways in which you must care for the car. We will, of course, reimburse you for any ordinary expenses associated with maintaining the vehicle.

9:3   Telephones

It's a good idea to let employees know that you expect them to use work phones for company business only, except in case of emergencies or quick calls. It isn't reasonable to prohibit all personal calls, as long as they are brief and infrequent—certainly you can allow an employee to tell a spouse that he or she will be home late or to make sure that his or her kids made it home from school. But without a policy limiting personal calls, some employees may take advantage.

Telephone System

The Company's telephone system is for business use only. Employees are expected to keep personal calls to a minimum. If you must make or receive a personal call, please keep your conversation brief. Extensive personal use of Company phones is grounds for discipline.

   See Section _____ of this Handbook for information on privacy and telephones.

9:3   Telephone System

CD File: 09_Company Property.rtf

Include This Policy?
☐ Yes
☐ No
☐ Use our existing policy
☐ Other _____

Alternate Modifications
None

Additional Clauses
None

Related Policies
For policies on personal use of the telephone and voicemail systems, see Chapter 14.

Notes
_____
_____
_____
_____
_____
_____
_____
_____
_____
_____
_____
_____
_____
_____
_____
_____
_____
_____
_____
_____
_____

9:4   Return of Company Property
CD File: 09_Company Property.rtf
Include This Policy?
☐ Yes
☐ No
☐ Use our existing policy
☐ Other _____
Alternate Modifications
None
Additional Clauses
Garnish Final Paycheck
Insert?: ☐ Yes   ☐ No
Related Policies
None
Notes

9:4   Return of Company Property

No employment relationship lasts forever, and when an employee leaves—whether through termination, layoff, or resignation—one of the loose ends to tie up is company property.

Return of Company Property

When your employment with this Company ends, we expect you to return Company property—and to return it clean and in good repair. This includes this Employee Handbook, all manuals and guides, documents, phones, computers, equipment, keys, and tools.

We reserve the right to take any lawful action to recover or protect our property.

Additional Clause to Garnish Final Paycheck

Some states allow for employers to garnish an employee's final paycheck to pay for lost, stolen, or damaged company property. Other states expressly do not allow employers to do this. To find out whether your state allows garnishment, contact your state labor department. (See Appendix A for contact information.)

If you live in a state that allows garnishment, consider adding the following paragraph to your policy.

Additional Clause

If you do not return a piece of property, we will withhold from your final paycheck the cost of replacing that piece of property. If you return a piece of property in disrepair, we will withhold from your final paycheck the cost of repair. We also reserve the right to take any other lawful action necessary to recover or protect our property.

■

10

Leave and Time Off

A little time off is a good thing, for employer and employee alike. Workers get a chance to have fun; deal with personal, civic, and family obligations; and recharge their batteries. Your company benefits, too—the business will be more productive if employees are healthy, rested, and focused on their jobs.

Although many employers believe otherwise, no law requires businesses to offer their employees paid vacation or sick leave (although California recently passed a law to require paid sick leave in certain circumstances, which went into effect in July 2004). By now, however, it's a nationwide standard. Also, an employer may be legally required to let employees take unpaid leave in certain circumstances. No matter what type of leave program your company decides to adopt, the policies in this chapter will help you set rules that are consistent, sensible, and easy to follow.

10:1   Vacation

CD File: 10_Time Off.rtf

Include This Policy?
☐ Yes
☐ No
☐ Use our existing policy
☐ Other _____

Alternate Modifications
None

Additional Clauses
Cap Accrual of Vacation Time
  Insert?: ☐ Yes ☐ No

Pay Unused Vacation at
Termination
  Insert?: ☐ Yes ☐ No

Related Policies
None

Notes

_____
_____
_____
_____
_____
_____
_____
_____
_____
_____
_____
_____
_____
_____
_____
_____
_____
_____
_____

10:1 Vacation

Most employers offer paid vacation benefits to at least some of their employees, even though they aren't legally required to do so. Paid vacation has become standard business practice in this country—employers who don't offer some paid days off for rest and relaxation will almost certainly have trouble attracting and retaining good employees.

Your vacation policy should explain who is eligible for vacation, how vacation time accrues, and how the employee can schedule time off.

Vacation

Our Company recognizes that our employees need to take time off occasionally, to rest and relax, to enjoy a vacation, or to attend to personal matters. That's why we offer a paid vacation program. _____
_____ employees are eligible to participate in the paid vacation program.

Eligible employees accrue vacation time according to the following schedule [*insert schedule here*]:

Years of Employment	Vacation Accrual
_____	_____
_____	_____
_____	_____
_____	_____
_____	_____
_____	_____
_____	_____
_____	_____
_____	_____

Employees must schedule their vacations in advance, with their supervisor. We will try to grant every employee's vacation request for the days off of their choice. However, we must have enough workers to meet our day-to-day needs—which means we might not be able to grant every vacation request, especially during holiday periods.

How to Complete This Policy

In the first blank space, indicate which employees will be eligible to participate in the vacation program. Some employers limit these benefits to full-time employees or require employees to complete a waiting period before they can accrue or use vacation benefits. For information and policies on these employee classifications, see Chapter 5.

In the second blank, write in the schedule by which employees will accrue benefits. Many employers provide increases in benefits to employees who stay with the company over time. For example, a worker might accrue ten days of vacation during the first year or two of employment, then move up to 15 the next year, then 20. Once you figure out how many days of vacation employees will accrue, divide that number by 12 to figure out how many days of vacation they accrue each month. The sample accrual schedule below allows employees to accrue ten days of vacation during their first and second years of employment, 15 during their third and fourth years, and 20 during each year thereafter.

SAMPLE POLICY LANGUAGE

Years of Employment	Vacation Accrual
0-2	10 days per year, at the rate of $5/6$ of a day per month
2-4	15 days per year, at the rate of $1\frac{1}{4}$ days per month
4 or more	20 days per year, at the rate of $1\frac{2}{3}$ days per month

Additional Clause to Cap Accrual of Vacation Time

Your company can encourage employees to use their vacation regularly—and avoid having employees out for months of collected vacation at a time—by capping how much vacation time employees can accrue. Employees who reach this limit won't earn any more vacation time until they take some vacation and bring themselves back down below the cap. To cap how much vacation time an employee can accrue, add this clause to your policy immediately after the accrual schedule. In the blank space, insert the cap—how many hours or days of vacation time an employee will be allowed to accrue.

Additional Clause

> Employees may not accrue more than _____
> of vacation time. Once an employee's vacation balance reaches
> this limit, an employee may accrue more vacation only by taking
> some vacation time to bring the employee's balance back below
> the limit.

⚠ **"Use it or lose it" policies are illegal in some states.** An employer is legally entitled to cap how much vacation time an employee can accrue. However, some states forbid "use it or lose it" policies, by which an employee would have to forfeit accrued but unused vacation time over a certain limit or past a certain date. Because these states view earned vacation time as a form of compensation, which must be cashed out when the employee quits or is fired, a policy that takes vacation time away is seen as an illegal form of failing to pay employees money that they have already earned. Although the difference may seem merely technical, an accrual cap is legal in these states, because it prohibits the employee from earning vacation time in the first place, rather than taking away vacation time after the employee has earned it. Contact your state labor department to find out about your state's rules. (See Appendix A for contact information.)

Additional Clause to Pay Unused Vacation at Termination

Some states require employers to cash out unused, accrued vacation time when an employee quits or is fired. You can find out your state's rule by checking "State Laws That Control Final Paychecks" at the end of Chapter 21. If your company does business in a state that requires employers to pay unused vacation, you might consider modifying the policy to inform employees that they will receive payment for unused vacation. To do so, simply add the clause below as the final paragraph of the policy.

Additional Clause

> Employees will be paid for any accrued and unused vacation when their employment terminates.

10:2 Holidays

Most companies offer their employees paid time off on certain holidays, such as New Year's Day, Independence Day, and Thanksgiving. Your holiday policy should tell employees what holidays the company observes and what happens when a holiday falls on a weekend.

Holidays

Our Company observes the following holidays each year [*list*]:

_____

_____

_____

_____

_____

_____

_____

_____

_____

_____

_____

_____

If a holiday falls on a weekend, the Company will inform you when the holiday will be observed. Ordinarily, holidays falling on a Saturday will be observed the preceding Friday; holidays falling on a Sunday will be observed the following Monday.

How to Complete This Policy

In the blank space, list the holidays that your company observes. The days you choose will, of course, depend on when your company is open. Most employers offer some combination of the following paid holidays: New Year's Day, Martin Luther King Jr. Day, President's Day, Good Friday, Memorial Day, Independence Day, Labor Day, Columbus Day, Veterans' Day, Thanksgiving, the Friday following Thanksgiving, Christmas Eve, Christmas Day, and New Year's Eve.

10:2   Holidays

CD File: 10_Time Off.rtf

Include This Policy?
- ☐ Yes
- ☐ No
- ☐ Use our existing policy
- ☐ Other _____

Alternate Modifications
None

Additional Clauses
Allow Floating Holidays
Insert?:   ☐ Yes   ☐ No

Related Policies
None

Notes

_____

_____

_____

_____

_____

_____

_____

_____

_____

_____

_____

_____

_____

_____

_____

_____

Additional Clause to Allow Floating Holidays

Some employees may not observe the religious holidays your company chooses to offer—for example, Christmas or Good Friday—and may wish to take a holiday on a day of significance to their own religion. Employers are legally obligated to accommodate their workers' religious observations, which in some cases may require an employer to give these workers time off for important religious holidays. Rather than requiring workers to come to management with these requests, your company can make floating holidays available to all workers, to allow them to participate in religious activities or attend to other personal matters.

Some employers offer only one or two floating holidays per year; others offer more floating holidays but trim the list of company-recognized holidays accordingly. If your company will offer floating holidays, add the clause below as the second paragraph of the policy, immediately after the list of holidays your company observes. In the blank, insert the number of floating holidays employees will be allowed to take each year.

Additional Clause

Eligible employees are also entitled to take _____ floating holidays each year. These holidays may be used to observe a religious holiday, to celebrate your birthday, or simply to take a day off for personal reasons. You must schedule your floating holidays with your supervisor in advance. If you do not use your floating holidays during the year, you may not carry them over to the next year.

10:3 Sick Leave

Although employers are not legally required to provide paid sick days, it's common practice to do so. There are sound reasons to offer paid days off for workers who are ill: Paid sick days help workers who live paycheck to paycheck make ends meet, create fewer payroll hassles, and, perhaps most important, encourage sick workers to stay home rather than coming to work to infect the rest of the workforce or perform at a substandard level.

Your sick leave policy should explain who is eligible for leave, how much leave employees can take, and any notice requirements the company will impose.

Sick Leave

Our Company provides paid sick days to _____. (For information on employee classifications, see Section _____ of this Handbook.) Eligible employees accrue _____ sick days per year at the rate of _____ per month. The Company will not pay employees for sick days that have accrued but have not been used when employment ends.

Employees may use sick leave when they are unable to work due to illness or injury. Sick leave is not to be used as extra vacation time, personal days, or "mental health" days. Any employee who abuses sick leave may be subject to discipline.

You must report to your supervisor if you will need to take sick leave. We ask that employees call in as soon as they realize that they will be unable to work, before the regular start of their work day. You must report to your supervisor by phone each day you are out on leave.

How to Complete This Policy

In the first blank, indicate who is eligible for paid sick leave. Some employers provide sick days only to certain employees—for example, only full-time employees, only full-time employees and part-time employees who work at least a minimum number of hours per week, or only employees who have been employed for at least a certain period of time. See Chapter 5 for more information and policies on these employee classifications.

In the second and third blanks, indicate the rate at which sick leave will accrue. For example, many employers provide that employees will accrue 12 paid sick days per year, at a rate of one per month. Others allow employees to accrue six or ten sick days per year, at a rate of the appropriate fraction of a day per month.

10:3   Sick Leave

CD File: 10_Time Off.rtf

Include This Policy?
☐ Yes
☐ No
☐ Use our existing policy
☐ Other _____

Alternate Modifications
None

Additional Clauses
Prohibit Carry Over or Cap Accrual of Sick Leave
Insert?: ☐ Yes   ☐ No
If yes, choose one: ☐ A   ☐ B

Allow Other Uses for Sick Leave
Insert?: ☐ Yes   ☐ No

Related Policies
None

Notes
_____
_____
_____
_____
_____
_____
_____
_____
_____
_____
_____
_____
_____
_____
_____
_____

Additional Clause to Prohibit Carry Over or Cap Accrual of Sick Leave

The policy above is silent on the issue of carry over—whether employees can simply keep accruing unused sick leave month after month, year after year. However, many employers either set a cap on how much sick leave an employee can accrue or don't allow employees to carry over sick leave from one year to the next at all. The problem with a flat "no carry over" policy is that an employee might get sick at the beginning of the year, before enough sick leave hours have accrued to cover the absence. And policies that zero out sick leave at the end of the year tend to encourage employees to take that leave before it disappears, whether they're sick or not—resulting in numerous cases of the "holiday flu."

In general, the better approach is simply to cap how many hours or days of sick leave an employee can accrue—for example, once an employee has 24 unused sick days, that employee accrues no more sick leave until some of the accrued time is used.

To prohibit carry over of sick leave from year to year, use Additional Clause A, below. To limit sick leave accrual, use Additional Clause B, instead. In the blank space, insert the cap—the maximum number of sick days or hours that an employee may accrue. In either case, insert the additional clause at the end of the policy.

Additional Clause A: Prohibit Carry Over of Sick Leave

Employees may not carry over unused sick leave from one year to the next.

Additional Clause B: Cap Accrual of Sick Leave

Employees may accrue a maximum of _____ of sick leave. Once an employee has reached this limit, no more sick leave will accrue until the employee uses sick leave to reduce the accrued total below the maximum.

Additional Clause to Allow Other Uses for Sick Leave

Our policy indicates that employees can use sick leave when they are too injured or ill to work. However, many employers make sick leave available for other purposes—for example, to go to appointments with a doctor or dentist, to care for a sick family member, or to take a family member for medical care. And some state laws require employers to make sick leave available for particular purposes—usually, to care for a sick family member. These laws are summarized in "State Family and Medical Leave Laws" at the end of this chapter.

If your state requires employers to make sick leave available for additional purposes, or if your company wants to allow employees to use sick leave for additional reasons, add this clause immediately after the first sentence in the second paragraph of our sample policy. In the blank, indicate the additional uses of sick leave the company offers (for example, "care for a sick family member" or "attend necessary medical and dental appointments").

Additional Clause

Employees may also use sick leave to _____
_____
_____
_____
_____
_____
_____
_____
_____
_____ .

10:4 Paid Time Off

CD File: 10_Time Off.rtf

Include This Policy?
☐ Yes
☐ No
☐ Use our existing policy
☐ Other _____

Alternate Modifications
None

Additional Clauses
Cap Accrual of PTO
Insert?: ☐ Yes ☐ No

Pay Unused PTO at Termination
Insert?: ☐ Yes ☐ No

Related Policies
None

Notes

_____
_____
_____
_____
_____
_____
_____
_____
_____
_____
_____
_____
_____
_____
_____
_____
_____

10:4 Paid Time Off

Rather than adopting separate policies on vacation, sick leave, float-ing holidays, or other types of leave, many employers now adopt a single policy to give employees a certain number of paid days off per year, which the employees can use as they wish. Using a unified paid time off ("PTO") policy can benefit your company by reducing paperwork and record-keeping hassles and reducing the oversight management needs to exercise over employees, particularly regarding their use of sick leave. Because employees are entitled to take PTO for any reason, no one will have to make sure they are really sick—and they won't feel compelled to prove it ("(cough), I really caught a bad cold (sniffle)").

However, adopting a unified PTO policy can have significant drawbacks in some states. Because PTO is legally considered vacation time and sick leave, any state laws that regulate these issues apply to an employee's entire allotment of PTO. For example, some states require employers to pay an employee for accrued, unused vacation time when the employee quits or is fired—an em-ployer that has a PTO policy will have to pay out the entire unused allotment of PTO. If your company does business in one of these states, management should think twice—and perhaps consult with a lawyer—before adopting a PTO policy.

If your company adopts a PTO policy, remember that the policy takes the place of vacation, sick leave, and floating holiday policies—you should adopt one or the other, not both. Your PTO policy should explain which employees are eligible for PTO, how many days of PTO will be granted per year, and any procedures employees must follow to take PTO.

Paid Time Off

Instead of offering separate vacation, sick leave, and personal days or floating holidays, _____

_____ [*Company name*] offers a paid time off ("PTO") program that combines all of these benefits. We believe this program will give employees the flexibility to manage their time off as they see fit. Employees may use PTO for sickness, for vacation, to attend a child's school activities, to care for elderly or ill family members, to take care of personal errands or business, or simply to take a day off work.

You are eligible to participate in the PTO program if you

_____. (For information on employee classifications, see Section _____ of this Handbook.)

PTO accrues according to the following schedule:

Years of Employment	PTO Accrual
_____	_____
_____	_____
_____	_____
_____	_____
_____	_____
_____	_____
_____	_____
_____	_____

Employees must schedule time off in advance with their supervisors. We will try to grant every employee's PTO request for the days off they choose. However, we must have enough workers to meet our day-to-day needs—which means we might not be able to grant every PTO request, especially during holiday periods.

If circumstances, such as a medical or family emergency, prevent advance scheduling, you must inform your supervisor as soon as possible that you are taking paid time off.

Because PTO encompasses vacation and sick leave, employees must manage their PTO responsibly to ensure that they have time available for emergencies, such as personal or family illness. An employee who needs time off but has no accrued PTO may be eligible to take unpaid leave. The company will decide these requests on a case-by-case basis.

How to Complete This Policy

In the first blank, indicate which employees will be eligible to participate in the PTO program. Some employers limit these benefits to full-time employees or full-time employees and part-time employees who work a minimum number of hours per week, or institute a waiting period before employees may accrue or use benefits. For information and policies on these employee classifications, see Chapter 5.

In the second blank, write in the schedule by which employees will accrue benefits. Many employers provide higher benefits to employees who have been with the company longer. For example, a worker might accrue 20 days of PTO during the first year or two of employment, then move up to 25, then 30. Once you figure out how many days of PTO employees will accrue, divide that number by 12 to figure out how many days of PTO employees accrue each month. The sample accrual schedule below allows employees to accrue 20 days of PTO during their first year of employment, 25 during their second year, and 30 during each year thereafter

SAMPLE POLICY LANGUAGE

Years of Employment	PTO Accrual
0-1	20 days per year, at the rate of $1^2/_3$ days per month
1-2	25 days per year, at the rate of $2^1/_{12}$ days per month
2 or more	30 days per year, at the rate of $2^1/_2$ days per month

Additional Clause to Cap Accrual of PTO

Some employers place an upper limit on the amount of PTO an employee can accrue. An employee who reaches this limit does not accrue any more PTO until he or she takes some time off. Imposing this type of cap can prevent employees from going months, or even years, without taking enough time off to prevent burnout. It can also help the company guard against having an employee gone for months at a time. If you wish to place a cap on PTO accrual, add this clause to the policy. In the blank, insert the maximum number of PTO days or hours an employee can accrue.

Additional Clause

Employees may not accrue more than _____
of PTO. Once an employee's PTO balance reaches this limit, an
employee may accrue more PTO only by taking some PTO to
bring the employee's balance back below the limit.

Additional Clause to Pay Unused PTO at Termination

In those states that require employers to cash out unused accrued
vacation time when an employee quits or is fired (see Policy 10:1,
above), employers will generally have to pay an employee for unused, accrued PTO on termination. If your company does business
in one of these states, consider modifying the policy to inform
employees that they will receive payment for unused PTO. To do
so, simply add the clause below as the final paragraph of the policy.

If your state requires employers to cash out vacation pay,
you might be better off with separate policies on vacation,
sick leave, and floating holidays. Talk to a local lawyer who knows
about your state's employment laws to determine the best choice
for your company.

Additional Clause

Employees will be paid for any accrued and unused PTO
when their employment ends.

10:5 Family and Medical Leave
CD File: 10_Time Off.rtf

Include This Policy?
☐ Yes
   Choose one: ☐ A ☐ B
☐ No
☐ Use our existing policy
☐ Other _____

Alternate Modifications
None

Additional Clauses
Policy A only: Continue Health
Insurance
   Insert?: ☐ Yes ☐ No

Related Policies
None

Notes

_____
_____
_____
_____
_____
_____
_____
_____
_____
_____
_____
_____
_____
_____
_____
_____
_____
_____
_____

10:5 Family and Medical Leave

Working people have always had a tough time balancing the demands of a job with personal and family needs. Today, with large numbers of women in the workforce and many workers having to care for young children and aging parents, the stresses created by this juggling act have become more acute than ever.

In response to this problem, Congress passed the Family and Medical Leave Act ("FMLA"), a federal law that requires employers who have at least 50 employees to allow eligible workers to take up to 12 weeks of unpaid leave per year in the following circumstances:

- for the arrival of a new child—through birth, adoption, or foster care
- to care for a family member who is suffering from a serious health condition, or
- when the employee suffers from a serious health condition that makes it impossible to work.

Many states have passed laws similar to the FMLA—and some of these laws apply to employers with fewer than 50 employees. Some state laws require employers to provide leave for a wider variety of circumstances than the FMLA—for example, to attend school activities relating to an employee's child, to take a child or parent to necessary medical and dental appointments, or to donate bone marrow. And some of these laws provide for more than 12 weeks of leave per year. You can find information on these laws in "State Family and Medical Leave Laws" at the end of this chapter.

A company that does business in a state that has a family and medical leave law must follow whichever law it is covered by (based on its number of employees) that gives its employees more rights and protections in a given situation—either the state law, the FMLA, or both. Because of these potential overlaps between federal and state law, an employer might find itself in one of four situations, any of which may require it to have a different family and medical leave policy:

1. The employer has fewer than 50 employees and either does not do business in a state with a family and medical leave law or does not have to comply with the state's law because the employer is too small. These employers are free to offer family and medical leave but are not legally required to do so.

2. The employer has fewer than 50 employees and does business in a state with a family and medical leave law that applies to it. These employers must comply with their state's law but not with the FMLA.

3. The employer has at least 50 employees but does not do business in a state with a family and medical leave law. These employers comply with the FMLA only.

4. The employer has at least 50 employees and does business in a state with a family and medical leave law. These employers must comply with both the FMLA and their state's law.

Because of the intricacies of state family and medical leave laws—and the sometimes complicated ways they interact with the FMLA—we cannot address the needs of employers who find themselves in groups 2 or 4 here. If the chart at the end of this chapter indicates that your company has to follow a state family and medical leave law, either alone or in conjunction with the FMLA, consult a lawyer who can help you work out a family and medical leave policy that meets your state's requirements.

We offer two alternate policies below. The first is for employers who have to comply with the FMLA only (group 3). The second is for smaller employers—those who, because they have fewer than 50 employees, do not have to comply with the FMLA (group 1)—who wish to adopt a family and medical leave policy.

Alternate Policy A: For Employers Who Must Comply With the FMLA Only

Family and Medical Leave

Employees who have worked for our Company for at least a full year, and have worked an average of at least 25 hours per week during that time, are eligible to take unpaid family and medical leave for one or more of these purposes:

- because the employee's own serious health condition makes the employee unable to work
- to care for a spouse, child, or parent who has a serious health condition, or
- to care for a newborn, newly adopted child, or recently placed foster child.

Leave Available

Eligible employees may take up to 12 weeks of unpaid leave per calendar year for any of the above purposes. For purposes of calculating available family and medical leave, the year starts on

_____ .

A parent who takes leave to care for a newborn, newly adopted child, or recently placed foster child must begin this leave within a year after the birth, adoption, or placement.

Notice Requirements

Employees are required to give notice at least 30 days in advance of their need for a family and medical leave, if their need for leave is foreseeable. In emergencies and unexpected situations, employees must give as much notice as is practicable under the circumstances.

Reinstatement Rights

When you return from an approved family and medical leave, you have the right to return to your former position or an equivalent position, except:

- You have no greater right to reinstatement than you would have had if you had not been on leave. If your position is eliminated for reasons unrelated to your leave, for example, you have no right to reinstatement.
- The Company is not obligated to reinstate you if you are a key employee—that is, you are among the highest-paid 10% of our workforce and holding your job open during your leave would cause the Company substantial economic harm. If the Company classifies you as a key employee under this definition, you will be notified when you request leave.

Substitution of Paid Leave

An employee who has accrued paid time off _____ [*"must" or "may"*] use these benefits to receive pay for all or a portion of family and medical leave.

Medical Certification

The Company may ask employees who take leave for their own serious health condition or to care for a spouse, parent, or child with a serious health condition to provide a doctor's form certifying the need for leave. The Company is also entitled to seek a second opinion and periodic recertifications. In some cases, the Company may ask employees who take leave because of their own serious health condition to provide a fitness-for-duty report from their doctors before they return to work.

Intermittent Leave

If you will need to take family and medical leave on an intermittent basis—that is, a day or two at a time rather than all at once—for your own serious health condition or to take care of a family member with a serious health condition, you will be allowed to do so. However, the Company may temporarily reassign you to a different position with equivalent pay and benefits to accommodate the intermittent schedule.

The Company will consider requests for intermittent leave to care for a new child on a case-by-case basis.

How to Complete This Policy

The FMLA allows eligible employees to take up to 12 weeks of unpaid leave per 12-month period. In the blank space, indicate what method your company will use to measure this 12-month period. There are four methods from which you can choose, using either:

- the calendar year (insert January 1)
- a fiscal year or a year that starts on an employee's anniversary date (insert the date your fiscal year begins or the date when the employee started work)
- a year that begins on the date the employee first takes FMLA leave (insert the date an employee first takes FMLA leave), or
- a year measured backward from the date the employee uses any FMLA leave (insert one year before an employee uses any FMLA leave).

In the second blank, insert either "may" or "must." The FMLA allows employers to require employees to use paid time off—such as vacation leave or personal days—during any FMLA leave, and also paid sick days during an FMLA leave for the employee's own serious health condition. This prevents employees from taking 12 weeks of unpaid leave and then tacking on available vacation or sick days. If you choose this option, insert "must." Even if an employer does not require employees to use paid time off, the FMLA always gives employees this option—so if your company doesn't require your employees to use paid time off, insert "may."

Additional Clause to Continue Health Insurance (Policy A Only)

The FMLA requires employers who provide a health insurance benefit to continue that benefit while employees are on leave. Employers must continue to pay whatever portion of the premium the employer would pay if the employee were not on leave. However, if the employee does not return from leave, the employer can require the employee to pay back the employer—unless the employee doesn't return for reasons beyond the employee's control (for example, a serious health condition that does not improve sufficiently to allow the employee to return to the job).

If your company offers health insurance, add the following clause to the policy, immediately after the "Substitution of Paid Leave" section.

Additional Clause

Health Insurance During Leave

Your health insurance benefits will continue during leave. You will be responsible for paying any portion of the premium that you ordinarily pay while you are working, and you must make arrangements to make these payments while you are out. Employees who do not return from family and medical leave may be required to reimburse the Company for any premiums paid on the employee's behalf during the leave.

Alternate Policy B: For Employers Who Don't Have to Comply With the FMLA

Family and Medical Leave

Because of our small size, our Company is not required to comply with the federal Family and Medical Leave Act (FMLA). However, we recognize that our employees may occasionally need to take unpaid leave to care for a new child, to care for a seriously ill family member, or to handle an employee's own medical issues.

If you anticipate that you might need time off to deal with family and medical issues, please talk to your supervisor. We can't guarantee that we'll grant every request, but we will seriously consider every request on a case-by-case basis. Among other things, we may consider our staffing needs, your position at the Company, the reason why you need leave, and how long you expect your leave to last.

For more information on the FMLA, see *Federal Employment Laws: A Desk Reference*, by Amy DelPo and Lisa Guerin (Nolo). You can find fact sheets, compliance assistance, and a workplace poster (which all employers covered by the FMLA are required to display) on the website of the U.S. Department of Labor, www.dol.gov. For detailed charts comparing the FMLA to state leave laws, go to www.dol.gov/esa/programs/whd/state/fmla and click on one of the states listed.

10:6 Bereavement Leave

Many employers offer their employees a few days off when a family member dies. These policies recognize that an employee who has experienced the death of a loved one will likely have both practical and personal issues that require attention. No law requires employers to offer bereavement leave, and some employers choose to let their employees take sick or vacation leave for this purpose. By offering bereavement leave, however, an employer communicates sensitivity and concern for its employees' well-being.

Your bereavement policy should explain who is eligible for leave, how many days of leave will be granted, and whether the leave will be paid or unpaid.

Bereavement Leave

If you suffer the death of an immediate family member, you are entitled to take up to _____ days off work. This leave will be _____ [*paid or unpaid*].

Immediate family members include _____

_____

_____

_____

_____ .

The Company will consider, on a case-by-case basis, requests for bereavement leave for the death of someone who does not qualify as an immediate family member under this policy.

How to Complete This Policy

In the first blank, insert the number of days employees can take off for bereavement leave. Many employers offer three days, although your company may choose to offer more or fewer.

In the second blank, indicate whether bereavement leave will be paid or unpaid.

In the third blank, list those who qualify as immediate family members. Some employers limit bereavement leave, particularly if it is paid, to parents, children, siblings, and spouses. A number of employers also make bereavement leave available to those who have lost their domestic partners, grandparents, aunts, uncles, or in-laws. You can also include any family member who lives with the employee.

10:6   Bereavement Leave

CD File: 10_Time Off.rtf

Include This Policy?
☐ Yes
☐ No
☐ Use our existing policy
☐ Other _____

Alternate Modifications
None

Additional Clauses
None

Related Policies
None

Notes

_____

_____

_____

_____

_____

_____

_____

_____

_____

_____

_____

_____

_____

_____

_____

_____

_____

_____

_____

_____

10:7   Military Leave

CD File: 10_Time Off.rtf

Include This Policy?
☐ Yes
☐ No
☐ Use our existing policy
☐ Other _____

Alternate Modifications
None

Additional Clauses
Paid Time Off
Insert?: ☐ Yes   ☐ No

Health Benefits
Insert?: ☐ Yes   ☐ No

Related Policies
None

Notes
_____
_____
_____
_____
_____
_____
_____
_____
_____
_____
_____
_____
_____
_____
_____
_____
_____
_____
_____

10:7 Military Leave

The federal Uniformed Services Employment and Reemployment Rights Act of 1994 ("USERRA") requires all employers, regardless of size, to reinstate employees who take time off work to serve in the U.S. armed forces. USERRA protects employees who give proper notice before taking leave, spend no more than five years on leave, are released or discharged from service under honorable conditions, and report back or apply for reinstatement within specified time limits (which depend on the length of the employee's service). When employees return from military leave, the employer must reinstate them to the same position they would have held had they been continuously employed throughout their leave, as long as they are otherwise qualified for the job—including any pay raises, promotions, or additional job responsibilities they would have received had they never taken a leave.

Almost every state has a law prohibiting discrimination against those in the state's militia or National Guard, and many of these laws also require employers to grant leave for certain types of military service. These state laws are summarized in "State Laws on Military Leave" at the end of this chapter.

Your policy on military leave should include an explanation of eligibility and notice requirements and a description of employees' reinstatement rights when their military service ends.

Military Leave

Our Company supports those who serve in the armed forces to protect our country. In keeping with this commitment, and in accordance with state and federal law, employees who must be absent from work for military service are entitled to take a military leave of absence. This leave will be _____ [*paid or unpaid*].

When an employee's military leave ends, that employee will be reinstated to the position he or she formerly held, or to a comparable position, as long as the employee meets the requirements of federal and state law.

Employees who are called to military service must tell their supervisors as soon as possible that they will need to take military leave. An employee whose military service has ended must return to work or inform the Company that he or she wants to be reinstated in accordance with these guidelines:

- For a leave of 30 or fewer days, the employee must report back to work on the first regularly scheduled workday after completing military service, allowing for travel time.
- For a leave of 31 to 180 days, the employee must request reinstatement within 14 days after military service ends.
- For a leave of 181 days or more, the employee must request reinstatement within 90 days after military service ends.

How to Complete This Policy

In the blank, indicate whether military leave will be paid or unpaid. USERRA requires employers to offer only unpaid leave; however, employers are free to offer paid leave if they wish. Because some military commitments can be lengthy, many employers who offer paid leave do so only for a limited number of days—two or three weeks, for example. If your company will offer a limited amount of paid leave, insert "paid for _____ days and unpaid after that," replacing the blank with the number of days for which you will provide pay.

Additional Clause for Employers Who Offer Paid Time Off

If your company, like most employers, offers any type of paid time off—such as vacation and/or personal days—you should modify this policy to allow employees to use this paid time during their military leaves, unless your company has chosen to pay employees for all military leaves. If your company offers paid time off and has decided that military leave will be unpaid or paid only for a limited number of days, add this sentence to the end of the first paragraph.

Additional Clause

> During this unpaid leave, employees are entitled to use applicable paid time off (vacation time or personal days).

Additional Clause for Employers Who Offer Health Benefits

If your company makes health insurance available to employees as a benefit (see Chapter 8), you should modify this policy to inform workers of the circumstances in which these benefits will continue during their military leave. USERRA requires employers to continue to offer health insurance to employees on leave for military service. Employees who return to work after an absence of 30 or fewer days are entitled to insurance continuation at the same cost, if any, paid by employees not on leave. Employees who are absent for more than 30 days must be offered the chance to continue their coverage, but they can be required to pay the full premium. If your company offers health insurance, modify the policy by adding the following clause to the end of the second paragraph.

Additional Clause

> The Company will continue your health insurance benefits during your leave, under these circumstances:
> - If you are absent for 30 or fewer days, you will be treated as any employee not on leave. The Company will continue to pay its share of the insurance premium, and you must continue to pay your usual share.
> - If your leave lasts longer than 30 days, you will have to pay the entire premium to continue your benefits.

For more information on USERRA and military leave, see *Federal Employment Laws: A Desk Reference*, by Amy DelPo and Lisa Guerin (Nolo). You'll also find lots of helpful materials at the Department of Labor's website (www.dol.gov) and at the website of the National Committee of Employer Support for the Guard and Reserve (www.esgr.org).

10:8 Time Off to Vote

The laws of almost every state take the responsibilities of citizenship very seriously. Most states prohibit employers from firing or disciplining employees for taking some time off work to cast their ballots, especially if their work schedules or commute make it difficult to vote outside of work hours. Some states require employers to pay employees for this time, and some states allow employers to require advanced notice or proof that the employee voted. These state laws are summarized in "State Laws on Taking Time Off to Vote" at the end of this chapter.

Your policy on voting leave should state how many hours employees can take off to vote, state whether employees will be paid for these hours, and describe any notice or other requirements employees must meet to qualify for voting leave.

Voting

Our Company encourages employees to exercise their right to vote. If your work schedule and the location of your polling place will make it difficult for you to get to the polls before they close, you are entitled to take up to _____ hours off work, at the beginning or end of your shift, to cast your ballot. This time will be_____ [*paid or unpaid*].

Employees who will need to take time off work to vote must inform their supervisors at least _____ day(s) in advance. Employees are expected to work with their supervisors to ensure that their absence doesn't negatively impact Company operations.

How to Complete This Policy

There are three spaces for you to fill in, based on your state's legal requirements and your company's preferences. In the first space, insert the number of hours employees can take off work in order to vote. Consult the chart at the end of this chapter to find out what your state requires; most states that mandate time off to vote require employers to provide two hours, although a few require more. If your state doesn't impose a requirement, your company can decide how many hours to allow.

In the second space, indicate whether this time off will be paid or unpaid. As you can see from the chart, some states require paid leave. If your company does business in one of these states, insert "paid" in the blank. If your state does not require employers to pay

---

10:8   Voting

CD File: 10_Time Off.rtf

Include This Policy?
- ☐ Yes
- ☐ No
- ☐ Use our existing policy
- ☐ Other _____

Alternate Modifications
None

Additional Clauses
Require Proof of Voting
Insert?:   ☐ Yes   ☐ No

Related Policies
None

Notes

_____

_____

_____

_____

_____

_____

_____

_____

_____

_____

_____

_____

_____

_____

_____

_____

_____

_____

employees for the time they take off work to vote, the company can choose either.

In the final space, insert the number of days' notice employees will have to give before taking time off to vote. The chart indicates whether your state requires employees to give notice. If your company does business in a state with a notice requirement, simply insert the number of days your state mandates (some states require only one day's notice). If your state has no rules about notice, your company can decide for itself how much notice to require, if any.

Additional Clause to Require Proof of Voting

A few states, including Hawaii and Maryland, allow employers to require employees to supply proof that they actually voted in order to claim leave time. If your company does business in one of these states, you can modify our policy to require such proof.

Your state may require employees to supply a certain type of proof—for example, a receipt or a state elections form. The sample addition, below, gives supervisors the authority to tell employees what types of proof are acceptable.

To inform employees of this proof requirement, simply add the following clause to the end of the policy.

Additional Clause

Employees who take time off to vote must supply their supervisor with proof that they actually voted. Your supervisor can tell you what types of proof of voting are acceptable.

10:9 Jury Duty

Almost every state prohibits employers from firing or disciplining employees for jury service. Generally, employers must allow employees to take time off for this purpose—and some states require employers to provide at least some pay for this time off. Check "State Laws on Jury Duty" at the end of this chapter to find out what your state requires.

Your policy on jury duty should let employees know whether jury service will be paid or unpaid, explain any notice requirements for employees called to jury duty, and clearly state that employees will not face discipline or retaliation for serving on a jury.

Jury Duty

If you are called for jury duty, you are entitled to take time off, as necessary, to fulfill your jury obligations. This leave will be _____ [*paid or unpaid*]. No employee will face discipline or retaliation for jury service.

You must immediately inform your supervisor when you receive your jury duty summons. If you are chosen to sit on a jury, you must inform your supervisor how long the trial is expected to last. You must also check in with your supervisor periodically during your jury service, so the Company knows when to expect you back at work.

How to Complete This Policy

In the blank, indicate whether leave to serve on a jury will be paid or unpaid. (Check "State Laws on Jury Duty" to find out whether your state requires paid leave for any employees.) Even if your state doesn't require paid leave, employers are free to provide it.

You will see that some states require paid leave only for full-time employees. If your company does business in one of these states, you can limit the policy accordingly by filling in the blank as follows: "paid for full-time employees only; part-time employees will not be paid for time taken off for jury service." If your state requires employers to pay only a certain number of days of jury duty leave, you can modify your policy to reflect this limit by using the Additional Clause to Limit Number of Paid Days of Leave, below.

10:9   Jury Duty

CD File: 10_Time Off.rtf

Include This Policy?
☐ Yes
☐ No
☐ Use our existing policy
☐ Other _____

Alternate Modifications
None

Additional Clauses
Limit Number of Paid Days of Leave
   Insert?:   ☐ Yes   ☐ No
Require Employees to Report Back to Work
   Insert?:   ☐ Yes   ☐ No

Related Policies
None

Notes

_____
_____
_____
_____
_____
_____
_____
_____
_____
_____
_____
_____
_____
_____
_____
_____
_____
_____

Additional Clause to Limit Number of Paid Days of Leave

Some states that require paid leave for jury duty allow employers to pay for only a certain number of days off. If your company does business in one of these states, or if your company offers paid leave even though your state law doesn't require it, you may want to limit how much paid leave an employee can take. If so, add the following sentence immediately after the second sentence of the standard policy. In the blank, indicate how many days of paid leave your company will offer.

Additional Clause

> You will be paid for up to _____ days of jury service; if your service extends beyond this period, the remainder of your leave will be unpaid.

Reality Check: Juror Fees Don't Pay the Bills

Many states pay jurors a fixed amount per day for serving on a jury. However, these stipends are usually meager—in some states, employees probably give their children a larger allowance than the court will pay for serving on a jury. In light of this sad state of affairs, many employers voluntarily take on the responsibility of paying their employees for time spent on jury duty.

But what if an employee gets called for the next "trial of the century" and is out of work for months? That's where the modification to limit how much paid leave the company will provide comes in. If your company chooses to compensate employees for jury duty, you can use this modification to put some outside limit on the obligation. Employers commonly adopt a policy limiting paid jury duty leave to ten to 20 workdays per year.

Additional Clause to Require Employees to Report Back to Work

Some employers require employees to call in on any day when jury service ends before the end of the workday, so that the employee can be asked to report back to work for the remainder of the day, if desired. To impose this requirement, add the sentence below to the end of the standard policy. If your company offers unpaid leave for jury duty, remember that employees are entitled to be paid for any time they actually spend working.

Additional Clause

On any day when your jury service ends before the end of your usual work day, you must check in with your supervisor to find out whether you need to return to work for that day.

State Family and Medical Leave Laws

This chart covers the basic aspects of state family and medical leave laws. Federal FMLA applies to all covered employers in every state. However, an employer must follow the state or federal laws that provide the most protection for employees.

We don't address every aspect of these laws (such as notice requirements, medical certifications, or reinstatement rules). For more information, contact your state's department of labor and be sure to check its website, where most states have posted their family leave rules. (See Appendix A for contact details.)

States that are not listed below do not have laws that apply to private employers or have laws that offer less protection than the FMLA.

California

Cal. Gov't. Code § 12945; Cal. Lab. Code §§ 230 and following; Cal. Unemp. Ins. §§ 3300 and following

Employers Covered: Employers with 5 or more employees must offer pregnancy leave; employers with 25 or more employees must offer leave for victims of domestic violence or sexual assault and school activity leave; employers with 50 or more employees must offer leave for domestic partners; employers whose employees contribute to state temporary disability insurance ("SDI") fund must allow employees to participate in state's paid family leave benefits program.

Eligible Employees: All employees for pregnancy leave, domestic violence, or school activity leave; employees eligible for leave under federal FMLA for domestic partners leave; employees who contribute to SDI fund for paid family leave benefits program.

Family Medical Leave: Up to 4 months for disability related to pregnancy (in addition to 12 weeks under state or federal FML if the employee is eligible). Up to 12 weeks of leave per year to care for seriously ill registered domestic partner. Employees who contribute to SDI fund may receive paid family leave benefits for up to 6 weeks of leave per year to care for a seriously ill family member (including a registered domestic partner) or bond with a new child. This leave is paid through employee contributions to the SDI fund; the employee will receive approximately 55% of regular earnings. Does not provide job protection unless the employee is otherwise covered by the state or federal FML.

School Activities: 40 hours per year.

Domestic Violence: Reasonable time for issues dealing with domestic violence or sexual assault, including health, counseling, and safety measures. Family member or domestic partner of a victim of a felony may take leave to attend judicial proceedings related to the crime.

Colorado

Colo. Rev. Stat. § 19-5-211, 24-34-402.7

Employers Covered: All employers who offer leave for birth of a child for adoption leave; employers with 50 or more employees for domestic violence leave.

Eligible Employees: All employees for adoption leave; employees with one year of service for domestic violence leave.

Family Medical Leave: Employee must be given same leave for adoption as allowed for childbirth (doesn't apply to stepparent adoption).

Domestic Violence: Up to 3 days leave to seek restraining order, obtain medical care or counseling, relocate, or seek legal assistance for victim of domestic violence, sexual assault, or stalking.

Connecticut

Conn. Gen. Stat. Ann. §§ 31-51kk to 31-51qq, 46a-51(10), 46a-60(7)

Employers Covered: Employers with 75 employees must offer childbirth, adoption, and serious health condition leave; with 3 employees, must offer maternity disability.

Eligible Employees: Any employee with one year and at least 1,000 hours of service in last 12 months.

Family Medical Leave: 16 weeks per any 24-month period for childbirth, adoption, employee's serious health condition, care for family member with serious health condition, or bone marrow or organ donation. "Reasonable" amount of maternity disability leave. May also use up to 2 weeks accumulated sick leave.

Family Member: Includes parents-in-law.

District of Columbia

D.C. Code Ann. §§ 32-501 and following, 32-1202

Employers Covered: Employers with at least 20 employees.

Eligible Employees: Employees who have worked at company for at least one year and at least 1,000 hours during the previous 12 months.

Family Medical Leave: 16 weeks per any 24-month period for childbirth, adoption, pregnancy/maternity, employee's serious health condition, or care for family

State Family and Medical Leave Laws (continued)

member with serious health condition.

School Activities: Up to 24 hours of leave per year.

Family Member: Includes anyone related by blood, custody, or marriage; anyone sharing employee's residence and with whom employee has a committed relationship (including a child for whom the employee assumes permanent parental responsibility).

Hawaii

Haw. Rev. Stat. §§ 398-1 to 398-11, 378-1, 378-71 to 378-74

Employers Covered: Employers with at least 100 employees must offer childbirth, adoption, and serious health condition leave; all employers must offer pregnancy leave and domestic violence leave.

Eligible Employees: Employees with 6 months of service are eligible for childbirth, adoption, and serious health condition benefits; all employees are eligible for pregnancy and maternity leave.

Family Medical Leave: 4 weeks per calendar year for childbirth, adoption, or care for family member with serious health condition; "reasonable period" of pregnancy/maternity leave required by discrimination statute and case law; may include up to 10 days accrued leave or sick leave.

Family Member: Includes reciprocal beneficiary, parents-in-law, grandparents, grandparents-in-law, stepparents.

Domestic Violence: Employer with 50 or more employees must allow up to 30 days unpaid leave per year for employee who is a victim of domestic or sexual violence or if employee's minor child is a victim. Employer with 49 or fewer employees must allow up to 5 days leave.

Illinois

820 Ill. Comp. Stat. §§ 147/1 and following, 180/1 and following

Employers Covered: Employers with 50 or more employees.

Eligible Employees: Employees who have worked at least half-time for 6 months.

School Activities: 8 hours per year (no more than 4 hours per day); required only if employee has no paid leave available.

Domestic Violence: Up to 12 weeks unpaid leave per 12-month period for employee who is a victim of domestic violence or sexual assault, or for employee with a family or household member who is a victim.

Iowa

Iowa Code § 216.6

Employers Covered: Employers with 4 or more employees.

Eligible Employees: All.

Family Medical Leave: Up to 8 weeks for disability due to pregnancy, childbirth, or legal abortion.

Kentucky

Ky. Rev. Stat. Ann. § 337.015

Employers Covered: All.

Eligible Employees: All.

Family Medical Leave: Up to 6 weeks for adoption of a child under 7 years old.

Louisiana

La. Rev. Stat. Ann. §§ 23:341 to 23:342, 23:1015 and following, 40:1299.124

Employers Covered: Employers with more than 25 employees must offer pregnancy/maternity leave; with at least 20 employees must comply with bone marrow donation provisions; all employers must offer leave for school activities.

Eligible Employees: All employees are eligible for pregnancy/maternity or school activities leave; employees who work 20 or more hours per week are eligible for leave to donate bone marrow.

Family Medical Leave: "Reasonable period of time" not to exceed four months for pregnancy/maternity leave, if necessary for pregnancy or related medical condition; up to 40 hours paid leave per year to donate bone marrow.

School Activities: 16 hours per year.

Maine

Me. Rev. Stat. Ann. tit. 26, §§ 843 and following

Employers Covered: All employers for domestic violence leave; employers with 15 or more employees at one location for family medical leave.

Eligible Employees: Employees with at least one year of service.

Family Medical Leave: 10 weeks in any two-year period for childbirth, adoption (for child 16 or younger), employee's serious health condition, or care for family member with serious health condition

Domestic Violence: "Reasonable and necessary" leave for employee who is victim of domestic violence, sexual assault, or stalking, or whose parent, spouse, or child is a victim, to prepare for and attend court, for medical treatment, and for other necessary services.

State Family and Medical Leave Laws (continued)

Maryland

Md. Code Ann., [Lab. & Empl.] § 3-802

Employers Covered: Employers that allow workers to take leave for the birth of a child.

Eligible Employees: All employees.

Family Medical Leave: Employee must be given same leave for adoption as allowed for childbirth.

Massachusetts

Mass. Gen. Laws ch. 149, §§ 52D, 105D; ch. 151B, § 1(5)

Employers Covered: Employers with 6 or more employees must provide maternity and adoption leave; employers with 50 or more employees must offer leave for school activities.

Eligible Employees: Full-time female employees who have completed probationary period, or 3 months of service if no set probationary period, are eligible for maternity and adoption leave; employees who are eligible under FMLA are eligible for all other leave.

Family Medical Leave: 8 weeks total for childbirth/maternity or adoption of child younger than 18 (younger than 23 if disabled); additional 24 hours total per year (combined with school activities leave) to accompany minor child or relative age 60 or older to medical and dental appointments.

School Activities: 24 hours per year total (combined with medical care under "other").

Minnesota

Minn. Stat. Ann. §§ 181.940 and following

Employers Covered: Employers with at least 21 employees at one site must provide childbirth/maternity and adoption leave; with at least 20 employees must allow leave to donate bone marrow; all employers must provide leave for school activities.

Eligible Employees: Employees who have worked at least half-time for one year are eligible for maternity leave; at least 20 hours per week are eligible for leave to donate bone marrow; at least one year are eligible for school activities.

Family Medical Leave: 6 weeks for childbirth/maternity or adoption; up to 40 hours paid leave per year to donate bone marrow; parent can use accrued sick leave to care for sick or injured child.

School Activities: 16 hours in 12-month period; includes activities related to childcare, preschool, or special education.

Montana

Mont. Code Ann. §§ 49-2-310, 49-2-311

Employers Covered: All.

Eligible Employees: All.

Family Medical Leave: "Reasonable leave of absence" for pregnancy/maternity and childbirth.

Nebraska

Neb. Rev. Stat. § 48-234

Employers Covered: Employers that allow workers to take leave for the birth of a child.

Eligible Employees: All employees.

Family Medical Leave: Employee must be given same leave as allowed for childbirth to adopt a child under 9 years old or a special needs child under 19. Does not apply to stepparent or foster parent adoptions.

Nevada

Nev. Rev. Stat. Ann. §§ 392.490, 613.335

Employers Covered: All.

Eligible Employees: Parent, guardian, or custodian of a child.

Family Medical Leave: Same sick or disability leave policies that apply to other medical conditions must be extended to pregnancy, miscarriage, and childbirth.

School Activities: Employers may not fire or threaten to fire a parent, guardian, or custodian for attending a school conference or responding to a child's emergency.

New Hampshire

N.H. Rev. Stat. Ann. § 354-A:7(VI)

Employers Covered: Employers with at least 6 employees.

Eligible Employees: All.

Family Medical Leave: Temporary disability leave for childbirth or related medical condition.

New Jersey

N.J. Stat. Ann. §§ 34:11B-1 to 34B:16

Employers Covered: Employers with at least 50 employees.

Eligible Employees: Employees who have worked for at least one year and at least 1,000 hours in previous 12 months.

Family Medical Leave: 12 weeks (or 24 weeks reduced leave schedule) in any 24-month period for pregnancy/maternity, childbirth, adoption, or care for family member with serious health condition.

State Family and Medical Leave Laws (continued)

Family Member: Includes parents-in-law; child includes legal ward; parent includes someone with visitation rights.

New York

N.Y. Lab. Law §§ 201-c, 202-a

Employers Covered: Employers that allow workers to take leave for the birth of a child must allow adoption leave; employers with at least 20 employees at one site must allow leave to donate bone marrow.

Eligible Employees: All employees are eligible for adoption leave; employees who work at least 20 hours per week are eligible for leave to donate bone marrow.

Family Medical Leave: Employees must be given same leave as allowed for childbirth to adopt a child of preschool age or younger, or no older than 18 if disabled; up to 24 hours leave to donate bone marrow.

North Carolina

N.C. Gen. Stat. § 95-28.3

Employers Covered: All employers.

Eligible Employees: All employees.

School Activities: Parents and guardians of school-aged children must be given up to 4 hours of leave per year.

Domestic Violence: Employer may not discipline or fire an employee who takes "reasonable" leave to get a protective order.

Oregon

Or. Rev. Stat. §§ 659A.150 and following, 659A. 190 and following, 659A.312; Or. Admin. R. §§ 839-009-0200 and following

Employers Covered: Employers of 25 or more employees must provide childbirth, adoption, and serious health condition leave; all employers must allow leave to donate bone marrow.

Eligible Employees: Employees who have worked 25 or more hours per week for at least 180 days are eligible for childbirth, adoption, and serious health condition leave; employees who work an average of 20 or more hours per week are eligible for leave to donate bone marrow.

Family Medical Leave: 12 weeks per year for pregnancy/ maternity, adoption, or childbirth; additional 12 weeks per year for serious health condition, care for family member with serious health condition, or care for child who has an illness, injury, or condition that requires home care; up to 40 hours or amount of accrued paid leave (whichever is less) to donate bone marrow.

Family Member: Includes parents-in-law, same-sex domestic partner, and domestic partner's parent or child.

Rhode Island

R.I. Gen. Laws §§ 28-48-1 and following

Employers Covered: Employers with 50 or more employees.

Eligible Employees: Employees who have worked an average of 30 or more hours a week for at least 12 consecutive months.

Family Medical Leave: 13 weeks in any two calendar years for childbirth, adoption of child up to 16 years old, employee's serious health condition, or care for family member with serious health condition.

Family Member: Includes parents-in-law.

School Activities: Up to 10 hours a year.

South Carolina

S.C. Code Ann. § 44-43-80

Employers Covered: Employers with 20 or more workers at one site in South Carolina.

Eligible Employees: Employees who work an average of at least 20 hours per week.

Family Medical Leave: Up to 40 hours paid leave per year to donate bone marrow.

Tennessee

Tenn. Code Ann. § 4-21-408

Employers Covered: Employers with at least 100 employees.

Eligible Employees: All female employees who have worked 12 consecutive months.

Family Medical Leave: Up to four months of unpaid leave for pregnancy/maternity and childbirth (includes nursing); employee must give 3 months' notice unless a medical emergency requires the leave to begin sooner; these laws must be included in employee handbook.

Vermont

Vt. Stat. Ann. tit. 21, §§ 471 and following

Employers Covered: Employers with at least 10 employees must provide parental leave for childbirth and adoption; with at least 15 employees must provide family medical leave to care for a seriously ill family member or to take a family member to medical appointments.

Eligible Employees: Employees who have worked an average of 30 or more hours per week for at least one year.

State Family and Medical Leave Laws (continued)

Family Medical Leave: 12 weeks per year for childbirth, adoption of child age 16 or younger, employee's serious health condition, or care for family member with a serious health condition; combined with school activities leave, additional 4 hours of unpaid leave in a 30-day period (up to 24 hours per year) to take a family member to a medical, dental, or professional well-care appointment or respond to a family member's medical emergency.

School Activities: Combined with leave described above, 4 hours total unpaid leave in a 30-day period (but not more than 24 hours per year) to participate in child's school activities.

Family Member: Includes parents-in-law.

Washington

Wash. Rev. Code Ann. §§ 49.78.010 and following, 49.12.265 and following, 49.12.350 and following; Wash. Admin. Code 296-130-010 and following, 162-30-020

Employers Covered: All employers must allow employees to use available paid time off to care for sick family members; employers with 8 or more employees must provide pregnancy/childbirth leave; employers with 100 or more employees must provide maternity, adoption, and terminally ill child leave.

Eligible Employees: All employees are eligible for family care leave; employees who have worked at least 35 hours per week for the previous year are eligible for

pregnancy/childbirth leave, maternity leave, and leave to care for a terminally ill child.

Family Medical Leave: In addition to any leave available under federal FMLA, employee may take leave for the period of time when she is sick or temporarily disabled due to pregnancy or childbirth; employers with 100 or more employees must allow up to 12 weeks during any 24-month period to care for a newborn or newly adopted child (under the age of 6), or to care for a terminally ill child under the age of 18; all employees can use any paid leave to care for a sick family member.

Family member: Includes parents-in-law, grandparents, and stepparents; in addition, may take 12 weeks during any 24-month period to care for a terminally ill child under 18.

Wisconsin

Wis. Stat. Ann. § 103.10

Employers Covered: Employers of 50 or more employees in at least six of the preceding 12 months.

Eligible Employees: Employees who have worked at least one year and 1,000 hours in the preceding 12 months.

Family Medical Leave: 6 weeks per 12-month period for pregnancy/maternity, childbirth, or adoption; additional 2 weeks per 12-month period to care for family member with a serious health condition.

Current as of February 2005

State Laws on Military Leave

Alabama

Alabama Stat. §§ 31-12-1 and following

State national guard and militia members called to active duty for at least 30 consecutive days or for federally funded duty for homeland security have the same leave and reinstatement rights and benefits guaranteed under USERRA.

Alaska

Alaska Stat. § 26.05.075

Employees called to active service in the state militia are entitled to unlimited unpaid leave and reinstatement to their former or a comparable position, with the pay, seniority, and benefits the employee would have had if not absent for service.

Arizona

Ariz. Rev. Stat. §§ 26-167, 26-168

Members of state military forces or national guard members called up by state for training or duty have the same leave and reinstatement rights and benefits guaranteed under USERRA. Employer may not dissuade employees from enlisting in state or national military forces by threatening economic reprisal.

Arkansas

Ark. Code Ann. § 12-62-413

Employees called by the Governor to active duty in the Arkansas National Guard or the state militia have the same leave and reinstatement rights and benefits guaranteed under USERRA.

California

Cal. Mil. & Vet. Code §§ 394, 394.5, 395.06

Employees who are called into service in the state military or naval forces have the same leave and reinstatement rights and benefits guaranteed under USERRA. Employees in the U.S. armed forces, National Guard, or Naval Militia are entitled to 17 days unpaid leave per year for training or special exercises. Employer may not terminate employee or limit any benefits or seniority because a of temporary disability (up to 52 weeks).

Colorado

Colo. Rev. Stat. § 28-3-609

Permanent employees who are members of Colorado National Guard or U.S. armed forces reserves are entitled to 15 days unpaid leave per year for training and reinstatement to their former or a similar position with the same status, pay, and seniority.

Connecticut

Conn. Gen. Stat. Ann. § 27-33a

Employees who are active or reserve members of the state militia or National Guard are entitled to take leave to attend meetings or drills that take place during regular working hours, without loss or reduction of vacation or holiday benefits. Employer may not discriminate in terms of promotion or continued employment.

Florida

Fla. Stat. Ann. §§ 250.482, 627.6692(h) to (j)

Employees who are members of the Florida National Guard and are called into active duty by the governor may not be penalized for absence from work. Employees not covered by COBRA whose employment is terminated while on active duty are entitled to a new 18-month benefit period beginning when active duty or job ends, whichever is later.

Georgia

Ga. Code Ann. § 38-2-280

Members of U.S. armed forces or Georgia National Guard called into active federal or state service are entitled to unlimited unpaid leave for active service, and up to 6 months leave in any 4-year period for service school or annual training. Employee is entitled to reinstatement with full benefits unless employer's circumstances have changed to make reinstatement impossible or unreasonable.

Hawaii

Haw. Rev. Stat. § 121-43

Employees serving in the state national guard have the same leave and reinstatement rights and benefits guaranteed under USERRA.

Idaho

Idaho Code §§ 46-224, 46-225, 46-407

Members of state national guard ordered to active duty by the Governor may take up to one year of unpaid leave and are entitled to reinstatement to former position. Returning employees may not be fired without cause for one year. Members of national guard and reserves may take up to 15 days leave per year for training; employee must give 90-days' notice of training dates.

Illinois

20 Ill. Comp. Stat. §§ 1805/30.1 to 1805/30.20; 330 Ill. Comp. State. § 60/4

State Laws on Military Leave (continued)

Members of Illinois State Guard and members of U.S. uniformed services who are called into state active duty in the Illinois National Guard have the same leave and reinstatement rights and benefits guaranteed under USERRA.

Indiana
Ind. Code Ann. §§ 10-17-4-1 to 10-17-4-5

Members of U.S. armed services reserves may take up to 15 days unpaid (or paid at employer's discretion) leave per year for training. Leave does not affect vacation, sick leave, bonus, or promotion rights. Employee must be reinstated to former or a similar position with no loss of seniority or benefits.

Iowa
Iowa Code § 29A.43

Members of national guard, reserves, or state military called into temporary duty are entitled to reinstatement to former or a similar position. Leave does not affect vacation, sick leave, bonuses, or other benefits. Employee must give employer proof of satisfactory completion of duty and of employee's qualifications to perform the job's duties.

Kansas
Kan. Stat. Ann. §§ 48-517, 48-222

Members of state military forces called into active duty by the state have the same leave and reinstatement rights and benefits guaranteed under USERRA. In addition to unlimited leave for active duty, employees are entitled to 5 to 10 days leave each year to attend state national guard training camp.

Kentucky
Ky. Rev. Stat. Ann. § 38.238

Members of Kentucky National Guard are entitled to unlimited unpaid leave for training and reinstatement to former position with no loss of seniority or benefits. Employer may not in any way discriminate against employee or threaten to prevent employee from enlisting in the Kentucky national guard or active militia.

Louisiana
La. Rev. Stat. Ann. §§ 29:38, 29:38.1, 29:410

Employees called into active duty in any branch of the state military forces have the same leave and reinstatement rights and benefits guaranteed under USERRA.

Maine
Me. Rev. Stat. Ann. tit. 37-B, § 342(5)

Employer may not discriminate against employee for membership or service in state military forces.

Maryland
Md. Code Ann. [Public Safety] § 13-705

Members of the national guard and militia called to active duty or training by the Governor have the same leave and reinstatement rights and benefits guaranteed under USERRA.

Massachusetts
Mass. Gen. Laws ch. 149, §§ 52A to 52A 1/2

Employees who are members of U.S. armed forces reserves or the state armed forces may take up to 17 days per year for training. Leave does not affect vacation, sick leave, bonus, or promotion rights. Employee who is qualified must be reinstated to former or a similar position. Veterans who want to participate in a Veterans Day or Memorial Day exercise, parade, or service must be given leave.

Michigan
Mich. Comp. Laws §§ 32.271 to 32.274

Members of state or U.S. uniformed services called into active state or federal duty may take unpaid leave; employee may also take unpaid leave to take a physical, enlist, be inducted, or attend training. Returning employee must be reinstated to former position. Employer may not in any way discriminate against employee or threaten to prevent employee from enlisting in the state armed forces.

Minnesota
Minn. Stat. Ann. § 192.34

Employer may not discharge employee, interfere with military service, or dissuade employee from enlisting by threatening employee's job. Applies to employees who are members of the U.S., Minnesota, or any other state military or naval forces.

Mississippi
Miss. Code Ann. § 33-1-19

Members of U.S. uniformed services and Mississippi armed forces are entitled to unpaid leave for active state duty or state training duty. If still qualified to perform job duties, employee entitled to reinstatement to previous or similar position.

Missouri
Mo. Rev. Stat. §§ 41.730, 557.021, 558.011, 560.016

Employer may not discharge employee, interfere with employee's military service, or threaten to dissuade

State Laws on Military Leave (continued)

employee from enlisting; applies to members of the state organized militia.

Montana
Mont. Code Ann. § 10-1-603

Members of the state organized militia called to active service during a state-declared disaster or emergency are entitled to unpaid leave for duration of service. Leave may not be deducted from sick leave, vacation, or other leave, although employee may voluntarily use that leave. Returning employee is entitled to reinstatement to same or similar position. Employer may not in any way discriminate against employee or dissuade employee from enlisting by threatening employee's job.

Nebraska
Neb. Rev. Stat. § 55-161

Employees who are members of the Nebraska National Guard and are called into active state duty have the same leave and reinstatement rights and benefits guaranteed under USERRA.

Nevada
Nev. Rev. Stat. Ann. §§ 412.139, 412.606, 683A.261

Employers may not discriminate against members of the Nevada National Guard and may not discharge any employee who is called into active service.

New Hampshire
N.H. Rev. Stat. Ann. §§ 110-B:65(II), 110-C:1

Members of the national guard or militia called to active duty have the same leave and reinstatement rights and benefits guaranteed under USERRA. Employer may not discriminate against employee because of connection or service with national guard; may not dissuade employee from enlisting by threatening job.

New Jersey
N.J. Stat. Ann. § 38:23C-20

An employee is entitled to take unpaid leave for active service in the U.S. or state military services. Upon return, employee must be reinstated to the same or a similar position, unless employer's circumstances have changed to make reinstatement impossible or unreasonable. Employee may not be fired without cause for one year after returning from service. Employee is also entitled to take up to three months leave for training or assemblies relating to military service.

New Mexico
N.M. Stat. Ann. §§ 28-15-1 to 28-15-3

Members of the state national guard or militia may take unpaid leave for service. Employee who is still qualified must be reinstated in former or similar position with no loss of status or seniority. Employee may not be fired without cause for one year after returning from service. Employer may not discriminate against or discharge employee because of membership in the national guard; may not prevent employee from performing military service.

New York
N.Y. Mil. Law § 317

Members of the state military forces called up by governor and members of U.S. uniformed services are entitled to unpaid leave for active service; reserve drills or annual training; service school; initial full-time or active duty training. Returning employee is entitled to reinstatement to previous position, or to one with the same seniority, status, and pay, unless the employer's circumstances have changed and reemployment is impossible or unreasonable.

North Carolina
N.C. Gen. Stat. §§ 127A-201 and following, 127B-14

Members of the North Carolina National Guard called to active duty by the governor are entitled to take unpaid leave. Returning employee must be restored to previous position or one of comparable seniority, status, and salary; if no longer qualified, employee must be placed in another position with appropriate seniority, status, and salary, unless the employer's circumstances now make reinstatement unreasonable. Employer may not deny employment, promotion, or any benefit because employee is a member or enlists or serves in the state national guard; employer may not discharge employee called up for emergency military service.

Ohio
Ohio Rev. Code Ann. §§ 5903.01, 5903.02

Employees who are members of the Ohio militia or national guard called for active duty or training; members of the commissioned public health service corps; or any other uniformed service called up in time of war or emergency have the same leave and reinstatement rights and benefits guaranteed under USERRA.

Oklahoma
Okla. Stat. Ann. tit. 44, §§ 71, 208

Employees called to state active duty in the Oklahoma National Guard have the same leave and reinstatement rights and benefits guaranteed under USERRA. Members

State Laws on Military Leave (continued)

of the national guard may take leave to attend state national guard training, drills, or ceremony. Employer may not fire employee or hinder or prevent employee from performing military service.

Oregon

Or. Rev. Stat. § 399.230

Members of state organized militia called into active duty by the governor may take unpaid leave for term of service. Returning employee is entitled to reinstatement with no loss of seniority or benefits including sick leave, vacation, or service credits under a pension plan.

Pennsylvania

51 Pa. Cons. Stat. Ann. §§ 7302, 7309

Employee who enlists or is drafted during a time of war or emergency called by the president or governor is entitled to unpaid military leave along with reservists called into active duty. Returning employee must be reinstated to same or similar position with same status, seniority, and pay. Employers may not discharge or discriminate against any employee because of membership or service in the military. Employees called to active duty are entitled to 30 days' health insurance continuation benefits at no cost.

Rhode Island

R.I. Gen. Laws §§ 30-11-2 to 30-11-6, 30-21-1

Members of state military forces and National Guard members on state active duty have the same leave and reinstatement rights and benefits guaranteed under USERRA. Employer may not discharge employee because of membership in the military, interfere with employee's military service, or dissuade employee from enlisting by threatening employee's job.

South Carolina

S.C. Code Ann. §§ 25-1-2310 to 25-1-2340

Members of the South Carolina National Guard and State Guard called to state duty by the governor are entitled to unpaid leave for service. Returning employee must be reinstated to previous position or one with same seniority, status, and salary; if no longer qualified, must be given another position, unless employer's circumstances make reinstatement unreasonable.

South Dakota

S.D. Codified Laws Ann. § 33-17-15.1

Members of the South Dakota National Guard ordered to active duty by the governor or president have the same leave and reinstatement rights and benefits

guaranteed under USERRA.

Tennessee

Tenn. Code Ann. § 58-1-604

Employer may not refuse to hire or terminate an employee because of national guard membership or because employee is absent for a required drill or annual training.

Texas

Tex. Gov't. Code Ann. § 431.006

Members of the state military forces called to active duty or training are entitled to unpaid leave. Returning employee is entitled to reinstatement to the same position with no loss of time, efficiency rating, vacation, or benefits unless employer's circumstances have changed so that reemployment is impossible or unreasonable.

Utah

Utah Code Ann. §§ 39-1-36

Members of U.S. armed forces reserves who are called to active duty, active duty for training, inactive duty training, or state active duty may take up to 5 years of unpaid leave. Upon return, employee is entitled to reinstatement to previous employment with same seniority, status, pay, and vacation rights. Employer may not discriminate against an employee based on membership in armed forces reserves.

Vermont

Vt. Stat. Ann. tit. 21, § 491

Permanent employees who are members of an organized unit of the national guard or the ready reserves and are called to active state duty or training with the U.S. military are entitled to unpaid leave. Employee must give 30 days' notice for U.S. training and as much notice as is practical for state duty. If still qualified, returning employee must be reinstated to former position with the same status, pay, and seniority, including any seniority that accrued during the leave of absence. Employer may not discriminate against an employee who is a member or an applicant for membership in the state or federal national guard.

Virginia

Va. Code Ann. §§ 44-93.2 to 44-93.4

Members of the Virginia National Guard, Virginia State Defense Force, or naval militia called to active state duty by the governor are entitled to take unpaid leave and may not be required to use vacation or any other

State Laws on Military Leave (continued)

accrued leave (unless employee wishes). Returning employee must be reinstated to previous position or one with same seniority, status, and pay. If position no longer exists, then to a comparable position, unless employer's circumstances would make reemployment unreasonable.

Washington

Wash. Rev. Code Ann. §§ 73.16.032 to 73.16.035

Permanent employees who are Washington residents or employed within the state and who volunteer or are called to serve in the uniformed services have the same leave and reinstatement rights and benefits guaranteed under USERRA.

West Virginia

W.Va. Code § 15-1F-8

Employees who are members of the organized militia in active state service have the same leave and reinstatement rights and benefits guaranteed under USERRA.

Wisconsin

Wis. Stat. Ann. § 45.50

Permanent employees who enlist, are inducted, or are called to serve in the uniformed services, or civilians requested to perform national defense work during an officially proclaimed emergency, may take up to 4 years leave for military service and/or training unless period

of service is extended by law. Returning employee is entitled to reinstatement to previous position, or to one with the same seniority, benefits, and pay, unless the employee is no longer qualified or the employer's circumstances have changed and reemployment is impossible or unreasonable. Employee may not be fired without cause for one year after returning from service.

Wyoming

Wyo. Stat. §§ 19-11-101 to 19-11-123

Employees who are members or who apply for membership in the uniformed services; employees who report for active duty, training, or a qualifying physical exam, or who are called to state duty by the governor, may take up to 4 years leave of absence. Employee may use vacation or any other accrued leave but is not required to do so. Returning employee is entitled to reemployment with the same seniority, rights, and benefits, plus any additional seniority and benefits that employee would have earned if there had been no absence, unless employer's circumstances have changed so that reemployment is impossible or unreasonable or would impose an undue hardship. Employee is entitled to complete any training program that would have been available to employee's former position during period of absence. Employee may not be terminated without cause for one year after returning to work.

Current as of February 2005

State Laws on Taking Time Off to Vote

Note: The states of Alabama, Connecticut, Delaware, District of Columbia, Florida, Idaho, Indiana, Louisiana, Maine, Michigan, Mississippi, Montana, New Hampshire, New Jersey, North Carolina, Oregon, Pennsylvania, Rhode Island, South Carolina, Vermont, and Virginia are not listed in this chart because they do not have laws or regulations on time off to vote that govern private employers. Check with your state department of labor if you need more information. (See Appendix A for contact list.)

Alaska
Alaska Stat. § 15.56.100
Time off work for voting: Not specified.
Time off not required if: Employee has 2 consecutive nonwork hours at beginning or end of shift when polls are open.
Time off is paid: Yes.

Arizona
Ariz. Rev. Stat. § 16-402
Time off work for voting: As much time as will add up to 3 hours when combined with nonwork time. Employer may decide when hours are taken.
Time off not required if: Employee has 3 consecutive nonwork hours at beginning or end of shift when polls are open.
Time off is paid: Yes.
Employee must request leave in advance: One day before election.

Arkansas
Ark. Code Ann. § 7-1-102
Time off work for voting: Employer must schedule work hours so employee has time to vote.
Time off is paid: No.

California
Cal. Elec. Code § 14000
Time off work for voting: Up to 2 hours at beginning or end of shift, whichever gives employee most time to vote and takes least time off work.
Time off not required if: Employee has sufficient time to vote during nonwork time.
Time off is paid: Yes (up to 2 hours).
Employee must request leave in advance: 2 working days before election.

Colorado
Colo. Rev. Stat. § 1-7-102
Time off work for voting: Up to 2 hours. Employer may decide when hours are taken, but employer must permit employee to take time at beginning or end of shift, if employee requests it.

Time off not required if: Employee has 3 nonwork hours when polls are open.
Time off is paid: Yes (up to 2 hours).
Employee must request leave in advance: Prior to election day.

Georgia
Ga. Code Ann. § 21-2-404
Time off work for voting: Up to 2 hours. Employer may decide when hours are taken.
Time off not required if: Employee has 2 nonwork hours at beginning or end of shift when polls are open.
Time off is paid: No.
Employee must request leave in advance: "Reasonable notice."

Hawaii
Haw. Rev. Stat. § 11-95
Time off work for voting: 2 consecutive hours excluding meal or rest breaks. Employer may not change employee's regular work schedule.
Time off not required if: Employee has 2 consecutive nonwork hours when polls are open.
Time off is paid: Yes.
Employee required to show proof of voting: Yes (voter's receipt). If employer verifies that employee did not vote, hours off may be deducted from pay.

Illinois
10 Ill. Comp. Stat. §§ 5/7-42, 5/17-15
Time off work for voting: 2 hours. Employer may decide when hours are taken.
Time off is paid: No.
Employee must request leave in advance: One day in advance (for general or state election). Employer must give consent (for primary).

Iowa
Iowa Code § 49.109
Time off work for voting: As much time as will add up to 3 hours when combined with nonwork time. Employer may decide when hours are taken.
Time off not required if: Employee has 3 consecutive nonwork hours when polls are open.
Time off is paid: Yes.
Employee must request leave in advance: In writing "prior to the date of the election."

Kansas
Kan. Stat. Ann. § 25-418
Time off work for voting: Up to 2 hours or as much time as will add up to 2 hours when combined with nonwork time. Employer may decide when hours are taken, but it may not be during a regular meal break.

State Laws on Taking Time Off to Vote (continued)

Time off not required if: Employee has 2 consecutive nonwork hours when polls are open.

Time off is paid: Yes.

Kentucky

Ky. Const. § 148; Ky. Rev. Stat. Ann. § 118.035

Time off work for voting: "Reasonable time," but not less than 4 hours. Employer may decide when hours are taken.

Time off is paid: No.

Employee must request leave in advance: One day before election.

Employee required to show proof of voting: No proof specified, but employee who takes time off and does not vote may be subject to disciplinary action.

Maryland

Md. Code Ann. [Elec. Law] § 10-315

Time off work for voting: 2 hours.

Time off not required if: Employee has 2 consecutive nonwork hours when polls are open.

Time off is paid: Yes.

Employee required to show proof of voting: Yes; also includes attempting to vote. Must use state board of elections form.

Massachusetts

Mass. Gen. Laws ch. 149, § 178

Time off work for voting: First 2 hours that polls are open. (Applies to workers in manufacturing, mechanical, or retail industries.)

Time off is paid: No.

Employee must request leave in advance: Must apply for leave of absence (no time specified).

Minnesota

Minn. Stat. Ann. § 204C.04

Time off work for voting: May be absent during the morning of election day.

Time off is paid: Yes.

Missouri

Mo. Rev. Stat. § 115.639

Time off work for voting: 3 hours. Employer may decide when hours are taken.

Time off not required if: Employee has 3 consecutive nonwork hours when polls are open.

Time off is paid: Yes (if employee votes).

Employee must request leave in advance: "Prior to the day of election."

Employee required to show proof of voting: None specified, but pay contingent on employee actually voting.

Nebraska

Neb. Rev. Stat. § 32-922

Time off work for voting: As much time as will add up to 2 consecutive hours when combined with nonwork time. Employer may decide when hours are taken.

Time off not required if: Employee has 2 consecutive nonwork hours when polls are open.

Time off is paid: Yes

Employee must request leave in advance: Prior to or on election day.

Nevada

Nev. Rev. Stat. Ann. § 293.463

Time off work for voting: If it is impracticable to vote before or after work: Employee who works 2 miles or less from polling place may take 1 hour; 2 to 10 miles, 2 hours; more than 10 miles, 3 hours.

Time off not required if: Employee has sufficient nonwork time when polls are open.

Time off is paid: Yes.

Employee must request leave in advance: Prior to election day.

New Mexico

N.M. Stat. Ann. § 1-12-42

Time off work for voting: 2 hours. (Includes Indian nation, tribal, and pueblo elections.)

Time off not required if: Employee's workday begins more than 2 hours after polls open or ends more than 3 hours before polls close.

Time off is paid: Yes.

New York

N.Y. Elec. Law § 3-110

Time off work for voting: As many hours at beginning or end of shift as will give employee enough time to vote when combined with nonwork time. Employer may decide when hours are taken.

Time off not required if: Employee has 4 consecutive nonwork hours at beginning or end of shift when polls are open.

Time off is paid: Yes (up to 2 hours).

Employee must request leave in advance: Not more than 10 or less than 2 working days before election.

North Dakota

N.D. Cent. Code § 16.1-01-02.1

Time off work for voting: Employers are encouraged to give employees time off to vote when regular work schedule conflicts with times polls are open.

Time off is paid: No.

State Laws on Taking Time Off to Vote (continued)

Ohio
Ohio Rev. Code Ann. § 3599.06
Time off work for voting: "Reasonable time."
Time off is paid: Yes.

Oklahoma
Okla. Stat. Ann. tit. 26, § 7-101
Time off work for voting: 2 hours, unless employee lives so far from polling place that more time is needed. Employer may decide when hours are taken or may change employee's schedule to give employee nonwork time to vote.
Time off not required if: Employee's workday begins at least 3 hours after polls open or ends at least 3 hours before polls close.
Time off is paid: Yes.
Employee must request leave in advance: One day before election.
Employee required to show proof of voting: Yes.

South Dakota
S.D. Codified Laws Ann. § 12-3-5
Time off work for voting: 2 consecutive hours. Employer may decide when hours are taken.
Time off not required if: Employee has 2 consecutive nonwork hours when polls are open.
Time off is paid: Yes.

Tennessee
Tenn. Code Ann. § 2-1-106
Time off work for voting: "Reasonable time" up to 3 hours.
Time off not required if: Employee's workday begins at least 3 hours after polls open or ends at least 3 hours before polls close.
Time off is paid: Yes.
Employee must request leave in advance: Before noon on the day before the election.

Texas
Tex. Elec. Code Ann. § 276.004
Time off work for voting: Employer may not refuse to allow employee to take time off to vote, but no time limit specified.
Time off not required if: Employee has 2 consecutive nonwork hours when polls are open.
Time off is paid: Yes.

Utah
Utah Code Ann. § 20A-3-103
Time off work for voting: 2 hours at beginning or end of shift. Employer may decide when hours are taken.

Time off not required if: Employee has at least 3 nonwork hours when polls are open.
Time off is paid: Yes.
Employee must request leave in advance: "Before election day."

Washington
Wash. Rev. Code Ann. § 49.28.120
Time off work for voting: Employer must either arrange work schedule so employee has enough nonwork time (not including meal or rest breaks) to vote, or allow employee to take off work for a "reasonable time," up to 2 hours.
Time off not required if: Employee has 2 nonwork hours when polls are open or enough time to get an absentee ballot.
Time off is paid: Yes.

West Virginia
W.Va. Code § 3-1-42
Time off work for voting: Up to 3 hours. (Employers in health, transportation, communication, production, and processing facilities may change employee's schedule so that time off doesn't impair essential operations but must allow employee sufficient and convenient time to vote.)
Time off not required if: Employee has at least 3 nonwork hours when polls are open.
Time off is paid: Yes (if employee votes).
Employee must request leave in advance: Written request at least 3 days before election.
Employee required to show proof of voting: None specified, but time off will be deducted from pay if employee does not vote.

Wisconsin
Wis. Stat. Ann. § 6.76
Time off work for voting: Up to 3 consecutive hours. Employer may decide when hours are taken.
Time off is paid: No.
Employee must request leave in advance: "Before election day."

Wyoming
Wyo. Stat. § 22-2-111
Time off work for voting: One hour, other than a meal break.
Time off not required if: Employee has at least 3 consecutive nonwork hours when polls are open.
Time off is paid: Yes (if employee votes).
Employee required to show proof of voting: None specified, but pay contingent on employee voting.

Current as of February 2005

State Laws on Jury Duty

Alabama
Ala. Code §§ 12-16-8 to 12-16-8.1

Paid leave: Full-time employees are entitled to usual pay minus any fees received from the court.

Notice employee must give: Must show supervisor jury summons the next working day; must return to work the next scheduled hour after discharge from jury duty.

Employer penalty for firing or penalizing employee: Liable for actual and punitive damages.

Alaska
Alaska Stat. § 09.20.037

Unpaid leave: Yes.

Additional employee protections: Employee may not be threatened, coerced, or penalized.

Employer penalty for firing or penalizing employee: Liable for lost wages and damages; must reinstate employee.

Arizona
Ariz. Rev. Stat. § 21-236

Unpaid leave: Yes.

Additional employee protections: Employee may not lose vacation rights, seniority, or precedence. Employer may not require employee to use annual, sick, or vacation hours.

Employer penalty for firing or penalizing employee: Class 3 misdemeanor, punishable by a fine of up to $500 or up to 30 days' imprisonment.

Note: Employers with 5 or fewer employees: Court must postpone an employee's jury service if another employee is already serving as a juror.

Arkansas
Ark. Code Ann. § 16-31-106

Unpaid leave: Yes.

Additional employee protections: Absence may not affect sick leave and vacation rights.

Employer penalty for firing or penalizing employee: Class A misdemeanor, punishable by a fine of up to $1,000 or up to one year's imprisonment.

California
Cal. Lab. Code §§ 230, 230.1

Unpaid leave: Employee may use vacation, personal leave, or comp time.

Additional employee protections: Victims of crime, domestic violence, or sexual assault are protected against discharge, discrimination, or retaliation for attending a court proceeding or seeking judicial relief.

Notice employee must give: Reasonable notice.

Employer penalty for firing or penalizing employee: Employer must reinstate employee with back pay and lost wages and benefits. Willful violation is a misdemeanor.

Colorado
Colo. Rev. Stat. §§ 13-71-126, 13-71-133 to 13-71-134

Paid leave: All employees (including part-time and temporary who were scheduled to work for the 3 months preceding jury service): regular wages up to $50 per day for first 3 days of jury duty. Must pay within 30 days of jury service.

Additional employee protections: Employer may not make any demands on employee which will interfere with effective performance of jury duty.

Employer penalty for firing or penalizing employee: Class 2 misdemeanor, punishable by a fine of $250 to $1,000 or 3 to 12 months' imprisonment, or both. May be liable to employee for triple damages and attorney's fees.

Connecticut
Conn. Gen. Stat. Ann. §§ 51-247 to 51-247c

Paid leave: Full-time employees: regular wages for the first 5 days of jury duty; after 5 days, state pays up to $50 per day.

Employer penalty for firing or penalizing employee: Criminal contempt: punishable by a fine of up to $500 or up to 30 days' imprisonment, or both. Liable for up to 10 weeks' lost wages for discharging employee.

Delaware
Del. Code Ann. tit. 10, § 4515

Unpaid leave: Yes.

Employer penalty for firing or penalizing employee: Criminal contempt: punishable by a fine of up to $500 or up to 6 months' imprisonment, or both. Liable to discharged employee for lost wages and attorney's fees.

District of Columbia
D.C. Code Ann. §§ 11-1913, 15-718

Paid leave: Full-time employees: regular wages for the first 5 days of jury duty.

Employer penalty for firing or penalizing employee: Criminal contempt: punishable by a fine of up to $300 or up to 30 days' imprisonment, or both, for a first offense; up to $5,000 or up to 180 days' imprisonment, or both, for any subsequent offense. Liable to discharged employee for lost wages and attorney's fees.

State Laws on Jury Duty (continued)

Florida
Fla. Stat. Ann. § 40.271

Unpaid leave: Yes.

Additional employee protections: Employee may not be threatened with dismissal.

Employer penalty for firing or penalizing employee: Threatening employee is contempt of court. May be liable to discharged employee for compensatory and punitive damages and attorney's fees.

Georgia
Ga. Code Ann. § 34-1-3

Unpaid leave: Yes.

Additional employee protections: Employee may not be discharged, penalized, or threatened with discharge or penalty for responding to a subpoena or making a required court appearance.

Notice employee must give: Reasonable notice.

Employer penalty for firing or penalizing employee: Liable for actual damages and reasonable attorney's fees.

Hawaii
Haw. Rev. Stat. § 612-25

Unpaid leave: Yes.

Employer penalty for firing or penalizing employee: Petty misdemeanor: punishable by a fine of up to $1,000 or up to 30 days' imprisonment. May be liable to discharged employee for up to 6 weeks' lost wages.

Idaho
Idaho Code § 2-218

Unpaid leave: Yes.

Employer penalty for firing or penalizing employee: Criminal contempt: punishable by a fine of up to $300. Liable to discharged employee for triple lost wages.

Illinois
705 Ill. Comp. Stat. § 310/10.1

Unpaid leave: Yes.

Additional employee protections: A regular night shift employee may not be required to work if serving on a jury during the day. May not lose any seniority or benefits.

Notice employee must give: Must give employer a copy of the summons within 10 days of issuance.

Employer penalty for firing or penalizing employee: Employer will be charged with civil or criminal contempt, or both; liable to employee for lost wages and benefits.

Indiana
Ind. Code Ann. § 35-44-3-10

Unpaid leave: Yes.

Additional employee protections: Employee may not be deprived of benefits or threatened with the loss of them.

Employer penalty for firing or penalizing employee: Class B misdemeanor: punishable by up to 180 days' imprisonment; may also be fined up to $1,000. Liable to discharged employee for lost wages and attorney's fees.

Iowa
Iowa Code § 607A.45

Unpaid leave: Yes.

Employer penalty for firing or penalizing employee: Contempt of court. Liable to discharged employee for up to 6 weeks' lost wages and attorney's fees.

Kansas
Kan. Stat. Ann. § 43-173

Unpaid leave: Yes.

Additional employee protections: Employee may not lose seniority or benefits. (Basic and additional protections apply to permanent employees only.)

Employer penalty for firing or penalizing employee: Liable for lost wages and benefits, damages, and attorney's fees.

Kentucky
Ky. Rev. Stat. Ann. § 29A.160

Unpaid leave: Yes.

Employer penalty for firing or penalizing employee: Class B misdemeanor: punishable by up to 90 days' imprisonment or fine of up to $250, or both. Liable to discharged employee for lost wages and attorney's fees. Must reinstate employee with full seniority and benefits.

Louisiana
La. Rev. Stat. Ann. § 23:965

Paid leave: Regular employee entitled to one day full compensation for jury service. May not lose any sick, vacation, or personal leave or other benefit.

Additional employee protections: Employer may not create any policy or rule that would discharge employee for jury service.

Notice employee must give: Reasonable notice.

Employer penalty for firing or penalizing employee: For each discharged employee: fine of $100 to $1,000; must

State Laws on Jury Duty (continued)

reinstate employee with full benefits. For not granting paid leave: fine of $100 to $500; must pay full day's lost wages.

Maine

Me. Rev. Stat. Ann. tit. 14, § 1218

Unpaid leave: Yes.

Additional employee protections: Employee may not lose or be threatened with loss of health insurance coverage.

Employer penalty for firing or penalizing employee: Class E crime: punishable by up to 6 months in the county jail or a fine of up to $1,000. Liable for up to 6 weeks' lost wages, benefits, and attorney's fees.

Maryland

Md. Code Ann., [Cts. & Jud. Proc.] § 8-105

Unpaid leave: Yes.

Massachusetts

Mass. Gen. Laws ch. 234A, §§ 48 and following

Paid leave: All employees (including part-time and temporary who were scheduled to work for the 3 months preceding jury service): regular wages for first 3 days of jury duty. If paid leave is an "extreme financial hardship" for employer, state will pay. After first 3 days state will pay $50 per day.

Michigan

Mich. Comp. Laws § 600.1348

Unpaid leave: Yes.

Additional employee protections: Employee may not be threatened or disciplined; may not be required to work in addition to jury service, if extra hours would mean working overtime or beyond normal quitting time.

Employer penalty for firing or penalizing employee: Misdemeanor, punishable by a fine of up to $500 or up to 90 days' imprisonment, or both. Employer may also be punished for contempt of court, with a fine of up to $250 or up to 30 days' imprisonment, or both.

Minnesota

Minn. Stat. Ann. § 593.50

Unpaid leave: Yes.

Employer penalty for firing or penalizing employee: Criminal contempt: punishable by a fine of up to $700 or up to 6 months' imprisonment, or both. Also liable to employee for up to 6 weeks' lost wages and attorney's fees.

Mississippi

Miss. Code Ann. § 13-5-23

Unpaid leave: Yes.

Additional employee protections: Employer may not threaten or intimidate, persuade, or attempt to persuade employee to avoid jury service.

Employer penalty for firing or penalizing employee: If found guilty of interference with the administration of justice: at least one month in the county jail or up to 2 years in the state penitentiary, or a fine of up to $500, or both. May also be found guilty of contempt of court, punishable by a fine of up to $1,000 or up to 6 months' imprisonment, or both.

Missouri

Mo. Rev. Stat. § 494.460

Unpaid leave: Yes.

Additional employee protections: Employer may not take or threaten to take any adverse action.

Employer penalty for firing or penalizing employee: Employer may be liable for lost wages, damages, and attorney's fees and ordered to reinstate employee.

Montana

Mont. Admin. R. 24.16.2520

Paid leave: No paid leave laws regarding private employers.

Nebraska

Neb. Rev. Stat. § 25-1640

Paid leave: Normal wages minus any compensation (other than expenses) from the court.

Additional employee protections: Employee may not lose pay, sick leave, or vacation or be penalized in any way; may not be required to work evening or night shift.

Notice employee must give: Reasonable notice.

Employer penalty for firing or penalizing employee: Class IV misdemeanor, punishable by a fine of $100 to $500.

Nevada

Nev. Rev. Stat. Ann. § 6.190

Unpaid leave: Yes.

Additional employee protections: Employer may not recommend or threaten termination; may not dissuade or attempt to dissuade employee from serving as a juror.

Notice employee must give: At least one day's notice.

State Laws on Jury Duty (continued)

Employer penalty for firing or penalizing employee:
Terminating or threatening to terminate is a gross misdemeanor, punishable by a fine of up to $2,000 or up to one year's imprisonment, or both; in addition, employer may be liable for lost wages, damages equal to lost wages, and punitive damages to $50,000 and must reinstate employee. Dissuading or attempting to dissuade is a misdemeanor, punishable by a fine of up to $1,000 or up to 6 months in the county jail, or both.

New Hampshire

N.H. Rev. Stat. Ann. § 500-A:14

Unpaid leave: Yes.

Employer penalty for firing or penalizing employee:
Employer may be found guilty of contempt of court; also liable to employee for lost wages and attorney's fees and must reinstate employee.

New Jersey

N.J. Stat. Ann. § 2B:20-17

Unpaid leave: Yes.

Employer penalty for firing or penalizing employee:
Employer may be found guilty of a disorderly persons offense, punishable by a fine of up to $1,000 or up to 6 months' imprisonment, or both. May also be liable to employee for economic damages and attorney's fees and may be ordered to reinstate employee

New Mexico

N.M. Stat. Ann. §§ 38-5-18 to 38-5-19

Unpaid leave: Yes.

Employer penalty for firing or penalizing employee:
Petty misdemeanor, punishable by a fine of up to $500 or up to 6 months in the county jail, or both.

New York

N.Y. Jud. Ct. Acts Law § 519

Unpaid leave: Yes.

Paid leave: Employers with more than 10 employees must pay first $40 of wages for the first 3 days of jury duty.

Notice employee must give: Must notify employer prior to beginning jury duty.

Employer penalty for firing or penalizing employee:
May be found guilty of criminal contempt of court, punishable by a fine of up to $1,000 or up to 6 months in the county jail, or both.

North Carolina

N.C. Gen. Stat. § 9-32

Unpaid leave: Yes.

Additional employee protections: Employee may not be demoted.

Employer penalty for firing or penalizing employee:
Liable to discharged employee for reasonable damages; must reinstate employee to former position.

North Dakota

N.D. Cent. Code § 27-09.1-17

Unpaid leave: Yes.

Additional employee protections: Employee may not be laid off, penalized, or coerced because of jury duty, responding to a summons or subpoena, serving as a witness, or testifying in court.

Employer penalty for firing or penalizing employee:
Class B misdemeanor, punishable by a fine of up to $1,000 or up to 30 days' imprisonment, or both. Liable to employee for up to 6 weeks' lost wages and attorney's fees and must reinstate employee.

Ohio

Ohio Rev. Code Ann. § 2313.18

Unpaid leave: Yes.

Notice employee must give: Reasonable notice. Absence must be for actual jury service.

Employer penalty for firing or penalizing employee:
May be found guilty of contempt of court, punishable by a fine of up to $250 or 30 days' imprisonment, or both, for first offense; a fine of up to $500 or 60 days' imprisonment, or both, for second offense; a fine of up to $1,000 or 90 days' imprisonment, or both, for third offense.

Oklahoma

Okla. Stat. Ann. tit. 38, §§ 34, 35

Unpaid leave: Yes.

Additional employee protections: Employee can't be required to use sick leave or vacation; may choose to take paid or unpaid leave.

Employer penalty for firing or penalizing employee:
Misdemeanor, punishable by a fine of up to $5,000. Liable to discharged employee for actual and exemplary damages; actual damages include past and future lost wages, mental anguish, and costs of finding suitable employment.

State Laws on Jury Duty (continued)

Oregon

Or. Rev. Stat. § 10.090

Unpaid leave: Yes (or according to employer's policy).

Employer penalty for firing or penalizing employee: Employer must reinstate discharged employee with back pay.

Pennsylvania

42 Pa. Cons. Stat. Ann. § 4563; 18 Pa. Cons. Stat. Ann. § 4957

Unpaid leave: Yes (applies to retail or service industry employers with 15 or more employees and to manufacturers with 40 or more employees).

Additional employee protections: Employee may not lose seniority or benefits. (Any employee who would not be eligible for unpaid leave will be automatically excused from jury duty.) Employee who must appear in court as a victim or witness, or as a family member of a victim or witness, must also be given unpaid leave.

Employer penalty for firing or penalizing employee: Liable to employee for lost benefits, wages, and attorney's fees; must reinstate employee.

Rhode Island

R.I. Gen. Laws § 9-9-28

Unpaid leave: Yes.

Additional employee protections: Employee may not lose wage increases, promotions, length of service, or other benefit.

Employer penalty for firing or penalizing employee: Misdemeanor punishable by a fine of up to $1,000 or up to one year's imprisonment, or both.

South Carolina

S.C. Code Ann. § 41-1-70

Unpaid leave: Yes.

Additional employee protections: Employee may not be demoted.

Employer penalty for firing or penalizing employee: For discharging employee, liable for one year's salary; for demoting employee, liable for one year's difference between former and lower salary.

South Dakota

S.D. Codified Laws Ann. §§ 16-13-41.1, 16-13-41.2

Unpaid leave: Yes.

Additional employee protections: Employee may not lose job status, pay, or seniority.

Employer penalty for firing or penalizing employee:

Class 2 misdemeanor, punishable by a fine of up to $200 or up to 30 days in the county jail, or both.

Tennessee

Tenn. Code Ann. § 22-4-108

Paid leave: Regular wages minus jury fees (does not apply to employers with fewer than 5 employees or to temporary employees who have worked less than 6 months).

Additional employee protections: Night shift employees are excused from shift work during and for the night before the first day of jury service.

Notice employee must give: Employee must show summons to supervisor the day after receiving it.

Employer penalty for firing or penalizing employee: Violating employee rights or any provisions of this law is a Class A misdemeanor, punishable by up to 11 months, 29 days' imprisonment or a fine up to $2,500, or both. Liable to employee for lost wages and benefits and must reinstate employee.

Texas

Tex. Civ. Prac. & Rem. Code Ann. §§ 122.001, 122.002

Unpaid leave: Yes.

Notice employee must give: Employee must notify employer of intent to return after completion of jury service.

Employer penalty for firing or penalizing employee: Liable to employee for not less than one year's nor more than 5 years' compensation and attorney fees. Must reinstate employee.

Utah

Utah Code Ann. § 78-46-21

Unpaid leave: Yes.

Additional employee protections: Employee may not be threatened or coerced and may not be requested or required to use annual or sick leave or vacation. Employer may not take any adverse employment action against employee.

Employer penalty for firing or penalizing employee: May be found guilty of criminal contempt, punishable by a fine of up to $500 or up to 6 months' imprisonment, or both. Liable to employee for up to 6 weeks' lost wages and attorney's fees.

Vermont

Vt. Stat. Ann. tit. 21, § 499

Unpaid leave: Yes.

State Laws on Jury Duty (continued)

Additional employee protections: Employee may not be penalized or lose any benefit available to other employees; may not lose seniority, vacation credit, or any fringe benefits. Protections also apply to an employee appearing as a witness in court or testifying before a board, commission, or tribunal.

Employer penalty for firing or penalizing employee: Fine of up to $200.

Virginia
Va. Code Ann. § 18.2-465.1

Unpaid leave: Yes.

Additional employee protections: Employee may not be subject to any adverse personnel action and may not be forced to use sick leave or vacation. If employee has to attend any future hearings, the same protections apply. As of 7/1/05, employee need not work on day of jury service.

Notice employee must give: Reasonable notice.

Employer penalty for firing or penalizing employee: Class 3 misdemeanor, punishable by a fine of up to $500.

Washington
Wash. Rev. Code Ann. § 2.36.165

Unpaid leave: Yes.

Additional employee protections: Employee may not be threatened, coerced, harassed, or denied promotion.

Employer penalty for firing or penalizing employee: Intentional violation is a misdemeanor, punishable by a fine of up to $1,000 or up to 90 days' imprisonment, or both; also liable to employee for damages and attorney's fees and must reinstate employee.

West Virginia
W.Va. Code § 52-3-1

Unpaid leave: Yes.

Additional employee protections: Employee may not be threatened or discriminated against; regular pay cannot be cut.

Employer penalty for firing or penalizing employee: May be found guilty of civil contempt, punishable by a fine of $100 to $500. Must reinstate employee. May be liable for back pay and for attorney's fees.

Wisconsin
Wis. Stat. Ann. § 756.255

Unpaid leave: Yes.

Additional employee protections: Employee may not lose seniority or pay raises; may not be disciplined.

Employer penalty for firing or penalizing employee: Fine of up to $200. Must reinstate employee with back pay.

Wyoming
Wyo. Stat. § 1-11-401

Unpaid leave: Yes.

Additional employee protections: Employee may not be threatened, intimidated, or coerced.

Employer penalty for firing or penalizing employee: Liable to employee for up to $1,000 damages, costs, and attorney's fees. Must reinstate employee with no loss of seniority.

Current as of February 2005

11

Performance

As the saying goes, a company is only as good as its employees or, more to the point, as its employees' performance. After all, the company hired them and pays them to do a job and do it well.

It makes sense, then, for you to say something about performance in the employee handbook. Employees need to see, in writing, that the company expects a certain level of performance from them and that it will accept no less. They also need to understand that how they perform affects everyone else at the company.

Of course, with all of the people doing all of the various jobs within your company, it's hard for one handbook policy to tell each employee what is expected. That is the stuff of performance evaluations. The policies in this chapter will let you establish a benchmark of excellence for employees to strive for, then refer employees to the performance evaluation system (if there is one) for more details.

11:1   Your Job Performance

CD File: 11_Performance.rtf

Include This Policy?
☐ Yes
☐ No
☐ Use our existing policy
☐ Other _____

Alternate Modifications
None

Additional Clauses
Specify Performance Standards
Insert?:   ☐ Yes   ☐ No

Related Policies
None

Notes
_____
_____
_____
_____
_____
_____
_____
_____
_____
_____
_____
_____
_____
_____
_____
_____
_____
_____
_____

11:1 Job Performance Expectations

Although it should be self-evident that employees should perform well, a job performance expectation policy reminds employees that your company expects them to perform well. It also warns them that if they don't perform well, your company may discipline or even terminate them. This policy lets employees know that the company takes their performance seriously and that it expects them to do so, too. It also points out to employees that their performance doesn't just affect company management but impacts their coworkers and them as well. As the fortunes of the company go, so go the fortunes of the employees.

Your Job Performance

Each and every employee at _____

_____ [*Company name*] contributes to the success or failure of our Company. If one employee allows his or her performance to slip, then all of us suffer. We expect everyone to perform to the highest level possible.

Poor job performance can lead to discipline, up to and including termination.

Additional Clause to Specify Performance Standards

Depending on the products or services your company provides, you may want to give more information about the type of performance you expect from your employees. For example, a software company might want to encourage innovation and "thinking outside the box," while a manufacturer might want to stress adherence to workplace rules.

If you would like to say more about your expectations, insert an additional paragraph after the first paragraph of the standard policy, above. Although we can't give you a standard modification to use, the following is an example of what you might write:

SAMPLE POLICY LANGUAGE
We believe our connection to our customers is of the utmost importance to our success. Therefore, every employee at Better Bread Bakery, from the accountant on up to the head baker, must make customer service a top priority. Excellent performance includes excellent customer service.

11:2 Job Performance Reviews

Rather than rely on casual feedback to keep their employees' performance on track, many companies have structured performance evaluation systems by which supervisors formally evaluate each employee's performance every so often (usually every six months or year).

If your company has such a system, then you should mention it in the handbook. To keep your flexibility, however, the following standard policy doesn't give a detailed description of how the system works. It simply alerts employees to the fact that there is a system for performance appraisal, and it states that the company requires employees to participate in it. You can give employees the details in other forms of communication, such as memoranda and company meetings.

Performance Reviews

Because our employees' performance is vital to our success, we conduct periodic reviews of individual employee performance. We hope that, through these reviews, our employees will learn what we expect of them, and we will learn what they expect of us.

We require all employees to participate in the review process. Failure to participate could lead to discipline, up to and including termination.

To learn more about our performance review system, contact

_____.

For more information on conducting performance reviews, including how to stay on top of this task and how to avoid legal missteps when writing evaluations, see *The Performance Appraisal Handbook: Legal & Practical Rules for Managers*, by Amy DelPo (Nolo).

11:2   Performance Reviews

CD File: 11_Performance.rtf

Include This Policy?
☐ Yes
☐ No
☐ Use our existing policy
☐ Other _____

Alternate Modifications
None

Additional Clauses
None

Related Policies
None

Notes

_____

_____

_____

_____

_____

_____

_____

_____

_____

_____

_____

_____

_____

_____

_____

_____

_____

_____

_____

_____

_____

12

Workplace Behavior

The Workplace Behavior section of a handbook is something of a grab bag of policies that define the minimum standards of conduct that your company expects from its employees. Other sections of the handbook will give more details about the various rules that employees must follow, but this section is where you set out the basics of how employees must behave while at work. It's also where you set out your company's discipline policy, if there is one.

<table>
<tr><td>

12:1   Please Act Professionally

CD File: 12_Work Behavior.rtf

Include This Policy?
- [ ] Yes
- [ ] No
- [ ] Use our existing policy
- [ ] Other _____

Alternate Modifications

None

Additional Clauses

Treatment of Customers

Insert?:   [ ] Yes   [ ] No

Related Policies

None

Notes

_____

_____

_____

_____

_____

_____

_____

_____

_____

_____

_____

_____

_____

_____

_____

_____

_____

_____

</td></tr>
</table>

12:1   Professional Conduct

Although you may not have articulated it before, your company probably expects from employees something more than mere work product. After all, they come into the workplace every day and interact with other employees, clients, and vendors. How they conduct themselves during these interactions is important to the smooth operation—indeed, to the success—of your business.

The following policy on professional conduct tells employees that you expect them to behave in a professional manner. It provides an explanation of professional conduct and informs employees that acting unprofessionally can be grounds for discipline.

Please Act Professionally

People who work together have an impact on each other's performance, productivity, and personal satisfaction in their jobs. In addition, how our employees act toward customers and vendors will influence whether those relationships are successful for our Company.

Because your conduct affects many more people than just yourself, we expect you to act in a professional manner whenever you are on Company property, conducting Company business, or representing the Company at business or social functions.

Although it is impossible to give an exhaustive list of everything that professional conduct means, it does, at a minimum, include the following:

- following all of the rules in this Handbook that apply to you
- refraining from rude, offensive, or outrageous behavior
- refraining from ridicule and hostile jokes
- treating coworkers, customers, and vendors with patience, respect, and consideration
- being courteous and helpful to others, and
- communicating openly with supervisors, managers, and coworkers.

Individuals who act unprofessionally will face discipline, up to and including termination.

Who Needs This Policy

A professional conduct policy can do no harm to a business, and it might even do it a lot of good. It encourages employees to "play nice," and it gives additional leeway in disciplining employees who behave unpleasantly but who don't violate a specific rule or let their performance or productivity drop.

Employee Conduct Outside of Work

The professional conduct policy in this chapter does not police employee conduct outside of work. Some companies believe that how employees act at all times—including during their private time—reflects on the company. Or maybe they prefer to employ only people with certain moral beliefs, so they allow employees' conduct outside of work to have an impact on their decisions about employees.

If your company is concerned about your employees' conduct outside of work, tread carefully—and consult with a lawyer. Many states have laws that protect employees from the prying eyes of their employer when they are not at work. These include laws protecting employees' right to privacy, laws prohibiting discrimination based on political activities, and laws prohibiting discrimination based on marital or family status.

Additional Clause Regarding Treatment of Customers

If employees have a great deal of contact with customers, you might want to add something to your professional conduct policy to emphasize how employees should treat customers. Does your company take the approach that "the customer is always right"? Does your company expect employees to do whatever it takes to make customers happy? Or are there limits to what your company expects employees to do for customers?

If you would like to include specific information about customer relations in this policy, add the following paragraph at the end of the sample policy (and complete it as appropriate for your company).

Additional Clause

The success of this Company depends in great part on the loyalty and good will of our customers. As a result, we expect our employees to behave in the following manner when interacting with customers:

- to treat all customers with courtesy and respect
- to always be helpful and cheerful toward customers
- to _____
  _____
- to _____
  _____, and
- to _____
  _____ .

12:2 Punctuality and Attendance

You may think it goes without saying that your company expects employees to show up to work consistently and on time. In these days of flexible schedules and telecommuting, however, prudent employers who care about punctuality and attendance specifically demand it. Otherwise, employees may think that it doesn't really matter what time they show up, as long as they get their work done. This policy makes it clear that it does matter—and that your company will discipline employees who take a lax attitude. It also sets out a process that employees can follow if they are unable to be at work or if they are going to be late.

Punctuality and Attendance

You are important to the effective operation of this business. When you are not here at expected times or on expected days, someone else must do your job or delay doing his or her own job while waiting for you to arrive. If you work with customers or vendors, they may grow frustrated if they can't reach you during your scheduled work times.

As a result, we expect you to keep regular attendance and to be on time and ready to work at the beginning of each scheduled workday. (In Section _____ of this Handbook, you can find a description of this Company's work hours, time keeping, and scheduling policies.)

Of course, things will sometimes happen that will prevent you from showing up to work on time. For example, you may be delayed by weather, a sick child, or car trouble. If you are going to be more than _____ minutes late, please call _____ _____ . If you cannot reach this person, please _____ . Please give this notice as far in advance as possible.

If you must miss a full day of work for reasons other than vacation, sick leave, or other approved leave (such as leave to serve on a jury or for a death in a family), you must notify _____ as far in advance as possible. If you cannot reach this person, _____ . (You can find information about this Company's vacation and leave policies in Handbook Section _____ .)

If you are late for work or fail to appear without calling in as required by this policy or by other policies in this Handbook, you will face disciplinary action, up to and including termination.

12:2   Punctuality and Attendance
CD File: 12_Work Behavior.rtf

Include This Policy?
☐ Yes
☐ No
☐ Use our existing policy
☐ Other _____

Alternate Modifications
None

Additional Clauses
None

Related Policies
None

Notes

_____
_____
_____
_____
_____
_____
_____
_____
_____
_____
_____
_____
_____
_____
_____
_____
_____
_____
_____
_____

How to Complete This Policy

To complete the policy you must decide three things:

- How much leeway will you give employees in terms of punctuality? That is, how many minutes late must they be before you require them to call in? This is something that you must decide based on the needs of your business. Typical periods range from 15 minutes to two hours.

- Whom do employees have to call if they are going to be late or miss work? Typically, this person is the employee's supervisor, but in some businesses this person might be the human resources manager or the office manager—whoever will be responsible for making sure the employee's duties are covered while the employee is out of the office.

- What should employees do if they can't reach the designated person? You might instruct employees to simply leave a voicemail for the individual, or you might require them to leave a message for that person with someone who holds a position that is always staffed—the office receptionist, for example.

12:3 Dress, Grooming, and Personal Hygiene

Workplace dress standards vary. Some employers ask only that their employees be clean and neat. Other employers have more specific policies—requiring a certain mode of dress or a uniform, for example.

We provide three alternate policies below, from which you can choose.

Policy A simply requires a clean and neat appearance from employees. It is very general and nonspecific. This allows you flexibility to set standards department by department, if you wish, through memos and instructions from supervisors. It also informs employees that your company will accommodate the needs of people with disabilities or people with specific religious or ethnic practices.

Policy B requires employees to wear a uniform. Most states have rules regarding who must pay for a work uniform: the employer or the employee. States also have rules as to who must pay for cleaning and repairing the uniform. If you require your employees to wear uniforms, be sure to check out your state's laws on these issues. Once you do so, you can add that information to the policy. For more information, contact your state labor department. (See Appendix A for contact information.)

Policy C requires employees to dress professionally, in addition to maintaining a neat and clean appearance.

Alternate Policy A

Employee Appearance and Dress

We ask all employees to use common sense when they dress for work. Please dress appropriately for your position and job duties, and please make sure you are neat and clean at all times.

If you have any questions about the proper attire for your position, please contact _____ _____ . We will try to reasonably accommodate an employee's special dress or grooming needs that are the result of religion, ethnicity, race, or disability.

12:3 Employee Appearance and Dress

CD File: 12_Work Behavior.rtf

Include This Policy?
- ☐ Yes
    Choose one: ☐ A ☐ B ☐ C
- ☐ No
- ☐ Use our existing policy
- ☐ Other _____

Alternate Modifications
None

Additional Clauses
Safety Concerns
    Insert?: ☐ Yes ☐ No

Policy C only: Allow Casual Dress on Fridays
    Insert?: ☐ Yes ☐ No

Related Policies
None

Notes

_____
_____
_____
_____
_____
_____
_____
_____
_____
_____
_____
_____
_____
_____
_____
_____

Alternate Policy B

Employees must wear a uniform during work hours. Please make sure you are neat and clean at all times, and please keep your uniform clean and in good condition.

If you have any questions about your uniform or about our appearance standards, please contact _____

_____ .

Alternate Policy C

We believe that a professional image enhances our work product and makes us more competitive in the marketplace. In part, we convey that image through the appearance of our employees. We ask all employees to use their common sense when dressing for work and to wear attire that is professional and appropriate. We also ask our employees to maintain a neat and clean appearance at all times.

Who Needs This Policy

Whether you need this policy will depend on your company culture and image and on the amount of contact that employees have with outsiders. The more formal or professional the culture and the more that employees interact with people outside the company, the more you will need a policy governing dress and appearance.

Additional Clause to Allow Casual Dress on Fridays

Many employers allow professional employees to "dress down" on Fridays. For some, this means that employees still have to dress up but that they can forgo the suit and tie. For others, it means T-shirts and blue jeans.

If you require professional dress during the week but would like to allow your employees to relax more on Fridays, add the following paragraph to Policy C. In the first blank, list the types of clothing you find acceptable on casual Fridays—such as slacks, collared shirts, jeans, dress shorts, and sandals. In the second blank, list clothing you do not find acceptable, even on Fridays—for example, T-shirts, tank tops, short or athletic shorts, or clothing that is torn, sheer, or see-through.

Additional Clause

Although we require professional attire Monday through Thursday, we celebrate Fridays here by allowing employees to dress casually. Acceptable casual clothing includes _____

_____

_____

_____

_____

[*list acceptable types of clothing*]. Unacceptable casual clothing includes _____

_____

_____

_____

_____

[*list unacceptable types of clothing*]. Even on Fridays, however, we ask employees to use good judgment and to maintain a neat and clean appearance.

Additional Clause Regarding Safety Issues

In some workplaces, employees cannot wear certain clothing or wear their hair in a certain style because of safety concerns. For example, most food service companies require employees to wear hair nets, and many companies in the manufacturing industry prohibit loose-fitting clothes and jewelry, which could get caught in machinery.

If there are health and safety reasons for dress and grooming standards, you should detail those either in the health and safety chapter of the handbook or through memos and instructions from supervisors. In this policy, you can simply refer employees to those rules by adding the following paragraph to your policy.

Additional Clause

We place specific restrictions on the dress and appearance of some employees for safety reasons. To learn about those restrictions, refer to _____

_____ .

Reality Check: Avoid Discriminatory Dress Codes

For the most part, the law will allow your company to govern how employees appear at work. Be careful, however, that you don't bump up against antidiscrimination laws when demanding certain modes of dress or appearance. Particular areas to watch out for include the following:

- **Sexual harassment.** If you require employees of a certain gender to dress in a sexually provocative way (for example, requiring female employees to wear tight, low-cut tops or short skirts), you may be accused of harassing those employees or of encouraging other people to harass them.

- **Sex discrimination.** Demanding different modes of dress for female and male employees leaves your company vulnerable to claims of gender discrimination. In addition, some states specifically prohibit employers from requiring female employees to wear skirts.

- **Race discrimination.** Some grooming policies disproportionately affect members of one race. For example, requiring that all men be clean-shaven can have a negative impact on African-American men, many of whom have a physical sensitivity to shaving.

- **Religious discrimination.** Some religions impose certain dress and grooming requirements on their members. For example, some Native Americans can't cut their hair; some Muslims must wear long beards and certain garments. If your company's grooming or dress policies force people to violate the tenets of their religion, the company could open itself up to claims of religious discrimination.

Although it's good to watch out for these issues, antidiscrimination laws do not mean that you can't require certain modes of dress; they just mean you must have a really good reason for doing so. If your company has a good reason for wanting to impose a grooming or dress standard that might raise discrimination issues, consult a lawyer for help.

12:4 Pranks and Practical Jokes

Most employers understand that employees who enjoy their work tend to be better and more productive performers. In some workplaces, however, employees carry enjoyment too far by playing pranks and practical jokes on each other. Although this may seem harmless at first blush, pranks and practical jokes can lead to real trouble.

For example, some pranks that employees think are harmless have racial or sexual undertones. For the victim of the prank, this may feel more like harassment or discrimination than innocent fun—and the employee may take up the issue with an attorney.

Even if the prank or joke doesn't cross the legal line, it may have the effect of disrupting the workplace and lowering the morale of the individual who was on the receiving end of the so-called humor.

This policy prohibits all pranks and practical jokes. It warns employees that they might face disciplinary action if they engage in such behavior.

Pranks and Practical Jokes

Although we want our employees to enjoy their jobs and have fun working together, we cannot allow employees to play practical jokes or pranks on each other. At best, these actions disrupt the workplace and dampen the morale of some; at worst, they lead to complaints of discrimination, harassment, or assault.

If you have any questions about this policy, contact _____ _____.

Employees who play pranks or practical jokes will face disciplinary action, up to and including termination.

Who Needs This Policy

Although this type of conduct occurs in all types of workplaces—from corporate law firms to longshoring operations—it does tend to be more prevalent in male-dominated and blue-collar industries. If you operate a business in these industries, or if your company has had problems with pranks and practical jokes in the past, you should consider having a policy explicitly prohibiting such activity.

On the other hand, if your employees do not tend to engage in such behavior, you can probably forgo this policy. Your policies regarding professional conduct, discrimination, and harassment should help you deal with any situations that arise.

12:4 Pranks and Practical Jokes
CD File: 12_Work Behavior.rtf

Include This Policy?
☐ Yes
☐ No
☐ Use our existing policy
☐ Other _____

Alternate Modifications
None

Additional Clauses
None

Related Policies
None

Notes

12:5 Threatening, Abusive, or Vulgar Language

Despite the old playground taunt, words can hurt you. They can lead to harassment and discrimination lawsuits, lower the morale and productivity of employees, and destroy the congenial atmosphere of the workplace.

In addition, employee violence is often preceded by threatening and abusive language. If an employee says something threatening or abusive, don't treat the situation lightly simply because the incident involves only words. Not only could your company be held legally liable if the employee later becomes violent (under a theory of law called "negligent retention"), but you or an employee could be injured or worse. Having a policy against this sort of language is a good first step in protecting a workplace from potential violence— and it can lay the groundwork for nipping a bad situation in the bud.

Threatening, Abusive, or Vulgar Language

We expect our employees to treat everyone they meet through their jobs with courtesy and respect. Threatening, abusive, and vulgar language has no place in our workplace. It destroys morale and relationships, and it impedes the effective and efficient operation of our business.

As a result, we will not tolerate threatening, abusive, or vulgar language from employees while they are on the worksite, conducting Company business, or attending Company-related business or social functions.

If you have any questions about this policy, contact _____ _____.

Employees who violate this policy will face disciplinary action, up to and including termination.

12:5 Threatening, Abusive, or Vulgar Language

CD File: 12_Work Behavior.rtf

Include This Policy?
- ☐ Yes
- ☐ No
- ☐ Use our existing policy
- ☐ Other _____

Alternate Modifications
None

Additional Clauses
None

Related Policies
None

Notes

_____

_____

_____

_____

_____

_____

_____

_____

_____

_____

_____

_____

_____

_____

_____

_____

_____

_____

_____

_____

12:6 Horseplay

Horseplay is boisterous physical interaction that disrupts the ordinary operation of a workplace. It usually begins innocently enough, arising from employees' more juvenile and playful impulses. Initially, it does not involve malice, ill will, or anger—it's just a matter of employees goofing off.

That being said, such aggressive playful conduct can often get out of hand, and what started out as innocent, yet loud, fun can turn into a fight or a brawl. Depending on the circumstances, it can also turn into discrimination, harassment, or assault. It's also a safety hazard.

Because horseplay is disruptive and can often lead to trouble, many employers ban it outright.

Horseplay

Although we want our employees to have fun while they work, we don't allow employees to engage in horseplay—which is fun that has gotten loud and boisterous and out of control. Horseplay disrupts the work environment and can get out of hand, leading to fighting, hurt feelings, safety hazards, or worse.

Employees who engage in horseplay will face disciplinary action, up to and including termination.

12:6 Horseplay

CD File: 12_Work Behavior.rtf

Include This Policy?
- ☐ Yes
- ☐ No
- ☐ Use our existing policy
- ☐ Other _____

Alternate Modifications

None

Additional Clauses

None

Related Policies

None

Notes

_____
_____
_____
_____
_____
_____
_____
_____
_____
_____
_____
_____
_____
_____
_____
_____
_____
_____

12:7   Fighting

CD File: 12_Work Behavior.rtf

Include This Policy?
- ☐ Yes
- ☐ No
- ☐ Use our existing policy
- ☐ Other _____

Alternate Modifications

None

Additional Clauses

None

Related Policies

None

Notes

_____
_____
_____
_____
_____
_____
_____
_____
_____
_____
_____
_____
_____
_____
_____
_____
_____
_____
_____

12:7 Fighting

Fights among employees not only injure the people involved but also damage collegiality among workers, disrupt the workplace, and can lead to more violence, physical and emotional injuries, and lawsuits. This policy prohibits fighting among employees and promises disciplinary action to those who engage in it. Verbal fighting can be just as damaging as physical fighting and is therefore encompassed by this policy.

Fighting

Verbal or physical fighting among employees is absolutely prohibited. Employees shall not engage in, provoke, or encourage a fight. Those who violate this policy will be disciplined, up to and including termination.

12:8 Sleeping on the Job

Depending on the type of business, employees who sleep on the job can create anything from a nuisance to a safety hazard. Most employers ban sleeping on the worksite outright, but some employers who schedule employees for exceptionally long shifts (for example, 24 hours) will expressly allow employees to sleep during designated times.

The following policy prohibits sleeping entirely and is designed for a business in which sleeping employees do not pose a safety hazard. If you would like to allow employees to sleep at designated times, or if you would like to emphasize the unsafe nature of sleeping, see the optional additional clauses that follow.

Sleeping on the Job

When our employees arrive at work, we expect them to be physically prepared to work through their day. Employees who sleep on the job dampen morale and productivity and deprive us of their work and companionship.

As a result, we do not allow any employees to sleep while at work. Employees who feel sick or unable to finish the day because of weariness should talk to _____ _____ about using sick leave to take the rest of the day off. (See Section _____ of this Handbook for information about our sick leave policy.)

Additional Clause to Allow Employees to Sleep Sometimes

If you would like to allow your employees to sleep at certain times, add the following clause at the end of the sample policy.

Additional Clause

We make an exception to this policy for certain employees who _____.

To find out if you fit within this exception, contact _____ _____.

12:8   Sleeping on the Job

CD File: 12_Work Behavior.rtf

☐ Yes

☐ No

☐ Use our existing policy

☐ Other _____

Alternate Modifications

None

Additional Clauses

Allow Employees to Sleep Sometimes

Insert?: ☐ Yes   ☐ No

Emphasize the Safety Hazard of Sleeping

Insert?: ☐ Yes   ☐ No

Related Policies

None

Notes

Additional Clause to Emphasize the Safety Hazard of Sleeping

If employees who sleep on the job pose a safety risk (either to themselves or to others), add the following paragraph between the first and second paragraphs of the sample policy. In the blank, insert a description—either by job department or job title—of which employees pose a safety hazard when they sleep.

Additional Clause

> For certain employees, sleeping on the job creates a safety hazard. Employees who work in _____
> _____
> _____
> _____
>
> [*list applicable job department(s) or titles*] create unacceptable risks to their own safety and the safety of others when they fail to be attentive and alert while working. For these employees, sleeping on the job violates both this policy and our safety policies. (See Section _____ of this Handbook for information about our safety program.)

12:9 Insubordination

Employee insubordination comes in two forms: (1) refusing to obey direct orders or instructions and (2) undermining authority through words and conduct. Insubordination is a particularly destructive force in the workplace, because it interferes with one of an employer's most basic rights: to operate the business as it sees fit. This means telling employees what jobs need to be done and how—and expecting them to do so. It also means directing and controlling a company's business and culture.

Of course, not every time an employee refuses to follow an order is insubordination. Under federal law and the laws of most states, employees have a right to refuse to work in unsafe conditions. They also have a right to refuse to do anything illegal.

These legal issues aren't the only reason to have an insubordination policy with some flexibility in it. Sometimes, employees might have ideas about how jobs can be done better and more efficiently. You don't want to squelch employee opinions and innovation by turning workers into robots who unthinkingly follow orders.

The policy below prohibits insubordination while explaining how employees may disobey orders acceptably if necessary.

Insubordination

This workplace operates on a system of mutual respect between supervisors and employees. Supervisors must treat their employees with dignity and understanding, and employees must show due regard for their supervisors' authority.

Insubordination occurs when employees unreasonably refuse to obey the orders or follow the instructions of their supervisors. It also occurs when employees, through their actions or words, show disrespect toward their supervisors.

Insubordinate employees will face discipline, up to and including termination.

We understand, however, that there will be times when employees have valid reasons for refusing to do as their supervisor says. Perhaps the employee fears for his safety or the safety of others. Perhaps the employee believes that following instructions will violate the law or pose some other problem for this Company. Or maybe the employee thinks that there is a better way to accomplish a goal or perform a task. When these issues arise, we do not ask that employees blindly follow orders. Instead, we ask that employees explain the situation to their supervisor. If, after hearing the employee's side, the supervisor continues to give the same order or rule, the employee must either obey or use the complaint procedures described in Section _____ of this Handbook.

12:9 Insubordination
CD File: 12_Work Behavior.rtf

Include This Policy?
☐ Yes
☐ No
☐ Use our existing policy
☐ Other _____

Alternate Modifications
None

Additional Clauses
None

Related Policies
None

Notes

_____

_____

_____

_____

_____

_____

_____

_____

_____

_____

_____

_____

_____

_____

_____

_____

12:10 Progressive Discipline

CD File: 12_Work Behavior.rtf

Include This Policy?
- [ ] Yes
- [ ] No
- [ ] Use our existing policy
- [ ] Other _____

Alternate Modifications

None

Additional Clauses

None

Related Policies

None

Notes

_____
_____
_____
_____
_____
_____
_____
_____
_____
_____
_____
_____
_____
_____
_____
_____

12:10 Progressive Discipline

In a progressive discipline system, employers use a range of disciplinary actions and counseling sessions to motivate employees to improve their conduct. In such a system, the goal of the discipline is not punitive, but rather it is communicative. A progressive discipline system can be a valuable tool in improving employee performance and productivity. It can also protect a company from lawsuits by ensuring that the company is fair to employees and by forcing it to document employee misconduct and the company's response.

If you have a progressive discipline system at your workplace, you should explain it to employees in general terms in the handbook.

Progressive discipline systems vary greatly from workplace to workplace. As a result, we cannot provide standard policy language. An example of what a progressive discipline policy might look like is provided below.

Reality Check: Follow Your Disciplinary Policy

If a company puts a written progressive discipline policy in the handbook, it must follow the policy—even when it doesn't want to. From an employee relations standpoint, a company's failure to follow its own policies will only make the company's personnel decisions look arbitrary and unfair. In addition, a company might have trouble convincing employees to follow rules when it fails to do so itself.

From a legal standpoint, a company's failure to follow its own progressive discipline policy leaves the company vulnerable to lawsuits. Even there is a good reason for firing someone, the company will have trouble proving it if it didn't follow the policy. In addition, some courts might view a written policy as a type of contract between the company and its employees. In such a situation, the court might view failure to follow the policy as a breach of contract.

SAMPLE POLICY LANGUAGE

Any employee conduct that, in the opinion of the Company, interferes with or adversely affects our business is sufficient grounds for disciplinary action.

Disciplinary action can range from oral warnings to immediate discharge. Our general policy is to take disciplinary steps in the following order:

- oral warning(s)
- written reprimand(s)

- suspension, and
- termination.

However, we reserve the right to alter the order described above, to skip disciplinary steps, to eliminate disciplinary steps, or to create new and/or additional disciplinary steps.

In choosing the appropriate disciplinary action, we may consider any number of the following things:

- the seriousness of your conduct
- your history of misconduct
- your employment record
- your length of employment with this Company
- the strength of the evidence against you
- your ability to correct the conduct
- your attitude about the conduct
- actions we have taken for similar conduct by other employees
- how your conduct affects this Company, its customers, and your coworkers, and
- any other circumstances related to the nature of the misconduct, to your employment with this Company, and to the effect of the misconduct on the business of this Company.

We will give those considerations whatever weight we deem appropriate. Depending on the circumstances, we may give some considerations more weight than other considerations—or no weight at all.

Some conduct may result in immediate termination. Here are some examples:

- theft of company property
- excessive tardiness or absenteeism
- arguing or fighting with customers, coworkers, managers, or supervisors
- brandishing a weapon at work
- threatening the physical safety of customers, coworkers, managers, or supervisors
- physically or verbally assaulting someone at work
- any illegal conduct at work
- using or possessing alcohol or illegal drugs at work
- working under the influence of alcohol or illegal drugs
- failing to carry out reasonable job assignments
- insubordination
- making false statements on a job application
- violating Company rules and regulations, and
- unlawful discrimination and harassment.

Of course, it is impossible to compile an exhaustive list of the types of conduct that will result in immediate termination. The ones listed above are merely illustrations.

You should remember that your employment is at the mutual consent of you and this Company. This policy does not change this fact. This means that you or this Company can terminate our employment relationship at will, at any time, with or without cause, and with or without advance notice.

As a result, this Company reserves its right to terminate your employment at any time, for any lawful reason, including reasons not listed above. You also have the right to end your employment at any time.

■

13

Health and Safety

Workplace safety is of paramount concern to savvy employers—and for good reason. Dangerous situations, accidents, violence, or breaches of security can have disastrous workplace consequences, including lost productivity, raised insurance premiums, stolen or damaged equipment, employee injuries, or even deaths.

What's more, the government regulates workplace safety issues very heavily. Both federal and state laws require employers to provide a workplace free of hazards that could cause serious harm to their employees. These laws also require employers to investigate and report workplace accidents, provide employees with safety training for their jobs, and keep records on workplace safety. Depending on the type of business an employer runs, virtually every aspect of its operations may be subject to detailed safety rules.

Although no employer can guarantee an accident-free workplace, policies that promote workplace safety are a good start.

13:1   Safety Policy

CD File: 13_Health Safety.rtf

Include This Policy?
- ☐ Yes
- ☐ No
- ☐ Use our existing policy
- ☐ Other _____

Alternate Modifications

None

Additional Clauses

Give Specific Safety Instructions

Insert?:   ☐ Yes   ☐ No

Related Policies

Chapter 12 provides policies on workplace behavior—including horseplay, fighting, and professional conduct.

Notes

_____

_____

_____

_____

_____

_____

_____

_____

_____

_____

_____

_____

_____

_____

_____

_____

_____

13:1 Workplace Safety

A basic safety policy is a must for every employer, in every type of business. Federal and state laws require employers to keep their workplace free of hazards, investigate accidents quickly, and keep proper safety records. An employer cannot meet these legal requirements unless its employees follow safe work habits and report workplace accidents and injuries—as our sample policy directs them to do.

Your workplace safety policy should tell employees that safety is a top concern for your company, let employees know about safety rules, and explain how to report accidents or injuries.

Some states require particular policy language. The federal law that regulates health and safety on the job is called the Occupational Safety and Health Act, or OSHA (29 U.S.C. §§ 651 and following). In addition, almost half of the states have adopted their own workplace safety laws that are at least as strict as OSHA. Although OSHA doesn't require employers to adopt a written workplace safety policy, some of these state laws do. For example, California employers must adopt a written "injury and illness prevention program." To find out what your state requires, contact your state labor department (see Appendix A for contact information) or consult with an experienced employment attorney.

Safety Policy

Our Company takes employee safety very seriously. In order to provide a safe workplace for everyone, every employee must follow our safety rules:

- Horseplay, roughhousing, and other physical acts that may endanger employees or cause accidents are prohibited.
- Employees must follow their supervisors' safety instructions.
- Employees in certain positions may be required to wear protective equipment, such as hair nets, hard hats, safety glasses, work boots, ear plugs, or masks. Your supervisor will let you know if your position requires protective gear.
- Employees in certain positions may be prohibited from wearing dangling jewelry or apparel, or may be required to pull back or cover their hair, for safety purposes. Your supervisor will tell you if you fall into one of these categories.
- All equipment and machinery must be used properly. This means all guards, restraints, and other safety devices must be used at all times. Do not use equipment for other than its intended purpose.
- All employees must immediately report any workplace condition that they believe to be unsafe to their supervisor. The Company will look into the matter promptly.
- All employees must immediately report any workplace accident or injury to _____

_____ .

Additional Clause to Give Specific Safety Instructions

Every type of industry has its own unique safety hazards. Our basic standard policy can be modified to include safety rules particular to your company. For example, you might want to include rules on the proper use of certain types of equipment and machinery; proper techniques for physical labor, such as lifting and carrying heavy objects; or ergonomic rules for those who operate computers or cash registers or perform other types of repetitive motions. If so, simply add these rules to the end of the policy.

<table>
<tr><td>

13:2   Workplace Security

CD File: 13_Health Safety.rtf

Include This Policy?
☐ Yes
☐ No
☐ Use our existing policy
☐ Other _____

Alternate Modifications
None

Additional Clauses
Require Escorts for Visitors
Insert?: ☐ Yes ☐ No

Require Badges for Visitors
Insert?: ☐ Yes ☐ No

Instructions for Employees
Who Are the Last to Leave the
Workplace
Insert?: ☐ Yes ☐ No

Related Policies
None

Notes

_____
_____
_____
_____
_____
_____
_____
_____
_____
_____
_____
_____
_____
_____

</td></tr>
</table>

13:2 Workplace Security

A workplace security policy explains what measures the company expects employees to take to keep its premises and property safe from intruders. Clearly, what you include in the policy will depend on the nature of your workplace: An office building in a bustling metropolis will have different security concerns from a farming operation. However, any security policy should include rules on securing the premises (locking up, closing gates, shutting off machinery, or securing tools, for example), rules on after-hours access to the workplace, and rules on workplace visitors.

Workplace Security

It is every employee's responsibility to help keep our workplace secure from unauthorized intruders. Every employee must comply with these security precautions.

When you leave work for the day, please do all of the following: _____
_____
_____ .

After-hours access to the workplace is limited to those employees who need to work late. If you are going to be working past our usual closing time, please let your supervisor know.

Employees are allowed to have an occasional visitor in the workplace, but workplace visits should be the exception rather than the rule. If you are anticipating a visitor, please let _____

know. When your visitor arrives, you will be notified.

How to Complete This Policy

In the first blank space, list all of the things employees are expected to do before they leave for the day. For example, the policy might tell employees to shut off their computers, turn off equipment, turn off lights, close and lock office windows, store and secure tools, lock and garage company vehicles, or lock any area that won't be used any more that day.

In the second blank space, list the position of the person who will greet visitors to your company. This might be a receptionist, security guard, or front desk attendant.

Additional Clause to Require Escorts or Badges for Visitors

Our sample policy allows employees to have visitors but asks them to keep visitors to a minimum. Some businesses, particularly large companies and companies that have industrial operations, put more restrictions on visitors in the workplace. Visitors might be required to wear a badge or other identification, or the employee who invited the visitor might be required to accompany the visitor at all times on company premises—including escorting the visitor to and from the entrance. If you wish to adopt either of these policies, simply add one or both of the modifications below to the policy paragraph on visitors.

Additional Clause

Visitors must wear an identification badge at all times when they are in our workplace. Visitors can get a badge at _____

_____ .

They must return the badge when they leave Company premises.

Additional Clause

Do not leave your visitor unattended in the workplace. If you have a visitor, you must accompany your visitor at all times. This includes escorting your visitor to and from the entrance to our Company.

Additional Clause to Give Instructions to Employees Who Are the Last to Leave the Workplace

In many companies, supervisors, managers, or the owner are always the last to leave the workplace. And some workplaces (such as 24-hour convenience stores or factories that operate round the clock) never close. However, if employees at your company are sometimes the last ones at work, you'll have to modify this policy to let them know how to secure the premises. Insert the sample modification, below, filling in the blank to tell employees what is expected of them. For example, the policy might direct employees to lock the building or security gates, set an alarm, make sure all windows are closed and locked, or turn off all equipment and lights.

Additional Clause

If you are the last to leave the workplace for the evening, you are responsible for doing all of the following: _____

_____

_____

_____

_____

_____ .

If you have questions about any of these responsibilities, please talk to your supervisor.

13:3 What to Do in an Emergency

Every business should have a written policy letting employees know what to do in case of emergency. Employees should be familiar with evacuation routes and procedures to ensure their safety should disaster strike. Employees should also be told where to congregate once they have left the workplace. This will help management—and rescue workers—figure out whether anyone is missing and may need assistance getting out of the workplace.

In this policy, you can describe evacuation plans, the location of emergency equipment (such as first aid supplies or fire extinguishers) kept on site, and where employees should go if they are forced to leave the workplace.

What to Do in an Emergency

In case of an emergency, such as a fire, earthquake, or accident, your first priority should be your own safety. In the event of an emergency causing serious injuries, IMMEDIATELY DIAL 9-1-1 to alert police and rescue workers of the situation.

If you hear a fire alarm or in case of an emergency that requires evacuation, please proceed quickly and calmly to the fire exits. The Company will hold periodic fire drills to familiarize everyone with the routes they should take. Remember that every second may count—don't return to the workplace to retrieve personal belongings or work-related items. Once you have exited the building, head towards the

_____

_____ .

(For our Company's policy on workplace violence, see Section _____ of this Handbook.)

Reality Check: Fire Drills Are Not Just for Kids

All of us probably remember the fire drills of grade school, but when was the last time your company held a fire drill? Emergency drills are vitally important for every business. They help workers learn emergency evacuation procedures, so they'll know what to do if a real disaster strikes. Of course, these drills disrupt business and may take 15 or 20 minutes to conduct. But if that advance planning later saves lives or prevents serious injuries, the inconvenience will seem a very small price to pay.

13:3   What to Do in an Emergency

CD File: 13_Health Safety.rtf

Include This Policy?
- ☐ Yes
- ☐ No
- ☐ Use our existing policy
- ☐ Other _____

Alternate Modifications
None

Alternate Modifications
None

Additional Clauses
Location of Emergency Supplies
Insert?: ☐ Yes   ☐ No

Related Policies
None

Notes

_____

_____

_____

_____

_____

_____

_____

_____

_____

_____

_____

_____

_____

_____

_____

_____

_____

_____

Additional Clause to Include Location of Emergency Supplies

Many businesses keep a store of emergency supplies in the workplace. If your company takes this very sensible precaution, modify the policy to let employees know where the supplies are kept. You can add the modification below, filling in the blanks to indicate the location of the supplies. If your company keeps additional types of supplies that are not listed below, add them on at the end.

Additional Clause

[*Company name*] keeps emergency supplies on hand. First aid kits are located _____

_____ .

Fire extinguishers can be found _____
_____ .

Earthquake preparedness kits are kept _____

_____ .

We also keep a supply of flashlights in _____ .
_____
_____ .

13:4 Smoking

Few workplace issues are as divisive as smoking. Smokers want the freedom to enjoy a cigarette without having to stand outside in the cold; nonsmokers want to work comfortably, without smoke irritating their eyes and throats. It is the employer's unfortunate job to decide how to balance these interests.

There are a few legal guidelines that can help. Most states allow employers to ban smoking in the workplace—so if your company wants to prohibit employees from lighting up, it can probably do so. However, if your company wants to allow smoking or allow it in certain areas, you will have to check your state and local laws to find out exactly what is allowed. These laws are summarized in "State Laws on Smoking in the Workplace" at the end of this chapter. Some states require employers to ban smoking, at least in certain kinds of businesses. For example, California bans smoking in the workplace, public or private. And other states prohibit smoking in certain kinds of business establishments, such as hospitals or restaurants.

Because of these variations, we offer you two sample policies to choose from. Policy A bans smoking altogether; Policy B allows smoking in designated areas.

Policy A

Smoking Is Prohibited

For the health, comfort, and safety of our employees, smoking is not allowed on Company property.

Policy B

Smoking Policy

To accommodate employees who smoke as well as those who do not, the Company has created smoking and nonsmoking areas. Smoking is allowed only in _____ _____ _____ .

The Company has posted signs designating smoking and nonsmoking areas. Employees who smoke are required to observe these signs and to smoke in designated areas only.

13:4   Smoking

CD File: 13_Health Safety.rtf

Include This Policy?
- ☐ Yes
  - *Choose one:* ☐ A   ☐ B
- ☐ No
- ☐ Use our existing policy
- ☐ Other _____

Alternate Modifications
None

Additional Clauses
Regulate When Employees May Smoke
   Insert?: ☐ Yes   ☐ No

Help Employees Quit Smoking
   Insert?: ☐ Yes   ☐ No
   If yes, choose one: ☐ A   ☐ B

Prohibit Discrimination Against Smokers
   Insert?: ☐ Yes   ☐ No

Related Policies
None

Notes

_____

_____

_____

_____

_____

_____

_____

_____

_____

_____

_____

_____

_____

Reality Check: Special Rules for Smoking Areas

States that allow smoking on the job often impose strict rules to prevent smoke from spreading to the rest of the workplace. Some require that any workplace smoking area have a separate ventilation system, so the smoky air does not recirculate to the rest of the office. Others require physical barriers—such as walls or partitions—to separate smoking and nonsmoking areas.

Even if your state does not impose these requirements, however, it's a good idea to keep smoking areas separate from the rest of the workplace. Nonsmokers who are physically troubled by smoke can complain to the Occupational Safety and Health Administration (OSHA) and may even have a legal claim under the Americans With Disabilities Act (ADA). There's no need to invite this kind of problem: If your company allows smoking, keep the air clean for nonsmokers by designating a smoking area that won't allow smoke to enter the rest of the workplace.

Who Needs This Policy

This is one of the few policies that is mandatory, at least in some states. If your company plans to allow smoking anywhere in the workplace, certain states—including Delaware, Florida, and New York—require employers to adopt a written smoking policy. In states that require a smoking policy, the rules vary as to what the policy must include. Check "State Laws on Smoking in the Workplace" at the end of this chapter to see what your state requires.

Additional Clause to Regulate When Employees May Smoke

"Smoking breaks" are a major source of workplace tension. Nonsmokers wonder why their smoking coworkers feel they have a right to take ten minutes off every hour or so to light up—and employers notice the lost work time (and resulting lost productivity). To combat this problem, some employers add language to their smoking policies reminding employees that they may smoke during scheduled or authorized breaks only. The modification below can be added to Policy A—you should add it to Policy B only if employees are required to smoke somewhere other than their workspaces (otherwise, they can smoke while working and need not take a break).

Additional Clause

> You may smoke during meal or rest breaks only. Employees may not take "smoking breaks" in addition to the regular breaks provided to every employee under our policies.
>
> (For our Company's policy on work and rest breaks, see Section _____ of this Handbook.)

Additional Clause to Help Employees Quit Smoking

It's no secret that employees who smoke tend to cost employers more money, on average, than nonsmokers. Smokers tend to have higher rates of absenteeism and higher health care costs. At the same time, we all know that smoking is a tough habit to give up—especially for those who try to quit on their own, without any support or encouragement.

Some employers offer to help their employees quit smoking by referring employees to, or paying for, smoking cessation programs. If your company offers health insurance to employees and your provider offers such a program, you can refer employees to that program by adding Additional Clause A, below, to the end of the policy. If not, your company may want to offer financial and other support to employees who want to enroll in such a program—add Additional Clause B, below, to the end of your policy to do so.

Additional Clause A

> Our Company encourages those who wish to quit smoking. Our health insurance provider offers a program to help employees stop smoking. If you are interested in this program, ask _____
>
> [the human resources department or benefits administrator] for more details. Or you can contact our insurance carrier directly.
>
> (For information on health insurance, see Section _____ of this Handbook.)

Additional Clause B

> Our Company encourages those who wish to quit smoking. If you are interested in getting help to stop smoking, the
>
> _____
>
> [*human resources department or benefits administrator*] can direct you to local smoking cessation programs. If you complete one of the programs on the Company's approved list, we will pay the cost of your participation.

Additional Clause to Prohibit Discrimination Against Smokers

Many states prohibit employment discrimination against smokers. Some of these laws apply only to smoking, while others protect any lawful activity in which the employee chooses to engage outside of work hours. Either way, in these states, employers may not make employment decisions based on the fact that an employee or applicant smokes. Check "State Laws on Smoking in the Workplace" at the end of this chapter to see whether your company needs to comply with this type of law.

If your state prohibits this kind of discrimination, you might want to add the following modification to the smoking policy to let employees know that your company will comply with the law.

Additional Clause

> We recognize that smoking tobacco products is legal and that employees have the right to smoke outside of work hours.
>
> _____
>
> [*Company name*] will not discriminate against any applicant or employee based on that person's choice to smoke.

13:5 Violence

Violence in the workplace is a frightening topic. The media reports stories about former employees, disgruntled clients or customers, or abusive spouses storming into a business and injuring or killing all who cross their paths. Of course, no policy can eliminate the risk that your company might face a violent incident. But a common-sense policy to prohibit violence—and to let employees know what to do if they fear or experience a violent incident—can go a long way toward making the workplace safer.

Violence Is Prohibited

We will not tolerate violence in the workplace. Violence includes physical altercations, coercion, pushing or shoving, horseplay, intimidation, stalking, and threats of violence. Any comments about violence will be taken seriously—and may result in your termination. Please do not joke or make offhand remarks about violence.

Who Needs This Policy

Including an antiviolence policy in your handbook provides several benefits. First, it lets employees know that the company will take all violent incidents seriously—and defines violence in a way that includes jokes about violence, roughhousing, or threats. This puts employees on notice that violence is no laughing matter. It should also minimize instances in which an employee alleged to have acted violently comes up with excuses like "I didn't mean it" or "I was only joking."

Second, it tells employees what to do if a violent incident occurs—to take steps to protect themselves and their co-workers immediately by calling emergency personnel if necessary, and to report less-serious incidents to company management. If managers aren't made aware of escalating aggressions in the workplace, they won't be able to intervene while the problem is still brewing. Encouraging employees to come forward will go a long way towards helping prevent more serious incidents.

And, third, it lays down the law on weapons in the workplace. (See "Alternate Modifications Regarding Weapons," below.)

13:5   Violence Is Prohibited

CD File: 13_Health Safety.rtf

Include This Policy?
☐ Yes
☐ No
☐ Use our existing policy
☐ Other _____

Alternate Modifications
Weapons Policy
Choose one: ☐ A   ☐ B

What to Do in Case of Violence
Choose one: ☐ A   ☐ B

Additional Clauses
None

Related Policies
None

Notes
_____
_____
_____
_____
_____
_____
_____
_____
_____
_____
_____
_____
_____
_____
_____
_____
_____
_____

Alternate Modifications Regarding Weapons

You will need to add policy language to address weapons in the workplace. We present two options below. Alternate Modification A prohibits weapons except for items required for work—and employees must get authorization even in this situation. Alternate Modification B is for companies that have at least a few employees who must carry weapons.

To Prohibit Weapons

Use this modification to prohibit all weapons in the workplace, except for items required for work. In any workplace, an employee might have to use an item that could be considered a weapon (such as a knife). Therefore, this modification allows employees to carry and use such items, if they are authorized to do so by their supervisor. Companies that do not require or allow employees to use weapons generally should use this modification.

Alternate Modification A

No Weapons

No weapons are allowed in our workplace. Weapons include firearms, knives, brass knuckles, martial arts equipment, clubs or bats, and explosives. If your work requires you to use an item that might qualify as a weapon, you must receive authorization from your supervisor to bring that item to work or use it in the workplace. Any employee found with an unauthorized weapon in the workplace will be subject to discipline, up to and including termination.

To Allow Weapons for Certain Employees

Some companies may require their employees to carry weapons. For example, a company that provides security services may require employees to carry a gun or nightstick. If a significant number of employees will need to carry weapons regularly, use this modification to specify who is authorized to do so and under what circumstances. In the blank space, list the positions for which workers are required to carry weapons—don't list the names of individual workers, as this will require you to update the policy every time you have a personnel change.

Alternate Modification B

Weapons in the Workplace

Weapons are generally not allowed in our workplace. Weapons include firearms, knives, brass knuckles, martial arts equipment, clubs or bats, and explosives.

However, some of our employees are required to carry weapons in order to perform their jobs. Weapons may be required in the following positions: _____

_____

_____

_____ .

If you hold one of these positions, ask your supervisor whether you will be required to carry a weapon. If your job requires you to carry a weapon, you must receive authorization from your supervisor to do so. You may be required to complete training courses, pass a safety test, and/or get a license in order to be authorized to carry a weapon.

Alternate Modifications on What to Do in Case of Violence

Some companies employ their own security personnel or do business in a building that has its own security force. If this is true for your company, you may want to ask employees to contact these security people—who are already on site and are familiar with the layout of the workplace—first. You can use Alternate Modification A, below, to accomplish this; in the first blank, insert the telephone number of the internal security personnel.

If your workplace does not have private security, you should tell employees to dial 9-1-1 when confronted with violence. You can use Alternate Modification B, below, to accomplish this.

In either modification, fill in the second blank with the person to whom employees should report violence that does not require an immediate response.

Alternate Modification A

What to Do in Case of Violence

If you observe an incident or threat of violence that is immediate and serious, call security personnel at _____
_____. If you are unable to reach someone at this number, IMMEDIATELY DIAL 9-1-1 and report the incident to the police.

   If the incident or threat does not appear to require immediate police intervention, please contact _____

_____

and report it as soon as possible, using the Company's complaint procedure. All complaints will be investigated and appropriate action will be taken. You will not face retaliation for making a complaint.

Alternate Modification B

What to Do in Case of Violence

If you observe an incident or threat of violence that is immediate and serious, IMMEDIATELY DIAL 9-1-1 and report it to the police.

   If the incident or threat does not appear to require immediate police intervention, please contact _____

_____

and report it as soon as possible, using the Company's complaint procedure. All complaints will be investigated and appropriate action will be taken. You will not face retaliation for making a complaint.

Reality Check: Stress Can Lead to Violence

Problems outside the workplace—such as money troubles, relationship problems, and drug or alcohol addictions—can lead to violence on the job. Many violent workplace incidents stem from domestic violence, for example. Your company can take great strides towards minimizing the chances of a violent incident—and improving the lives of its employees—by adopting an Employee Assistance Program (EAP).

EAPs can help employees with a variety of problems inside and outside the workplace. Common offerings include therapy for individuals or couples; help kicking a drug, alcohol, or smoking habit; advice on exercise and nutrition; anger management classes; assistance with estate planning; and debt management counseling. Talk to your company's insurance carrier for more information about EAPs. Many insurers offer EAP services as part of an overall mental health benefit.

For information on federal and state health and safety laws, go to the website of the Occupational Safety and Health Administration, the federal agency that administers workplace health and safety rules, at www.osha.gov. You'll find a number of helpful publications describing employers' legal obligations, as well as a list of state health and safety agencies.

For information on preventing and investigating workplace violence, see *Workplace Investigations*, by Lisa Guerin (Nolo). This step-by-step guide includes detailed information on investigating common workplace problems, including violence.

State Laws on Smoking in the Workplace

Note: The states of Alabama, Arizona, Arkansas, Georgia, Kansas, Michigan, New Mexico, Ohio, and Texas are not included in this chart because they do not have laws governing smoking in private workplaces. Different rules may apply to workplaces that are also public spaces, such as restaurants, bars, hotels, or casinos—we don't cover those rules here. Check with your state department of labor (see Appendix A for contact list) or with your state or local health department if you need more information.

Alabama

Ala. Code § 22-15A-4

Workplaces where laws apply: Enclosed places of employment with 5 or more employees.

Where smoking prohibited: Employer may prohibit smoking in all or part of workplace. Individual employee may designate his or her own work area as a nonsmoking area. No smoking in common work areas unless majority of workers in that area agree to designate it as a smoking area.

Where smoking permitted: Majority of workers in an area may decide to designate common work area as smoking area, unless employer prohibits.

Accommodations for nonsmokers: Employers must provide signs to post if an employee designates his or her own work area as nonsmoking.

Employer smoking policy: Written policy must meet minimum requirements and be communicated to all employees.

Alaska

Alaska Stat. §§ 18.35.300 and following

Workplaces where laws apply: Any private place of business that posts signs regulating smoking; restaurants serving more than 50.

Where smoking prohibited: Throughout workplace except in designated smoking area. Employer may designate entire site nonsmoking.

Where smoking permitted: Designated smoking area.

Smoking area requirements: Ventilated or separated to protect nonsmokers from active by-products of smoke.

Accommodations for nonsmokers: Reasonable accommodations to protect the health of nonsmokers.

California

Cal. Lab. Code § 6404.5

Workplaces where laws apply: Workplaces with more than 5 employees.

Exceptions: Designated lobby areas; meeting and banquet rooms when food is not being served; warehouses over 100,000 sq. ft. with fewer than 20 employees; truck cabs if no nonsmoking employees are present.

Where smoking prohibited: Employer may not knowingly or intentionally permit smoking in any enclosed workplace; must take reasonable steps to prevent nonemployees from smoking. May designate entire site nonsmoking.

Where smoking permitted: Breakrooms designated for smokers.

Smoking area requirements: Breakroom must be in a nonwork area. No employee may be required to enter room as part of job (does not apply to custodial work when room is unoccupied). Air must be exhausted directly outside with a fan and cannot recirculate to other areas of the building.

Accommodations for nonsmokers: If there is a breakroom for smokers, must be enough breakrooms for all nonsmokers.

Accommodations for smokers: None required. However, employers with 5 or fewer employees may permit smoking if:
- all the employees agree
- no minors are allowed in the smoking area, and
- no employee is required to enter smoking area.

Colorado

Colo. Rev. Stat. §§ 25-14-103, 24-34-402.5

Workplaces where laws apply: Any enclosed indoor workplace.

Exceptions: Offices occupied exclusively by smokers even if visited by nonsmokers. Restaurants.

Accommodations for nonsmokers: Employers encouraged to create physically separate nonsmoking work areas; must make effort to provide separate nonsmoking areas in employee lounges and cafeterias.

Protection from discrimination: Employee may not be fired for lawful conduct offsite during nonwork hours.

Connecticut

Conn. Gen. Stat. Ann. §§ 31-40q, 31-40s

Workplaces where laws apply: Enclosed facilities.

Where smoking prohibited: Employer may prohibit smoking throughout the workplace.

Smoking area requirements: Employers with fewer than 5 employees: Existing physical barriers and ventilation systems. Employers with 5 or more employees: Air must be exhausted directly outside with a fan and cannot

State Laws on Smoking in the Workplace (continued)

recirculate to other areas of the building; room must be in a nonwork area where no employee is required to enter.

Accommodations for nonsmokers: Employers with fewer than 5 employees: Employer must provide one or more clearly designated work areas for nonsmoking employees. Employers with 5 or more employees: If there are smoking rooms, employer must provide sufficient nonsmoking break rooms.

Protection from discrimination: Employer may not require employee to refrain from smoking as a condition of employment.

Delaware
Del. Code Ann. tit. 16, §§ 2902 to 2908

Workplaces where laws apply: Indoor areas.

Exceptions: Restaurants serving 50 or fewer.

Where smoking prohibited: Any place designated a smoke-free work area.

Smoking area requirements: Walls or other physical barriers that separate area.

Accommodations for nonsmokers: Employer must provide nonsmoking work area for every employee who requests one; must provide sufficient nonsmoking areas in lounges, lunchrooms, and cafeterias.

Accommodations for smokers: Employer may provide a smoking work area.

Protection from discrimination: Employer may not discriminate or retaliate against employee who files a complaint or testifies in a proceeding about workplace smoking laws.

Employer penalties and liabilities: $1,000 to $5,000 penalty for each discrimination violation.

Employer smoking policy: Must adopt and implement a written policy that outlines accommodations for nonsmokers and smokers.

District of Columbia
D.C. Code Ann. §§ 7-1701 & following, 7-1703.03

Workplaces where laws apply: Any private employer.

Where smoking prohibited: Throughout the workplace except for designated smoking area.

Where smoking permitted: Designated smoking area.

Smoking area requirements: Physical barrier or separate room.

Accommodations for smokers: Employer required to provide smoking area.

Protection from discrimination: Employee may not be fired or discriminated against in hiring, wages, benefits, or terms of employment because of being a smoker.

Employer smoking policy: Must have written policy that designates a smoking area; must notify each employee orally and post policy within 3 weeks after adopting it.

Florida
Fla. Stat. Ann. §§ 386.201 to 386.209

Workplaces where laws apply: All enclosed indoor workplaces (more than 50% covered and surrounded by physical barriers).

Exceptions: Private residences and standalone bars.

Where smoking prohibited: Smoking is prohibited throughout the workplace.

Employer smoking policy: Employer must develop and enforce a policy prohibiting smoking in the workplace. May post "No Smoking" signs to increase awareness.

Hawaii
Haw. Rev. Stat. §§ 328K-11 and following

Workplaces where laws apply: Any private business that receives state grants or subsidies.

Where smoking prohibited: Employer decides based on preferences of nonsmokers and smokers. If decision does not satisfy all employees, workers will vote to prohibit or permit smoking in their work area.

Where smoking permitted: Employer decides based on preferences of smokers and nonsmokers. If decision does not satisfy all employees, workers will vote to permit or prohibit smoking in their work area.

Smoking area requirements: Existing ventilation and partitions. No expenditures or structural changes required.

Accommodations for nonsmokers: If nonsmoker complains about smoke, employer must attempt reasonable accommodation between nonsmokers' and smokers' needs. If nonsmokers are not satisfied, a simple majority may appeal to the state director of health for a determination.

Accommodations for smokers: Employer must attempt reasonable accommodation between smokers' and nonsmokers' needs.

Employer smoking policy: Implement and maintain written policy that outlines accommodations for smokers and nonsmokers, procedures for voting and appeal. If employees vote to decide smoking and nonsmoking

State Laws on Smoking in the Workplace (continued)

areas, policy must be announced and posted within 2 weeks after vote.

Idaho

Idaho Code §§ 39-5501 and following

Workplaces where laws apply: Enclosed indoor area used by the general public, including restaurants that seat 30 or more, retail stores, and grocery stores.

Exceptions: Bowling alleys, bars.

Where smoking prohibited: Everywhere except designated smoking area.

Where smoking permitted: Employer or proprietor designates.

Accommodations for nonsmokers: "Good faith effort" to minimize effect of smoke on nonsmoking areas.

Illinois

410 Ill. Comp. Stat. §§ 80/3 and following; 820 Ill. Comp. Stat. § 55/5

Workplaces where laws apply: Any enclosed indoor workplace.

Exceptions: Offices occupied exclusively by smokers, even if visited by nonsmokers. Factories, warehouses, and other workplaces not visited by the public.

Where smoking prohibited: Entire workplace except for designated smoking area.

Where smoking permitted: Designated smoking area only.

Smoking area requirements: Existing ventilation systems and physical barriers to minimize smoke in nonsmoking areas.

Protection from discrimination: Employee may not be discriminated against for asserting rights under the clean indoor air laws. May not be refused a job, fired, or discriminated against in terms of compensation or benefits because of using lawful products outside of work. Different insurance rates or coverage for smokers are not discriminatory if:

- difference is based on cost to employer, and
- employees are given a notice of carriers' rates.

Indiana

Ind. Code Ann. §§ 22-5-4-1 and following

Protection from discrimination: Employer may not require prospective employee to refrain from using tobacco products outside of work in order to be hired or discriminate against employee who uses them in terms of wages, benefits, or conditions of employment.

Iowa

Iowa Code §§ 142B.1, 142B.2

Workplaces where laws apply: Enclosed indoor area at least 250 sq. ft.; restaurants serving more than 50 people.

Exceptions: Offices occupied exclusively by smokers, even if visited by nonsmokers. Factories, warehouses, and other workplaces not visited by the public.

Where smoking prohibited: Entire workplace except for designated smoking area.

Where smoking permitted: Designated smoking area only (may not be entire workplace).

Smoking area requirements: Existing physical barriers and ventilation systems to minimize toxic effect of smoke.

Accommodations for nonsmokers: Employee cafeteria in warehouse or factory must have nonsmoking area.

Kentucky

Ky. Rev. Stat. Ann. § 344.040(3)

Protection from discrimination: As long as employee complies with workplace smoking policy, employer may not:

- discharge employee or discriminate in terms of wages, benefits, or conditions of employment because of being a smoker or nonsmoker
- require employee to refrain from using tobacco products outside of work as a condition of employment.

Louisiana

La. Rev. Stat. Ann. §§ 40:1300.21 and following, 23:966

Workplaces where laws apply: Office workplaces of employers with more than 25 employees.

Exceptions: Offices occupied exclusively by smokers, even if visited by nonsmokers.

Where smoking prohibited: Employer designates.

Where smoking permitted: Employer designates.

Smoking area requirements: Existing ventilation systems and partitions; no expenditures or structural changes required.

Accommodations for nonsmokers: Law protects the right of nonsmoking workers to breathe smoke-free air in the workplace. If nonsmoker complains about smoke, employer must attempt reasonable accommodation between nonsmokers' and smokers' needs.

Accommodations for smokers: Law does not deny workers the right to smoke. Employer must attempt

State Laws on Smoking in the Workplace (continued)

reasonable accommodation between smokers' and nonsmokers' needs.

Protection from discrimination: Employer may not:

- require prospective employee to refrain from using tobacco products outside of work as a condition of employment
- discriminate against smokers or nonsmokers regarding termination, layoffs, wages, benefits, or other terms of employment.

Employer smoking policy: Implement and maintain written policy that outlines smoking area requirements and procedures for accommodation and complaint. Must be announced and posted within 3 months of being adopted.

Maine

Me. Rev. Stat. Ann. tit. 22, §§ 1580-A and following; tit. 26, § 597

Workplaces where laws apply: Structurally enclosed business facilities.

Exceptions: Workplaces where employer and all employees have agreed upon a smoking policy.

Where smoking prohibited: Employer may prohibit throughout entire workplace.

Where smoking permitted: Designated smoking area.

Protection from discrimination: Employer may not discriminate or retaliate against employee for assisting with enforcement of workplace smoking laws. As long as employee follows workplace smoking policy employer may not:

- discriminate in wages, benefits, or terms of employment because of use of tobacco products outside of work
- require employee to refrain from tobacco use as a condition of employment.

Employer penalties and liabilities: Failure to post or supervise implementation of policy, $100 fine.

Employer smoking policy: Written policy concerning smoking and nonsmoking rules. State bureau of health will assist employees and employers with creating policy.

Maryland

Md. Regs. Code 09.12.23.01 and following

Workplaces where laws apply: Indoor work areas. Employee lounges, restrooms, and cafeterias; work vehicle when occupied by more than one employee; conference or meeting room.

Where smoking prohibited: Entire workplace except for designated smoking area.

Where smoking permitted: Designated smoking area. Employer not required to provide one.

Smoking area requirements: May not be in location where any employee required to work (maintenance and cleaning to take place when no one is smoking in area). Must have:

- solid walls and closable door
- ventilation system that exhausts air outdoors
- no air recirculating to nonsmoking areas, and
- negative air pressure to prevent smoke migration.

Massachusetts

Mass. Gen. Laws ch. 270, § 22

Workplaces where laws apply: Any enclosed workspace.

Exceptions: Membership associations; guest rooms designated as smoking rooms; tobacco stores; smoking bars; part of nursing homes occupied by permanent residents; facilities doing scientific research about tobacco; religious services involving tobacco; facilities used for tobacco quality control; and private residences, except when used as a child care or health care facility

Where smoking is prohibited: Where employees work in an enclosed workspace.

Employer penalties and liabilities: $100 to $300 per day; possible loss of license.

Minnesota

Minn. Stat. Ann. §§ 144.411 and following, 181.938

Workplaces where laws apply: Enclosed indoor workplace.

Exceptions: Offices occupied exclusively by smokers, even if visited by nonsmokers. Factories, warehouses, and other workplaces not visited by the public; however, state commissioner of health will restrict smoking if smoke pollution affects nonsmokers.

Where smoking prohibited: Entire workplace except for designated smoking area.

Where smoking permitted: Designated smoking area (may not be entire workplace).

Smoking area requirements: Existing barriers and ventilation systems to minimize toxic effects of smoke.

Protection from discrimination: Employer may not refuse to hire, discipline, or discharge an employee for using lawful products offsite during nonwork hours; employer may restrict nonwork use if it is a genuine job

State Laws on Smoking in the Workplace (continued)

requirement. It is not discrimination to have an insurance plan with different premiums and coverage for smokers if difference reflects actual cost to employer.

Mississippi
Miss. Code Ann. § 71-7-33

Protection from discrimination: Employer may not make it a condition of employment for prospective or current employee to abstain from smoking during nonwork hours, as long as employee complies with laws or policies that regulate workplace smoking.

Missouri
Mo. Rev. Stat. §§ 191.765 and following, 90.145

Workplaces where laws apply: Enclosed indoor workplaces.

Where smoking prohibited: Entire workplace except for designated smoking area.

Where smoking permitted: Designated smoking area (may not be more than 30% of workplace).

Smoking area requirements: Existing physical barriers and ventilation systems that isolate area.

Protection from discrimination: Employer may not refuse to hire, discharge, or in any way discriminate against employee for lawful use of tobacco offsite during nonwork hours, unless use interferes with employee's or coworkers' performance or employer's business operations.

Montana
Mont. Code Ann. §§ 50-40-104, 39-2-313

Workplaces where laws apply: Enclosed rooms where more than one person works.

Where smoking prohibited: Employer designates; may designate entire workplace as a nonsmoking area.

Where smoking permitted: Employer designates; may designate entire workplace as a smoking area.

Protection from discrimination: Employer may not discharge, refuse to hire, or discriminate against employee in regard to compensation, promotion, benefits, or terms of employment because of lawful tobacco use offsite during nonwork hours. Use that affects job performance or other workers' safety or conflicts with a genuine job requirement is not protected. It is not discrimination to have different insurance rates or coverage for smokers if:
- difference is based on cost to employer, and
- employees are given a written statement of carriers' rates.

Nebraska
Neb. Rev. Stat. §§ 71-5702 to 71-5709

Workplaces where laws apply: Any enclosed indoor workplace.

Exceptions: Offices occupied exclusively by smokers, even if visited by nonsmokers. Factories, warehouses, and other workplaces not visited by the public; however, state health department will restrict smoking if smoke pollution affects nonsmokers.

Where smoking prohibited: Entire workplace except in designated smoking area.

Where smoking permitted: Designated smoking area (may not be entire workplace).

Smoking area requirements: Existing barriers and ventilation systems to minimize toxic effects of smoke.

Employer smoking policy: Employer must make reasonable effort to prevent smoking and minimize secondhand smoke.

Nevada
Nev. Rev. Stat. Ann. § 613.333

Protection from discrimination: Employer may not fail or refuse to hire, discharge, or discriminate in terms of compensation, benefits, or conditions of employment because of employee's lawful use of any product offsite during nonwork hours, unless use adversely affects job performance or the safety of other employees.

Employer penalties and liabilities: For discrimination, employee may sue for:
- lost wages and benefits
- reinstatement without loss of position, seniority, or benefits
- an offer of employment, and
- damages equal to lost wages and benefits.

New Hampshire
N.H. Rev. Stat. Ann. §§ 155:64 to 155.77, 275:37-a

Workplaces where laws apply: Enclosed workplaces where 4 or more people work.

Exceptions: Restaurants that seat fewer than 50.

Where smoking prohibited: Throughout the workplace except for designated smoking area. If smoking area cannot be effectively segregated, smoking will be totally prohibited. Employer may declare entire workplace nonsmoking.

Where smoking permitted: Designated smoking area.

Smoking area requirements: Effectively segregated so that smoke does not cause harm or enter nonsmoking

State Laws on Smoking in the Workplace (continued)

area. It must:

- be located as close as possible to exhaust vents
- have 200 sq. ft. minimum contiguous workspace
- have (1) a continuous, physical barrier at least 56 in. high, or (2) a buffer zone space at least 4 ft. wide separating area from nonsmoking area.

Accommodations for nonsmokers: Special consideration for employees with medically proven conditions adversely affected by smoke, as documented by an occupational physician.

Protection from discrimination: Employer may not require employee or applicant to refrain from using tobacco products outside of work as a condition of employment, as long as employee complies with workplace smoking policy. Employer may not retaliate or discriminate against any employee who exercises rights under smoking laws; however, laws do not give employee right to refuse to perform normal duties, even if duties require entering a smoking area.

Employer penalties and liabilities: For discrimination, misdemeanor with a fine of up to $1,000 and up to 1 year in prison.

Employer smoking policy: Written policy outlining either smoking prohibition or areas where smoking permitted. Policy must be handed out or posted; employees must receive policy orientation. If there is a designated smoking area, must be written training procedures for:

- enforcing smoking policy
- handling complaints and violations, and
- accommodating employees with medical conditions.

New Jersey

N.J. Stat. Ann. §§ 26:3D-23 and following, 34:6B-1

Workplaces where laws apply: Enclosed workspaces with 50 or more employees.

Where smoking prohibited: Entire workplace except for designated smoking area. Employer may designate entire workplace nonsmoking.

Where smoking permitted: Designated smoking area.

Protection from discrimination: Employer may not discharge or discriminate in terms of hiring, compensation, benefits, or conditions of employment because employee does or does not smoke, unless smoking or not smoking relates to work and job responsibilities.

Employer smoking policy: Written policy and procedures to protect employees from harmful

effects of tobacco smoke; must include designated nonsmoking areas and may include smoking areas. Employees must be given copy upon request.

New York

N.Y. Pub. Health Law §§ 1399-n and following; N.Y. Lab. Law § 201-d(2b),(6)

Workplaces where laws apply: Indoor workspaces.

Where smoking prohibited: Smoking is prohibited throughout the workplace, in copy machine and common equipment areas, and in company vehicles.

Protection from discrimination: Employee may not be discharged, refused employment, or discriminated against in terms of compensation or benefits because of lawful use of products offsite during nonwork hours when not using employer's equipment or property. It is not discrimination to offer insurance with different rates or coverage for smokers if:

- difference is based on cost to employer, and
- employees are given a written statement of carriers' rates.

Employer penalties and liabilities: For discrimination, employee may sue for relief and damages. For violation of smoking prohibition, employers may be subject to a fine of $1,000 or $2,000.

Employer smoking policy: Must post "No Smoking" signs; must make good faith effort to ensure that employees do not smoke.

North Carolina

N.C. Gen. Stat. § 95-28.2

Workplaces where laws apply: Discrimination laws apply to employers with 3 or more employees.

Protection from discrimination: Employer may not discharge, refuse to hire, or discriminate in regard to compensation, benefits, or terms of employment because of employee's use of lawful products offsite during nonwork hours. Use that affects employee's job performance or other workers' safety or conflicts with a genuine job requirement is not protected. It is not discrimination to offer insurance with different rates or coverage for smokers if:

- difference is based on cost to employer
- employees are given written notice of carriers' rates, and
- employer makes equal contribution for all employees.

Employer penalties and liabilities: For discrimination, employee may sue for lost wages and benefits,

State Laws on Smoking in the Workplace (continued)

reinstatement, or offer of employment. Employer liable for costs and attorney fees.

North Dakota

N.D. Cent. Code § 14-02.4-03

Protection from discrimination: Employer may not refuse to hire, discharge, or discriminate with regard to training, apprenticeship, tenure, promotion, compensation, benefits, or conditions of employment because of employee's lawful activity offsite during nonwork hours, unless it is in direct conflict with employer's essential business-related interests.

Oklahoma

Okla. Stat. Ann. tit. 40, §§ 500 to 503

Protection from discrimination: Employer may not:

- discharge or disadvantage employee in terms of compensation, benefits, or conditions of employment because of being a nonsmoker or smoking during nonwork hours, or
- require that employee abstain from using tobacco products during nonwork hours as a condition of employment.

Employer may restrict nonwork smoking if it relates to a genuine occupational requirement.

Employer penalties and liabilities: Employee may sue for lost wages and benefits. Employer may be liable for costs and attorney fees.

Oregon

Or. Rev. Stat. §§ 433.835 to 433.875, 659A.315

Workplaces where laws apply: All enclosed areas used by employees.

Where smoking prohibited: Entire workplace unless there are employee lounges designated for smoking.

Where smoking permitted: Employee lounges designated for smoking.

Smoking area requirements:

- Lounge must be inaccessible to minors.
- Lounge must be in a nonwork area.
- Air must be exhausted directly to the outside with a fan.
- Air may not recirculate to other areas of building.
- No employee may be required to enter lounge as part of job (does not apply to custodial work when lounge is unoccupied).

Accommodations for nonsmokers: If there is a lounge for smokers, must be enough lounges for nonsmokers.

Protection from discrimination: Employer may not

require that employee refrain from lawful use of tobacco products during nonwork hours as a condition of employment, unless there is a genuine occupational requirement.

Employer penalties and liabilities: For discrimination, employee may sue for employment or reinstatement, may be awarded damages.

Pennsylvania

35 Pa. Cons. Stat. Ann. § 1230.1

Workplaces where laws apply: Enclosed indoor workplaces.

Exceptions: Factories, warehouses, and other workplaces not visited by the public.

Where smoking prohibited: Employer designates.

Where smoking permitted: Employer designates.

Employer smoking policy: Must have policy that regulates smoking. Must post and provide copy to any employee upon request.

Rhode Island

R.I. Gen. Laws §§ 23-20.10-1 and following

Workplaces where laws apply: Smoking shall be prohibited in all enclosed facilities within places of employment. Required signs must be posted.

Exceptions: Certain businesses are exempt from the law: Private homes, unless licensed for child care or adult care; hotel or motel rooms designated as smoking rooms; tobacco stores and smoking bars; designated parts of assisted living facilities and nursing homes; certain facilities with Class C or D liquor licenses (until Oct. 1, 2006); licensed gaming facilities.

Where smoking permitted: Employer may designate outdoor area.

Smoking area requirements: Must be physically separate from enclosed workspace, to prevent smoke from getting into the workplace.

Protection from discrimination: Employers cannot prohibit the use of tobacco outside of work and cannot discriminate in compensation, terms, or benefits for tobacco use outside of work.

Employer penalties and liabilities: For violating restrictions on workplace smoking, penalties of $250 to $1,000 per day. For discrimination against smoker, treble damages, costs, and injunctive relief.

South Carolina

S.C. Code Ann. § 41-1-85

Protection from discrimination: Employer may not

State Laws on Smoking in the Workplace (continued)

take personnel actions, including hiring, discharge, demotion, or promotion, based on use of tobacco outside the workplace.

South Dakota

S.D. Codified Laws Ann. §§ 22-36-2 and following, 60-4-11

Workplaces where laws apply: Any enclosed indoor work area; employee cafeterias, lounges, and restrooms; conference and classrooms; hallways.

Where smoking prohibited: It is a petty offense to smoke in the workplace.

Protection from discrimination: Employer may not discharge employee because of using tobacco products offsite during nonwork hours, unless not smoking is a genuine occupational requirement. It is not discrimination to have insurance policies with different rates or coverage for smokers.

Employer penalties and liabilities: For discrimination, employee may sue for lost wages and benefits.

Tennessee

Tenn. Code Ann. § 50-1-304(e)

Protection from discrimination: Employee may not be fired for use of a lawful product during nonwork hours as long as employee observes workplace policy when at work.

Utah

Utah Code Ann. § 26-38-5

Workplaces where laws apply: Private workplaces.

Where smoking prohibited: Entire workplace except for designated smoking area. Employer may prohibit smoking entirely.

Where smoking permitted: Restricted to designated enclosed smoking area.

Smoking area requirements: Must be enclosed or may be unenclosed, if layout prevents smoke from reaching nonsmokers' work areas and ¾ of employees agree.

Employer smoking policy: Written policy that either prohibits smoking entirely or restricts to designated areas (need not be written if there are fewer than 10 full-time employees).

Vermont

Vt. Stat. Ann. tit. 18, §§ 1421 and following

Workplaces where laws apply: Enclosed structures not usually open to the public.

Where smoking prohibited: Throughout workplace except for designated smoking area. Employer may prohibit smoking entirely.

Where smoking permitted: Restricted to designated enclosed smoking area. Up to 30% of employee cafeteria and lounge areas may be designated.

Smoking area requirements: Must be area that non-smokers are not required to visit on a regular basis. Must be enclosed or may be unenclosed, if layout prevents smoke from irritating nonsmokers and ¾ of employees agree.

Protection from discrimination: Employer may not discharge, discipline, or otherwise discriminate against employee who assists in enforcement of workplace smoking laws.

Employer penalties and liabilities: For discrimination, employee may sue for reinstatement with back pay.

Employer smoking policy: Written policy that either prohibits smoking entirely or restricts it to designated areas (need be written only if employer has 10 or more employees working more than 15 hours a week).

Virginia

Va. Code Ann. § 15.2-2807

Workplaces where laws apply: No state laws regulate smoking in the workplace. However, if local ordinance permits, employer may:

- regulate smoking, if smoking and nonsmoking areas are designated by written agreement between employer and employees, or
- totally ban smoking, if a majority of the affected employees vote for it.

Washington

Wash. Admin. Code 296-800-240 and following

Workplaces where laws apply: Office environment: indoor or enclosed space used for clerical, administrative, or business work. Includes offices in manufacturing, food service, construction, and agricultural facilities.

Exceptions: Outdoor structures, gazebos, and lean-tos provided for smokers.

Where smoking prohibited: Employer must prohibit throughout workplace or restrict to designated enclosed smoking area. Smoking is also prohibited in employee cafeterias and lunchrooms, meeting rooms, rest rooms, halls, and stairways.

Where smoking permitted: Designated enclosed smoking area.

Smoking area requirements:
- may not be in common areas or places where nonsmokers work or visit

State Laws on Smoking in the Workplace (continued)

- no employee required to enter room when someone is smoking (cleaning and maintenance must take place when room is unoccupied)
- ventilation at rate of at least 60 cu. ft./min. per smoker
- negative air pressure to prevent smoke migration
- separate mechanical exhaust system to move air directly outside
- no air recirculating into nonsmoking areas
- if exhaust system not working, room use is prohibited until repaired.

Outdoor smoking areas may not be close to doorways, air intakes, or other openings that allow airflow into an office.

West Virginia

W.Va. Code § 21-3-19

Protection from discrimination: Employer may not refuse to hire, discharge, or penalize an employee with respect to compensation, conditions of employment, or other benefits for using tobacco products offsite during nonwork hours. It is not discrimination to have insurance policies with different rates or coverage for smokers if:

- difference is based on cost to employer, and
- employees are given a notice of carriers' rates.

Wisconsin

Wis. Stat. Ann. §§ 101.123, 111.31, 111.35

Workplaces where laws apply: Professional, clerical, or administrative services work offices.

Exceptions: Offices occupied exclusively by smokers, even if visited by nonsmokers. Manufacturing plants.

Where smoking prohibited: Throughout the workplace except in designated smoking area.

Where smoking permitted: Designated smoking area. Employer may not designate entire building a smoking area.

Smoking area requirements: Existing ventilation systems and physical barriers to minimize smoke in nonsmoking areas; no new construction required.

Accommodations for smokers: Employer must arrange seating to accommodate nonsmokers if they work adjacent to smoking areas.

Protection from discrimination: Employer may not discriminate against employee who uses or does not use lawful products offsite during nonwork hours. Use that impairs employee's ability to perform job or conflicts with a genuine occupational requirement is not protected. It is not discrimination to have insurance policies with different coverage and rates for smokers and nonsmokers if:

- difference is based on cost to employer, and
- each employee is given a written statement of carriers' rates.

Wyoming

Wyo. Stat. § 27-9-105(a,iv)

Protection from discrimination: Employer may not make use or nonuse of tobacco products outside of work a condition of employment unless nonuse is a genuine occupational qualification. May not discriminate regarding compensation, benefits, or terms of employment because of use or nonuse of tobacco products outside of work. It is not discrimination to offer insurance policies with different rates and coverage for smokers and nonsmokers if:

- difference reflects actual cost to employer, and
- employees are given written notice of carriers' rates.

Current as of February 2005

Employee Privacy

Sensibly, many companies are not inclined to monitor their employees' every move in the workplace. Most employers cannot afford to spend the time or money it would take to monitor their workers' every phone call or bathroom break, nor do they especially want to. There is rarely a need for extensive worker surveillance in most types of businesses. Moreover, keeping such close track of workers can breed resentment and anxiety.

On the other hand, some companies may, one day, have to take a closer look at what their employees are up to. If management learns or suspects that an employee has brought a weapon to work or stolen company property, for example, the company will have to investigate. This means that company officials may need to conduct a search or keep closer tabs on employees.

The policies in this chapter protect an employer's ability to search or monitor employees by telling them that their workspaces and workplace communications are not private—and warning them that the employer reserves the right to search or inspect them at any time. If company officials conduct searches without policies like these in place, the company will be open to lawsuits by angry employees claiming that their right to privacy was violated.

14:1   Search Policy

CD File: 14_Privacy.rtf

Include This Policy?
- ☐ Yes
    - *Choose one:* ☐ A ☐ B
- ☐ No
- ☐ Use our existing policy
- ☐ Other _____

Alternate Modifications
None

Additional Clauses
None

Related Policies
Chapter 15 provides policies on employee email and Internet use.

Notes

_____
_____
_____
_____
_____
_____
_____
_____
_____
_____
_____
_____
_____
_____
_____
_____
_____
_____
_____

Striking a Balance: How Privacy Laws Work

In many areas of employment law, the rules are fairly simple: The federal government or state legislature passes laws setting out the rights of employees and employers, and then everyone has to do what the law says. Once you enter the realm of privacy law, however, things get a bit more confusing. Although there are a few clear-cut rules, questions of privacy in the workplace are generally resolved on a case-by-case basis. Judges examine the reasons both sides acted as they did: why the employee expected privacy and why the employer searched or monitored. Judges then decide whose side of the argument seems more reasonable, in what is aptly called a "balancing test."

Clearly, an employer's goal is to tip the scales in its favor. Employers can do this by exercising restraint—never searching or monitoring employees without good reason. At the same time, an employer shouldn't give its employees reason to believe that their communications or workspaces are private. Adopting the policies in this chapter can help manage employees' expectations of how much privacy they are entitled to in the workplace, thereby taking some of the weight away from the employees' side of this balancing test scale. A written policy makes it much harder for employees to later argue that they had a reasonable expectation of privacy at work.

14:1 Workplace Privacy

Workplace searches are controversial and carry with them an element of legal risk. The reasons are obvious: Employees feel a sense of ownership toward their personal workspaces and, in fact, own their personal possessions. Most employees assume that no one can snoop into these areas without their permission. Searching calls up images of police and prison, not the enlightened American workplace. For these reasons, many companies neither want to nor do conduct workplace searches.

However, there may come a time when even the most reluctant employer has to poke around in a desk or locker. For example, if management learns that an employee has brought a gun or a pornography collection to work or has stolen company property, company officials will need to find out what's going on. And, unless the employee volunteers the contraband, there may be a need to search.

Policy A will put employees on notice that company officials may search in these worst-case scenarios. An employer doesn't have to start conducting random searches or doing a "locker check" every morning if it adopts this policy; it simply reserves the company's rights should the unfortunate need to search arise.

Policy B is a more aggressive policy—and it is probably more than most employers need. However, if your company deals in small, valuable items—such as jewelry or electronic components—or handles large amounts of cash, you may want to warn employees that the company reserves its right to find out what they are carrying out of the workplace.

Alternate Policy A

Company Property Is Subject to Search

Employees do not have a right to privacy in their workspaces or in any other property belonging to the Company. The Company reserves the right to search Company property at any time, without warning, to ensure compliance with our policies on employee safety, workplace violence, harassment, theft, drug and alcohol use, and possession of prohibited items. Company property includes, but is not limited to, lockers, desks, file cabinets, storage areas, and workspaces. If you use a lock on any item of Company property (a locker or file cabinet, for example), you must give a copy of the key or combination to

_____ .

Alternate Policy B

Company and Personal Property Are Subject to Search

Employees do not have a right to privacy in their workspaces, any other Company property, or any personal property they bring to the workplace. The Company reserves the right to search Company premises at any time, without warning, to ensure compliance with our policies on employee safety, workplace violence, harassment, theft, drug and alcohol use, and possession of prohibited items. The Company may search Company property, including but not limited to lockers, desks, file cabinets, storage areas, and workspaces. If you use a lock on any item of Company property (a locker or file cabinet, for example), you must give a copy of the key or combination to

_____ .

The Company may also search personal property brought onto Company premises, including but not limited to toolboxes, briefcases, backpacks, purses, and bags.

⚠️ **For policies allowing more intrusive searches or surveillance, talk to a lawyer.** Some employers want to adopt a search policy that allows them to search an employee's pockets, clothing, or body before the employee leaves work. Because we all have a strong expectation of privacy in our own bodies (and the clothing we wear on them), an employer will need a carefully drafted search policy before undertaking this type of search. (Your company will also need an *extremely* compelling reason to conduct the search—one that would arise only in a rare and unusual situation.) Similarly, some employers want to install security devices—such as hidden cameras or one-way mirrors—to keep an eye on customers and employees. These surveillance devices are highly controversial—and a growing number of states have adopted specific rules that limit an employer's right to use them. If your company wants to adopt a policy allowing surveillance or intrusive searches, talk to an employment lawyer in your state.

14:2 Telephone Monitoring

If your company will monitor employees' telephone calls, you must adopt a policy to let employees know about it. Federal law allows employers to monitor employee phone calls "in the ordinary course of business"—for example, to keep tabs on customer service. However, some states require the consent of at least one party to the conversation for monitoring to be legal. By adopting a policy and requiring employees to consent, in writing, to monitoring, your company will be protected from lawsuits claiming invasion of privacy.

Your telephone policy should let employees know whether the company plans to monitor calls on work telephones and under what circumstances.

Telephone Monitoring

The Company reserves the right to monitor calls made from or received on Company telephones. Therefore, no employee should expect that conversations made on Company telephones will be private.

Additional Clause to Designate Nonmonitored Phones

If your company chooses to monitor employee phone calls, it may want to designate specified phones that are not monitored for employees to use for personal calls. By doing this, an employer can avoid employee claims of invasion of privacy by giving them an opportunity to make personal calls that won't be overheard. Employees who fail to use the designated phones have no cause for complaint if their personal calls from nondesignated work phones are monitored.

To insert this additional clause, simply add this language to the end of your telephone policy.

14:2   Telephone Monitoring
CD File: 14_Privacy.rtf

Include This Policy?
☐ Yes
☐ No
☐ Use our existing policy
☐ Other _____

Alternate Modifications
None

Additional Clauses
Designate Nonmonitored Phones
  Insert?: ☐ Yes   ☐ No

Related Policies
Policy 9:3 covers employee use of company phones. See Chapter 9 for this policy and a related discussion.

Notes
_____
_____
_____
_____
_____
_____
_____
_____
_____
_____
_____
_____
_____
_____
_____
_____
_____

Additional Clause

The Company has designated telephones that employees may use for personal calls. Calls made from these phones will not be monitored. Employees may make personal calls during their breaks; if you must make a personal call during your work hours, you are expected to keep the conversation brief.

Telephones for personal calls are located _____

_____

[*state where the phones are, for example "in the main lobby of the building" or "in the employee lunch room"*].

Reality Check: How to Monitor Telephone Calls

If your company plans to monitor employee phone calls, it must make sure not to violate or the privacy of the employee or the person on the other end of the line. Although the law of telephonic monitoring is still in flux, a few clear guidelines have emerged:

- **Make a monitoring announcement.** We've all called a bank, utility company, or other institution and heard that "calls may be monitored for quality assurance." The purpose of this message is simple: to tell the person outside the company that their call may be recorded or overheard. Your company policy will let employees know what to expect, but the company must also tell the other party to the phone call that the conversation may be monitored. In fact, some states allow eavesdropping only if all parties to the call consent. A monitoring announcement lets everyone on the line know that they may have a silent partner.

- **If the call is personal, get off the line.** Federal law allows monitoring for clear business purposes. However, courts have held that employers no longer have a business purpose to monitor once they realize that they are listening in on a private conversation. Whoever is listening in should stop monitoring as soon as he or she finds out that a call is personal.

- **Choose monitors carefully.** The people who actually listen to employee phone calls must be discreet and professional. Even if an employer has a solid business reason for monitoring calls, it will be on shaky legal ground if its monitors blab what they overhear to all who care to listen. Choose monitors who can keep their mouths shut—and use as few monitors as possible.

Computers, Email, and the Internet

Computers can be an employer's best friend—or worst nightmare. On the one hand, computers can improve efficiency, allow employees to communicate with one another across great distances, and provide access to the vast ocean of information that is the World Wide Web. On the other hand, computers also give employees the opportunity to spend their days sending harassing or threatening email, downloading pornographic images or pirated software, and shopping online.

So how does a savvy employer get the benefits without the downside? By adopting comprehensive policies that govern how employees may use computer equipment—including email and Internet access. In this chapter, we show you how to create policies that tell employees how the company expects them to use its computer equipment and that will allow management to read email and monitor Internet traffic, to make sure that employees follow the rules.

15:1   Email

CD File: 15_Computers.rtf

Include This Policy?
- ☐ Yes
- ☐ No
- ☐ Use our existing policy
- ☐ Other _____

Alternate Modifications

Personal Use of Email
Choose one: ☐ A   ☐ B

Email Privacy
Choose one: ☐ A   ☐ B
☐ C   ☐ D

Additional Clauses

Email Rules and Style
Insert?: ☐ Yes   ☐ No

Related Policies

Chapter 14 explains privacy issues in detail.

Notes

_____

_____

_____

_____

_____

_____

_____

_____

_____

_____

_____

_____

_____

_____

_____

_____

_____

15:1 Email

Any company that makes electronic communications equipment available to employees is asking for trouble if it doesn't have a policy explaining the company's rules for email use and allowing the company to monitor messages sent on that equipment. Even an employer that has never read employee email and doesn't plan to set up a regular system of monitoring should protect its right to do so. If your company is ever faced with a problem involving employee email—an employee who sends sexually explicit images, proselytizes other employees to join a religious group, transmits trade secrets to a competitor, or gets involved in a "flame war" with a client, for example—a company official will have to read the messages involved to figure out what to do. If your company doesn't have a policy warning employees that the company can read their messages at any time, an employee might sue for violation of privacy.

Your email policy should tell employees what the company considers proper use of its email system, reserve the company's right to read employee email at any time, and establish a schedule for purging the email system.

⚠️ **Make sure employees know that their computer use is not private.** Perhaps the most important goal of computer policies is to reserve the company's right to monitor employee communications when necessary. The policies must tell employees that they should not expect their email or Internet use to be private.

Email

[*Company name*] provides employees with computer equipment, including an Internet connection and access to an electronic communications system, to enable them to perform their jobs successfully. This policy governs your use of the Company's email system.

Email Rules

All of our policies and rules of conduct apply to employee use of the email system. This means, for example, that you may not use the email system to send harassing or discriminatory messages, including messages with explicit sexual content or pornographic images; to send threatening messages; or to solicit others to purchase items for non-Company purposes.

We expect you to exercise discretion in using electronic communications equipment. When you send email using the Company's communications equipment, you are representing the Company. Make sure that your messages are professional and appropriate, in tone and content. Remember, although email may seem like a private conversation, email can be printed, saved, and forwarded to unintended recipients. You should not send any email that you wouldn't want your boss, your mother, or our Company's competitors to read.

Deleting Emails

Because of the large volume of emails our Company sends and receives, we discourage employees from storing large numbers of email messages. Please make a regular practice of deleting emails once you have read and/or responded to them. If you need to save a particular email, you may print out a paper copy, archive the email, or save it on your hard drive or disk. The Company will purge email messages that have not been archived after _____ days.

Violations

Any employee who violates this policy can be subject to discipline, up to and including termination.

How to Complete This Policy

Many email policies provide that messages will be purged every 60 days. (For more on the importance of purging email, see "Reality Check: Don't Fight the Urge to Purge Email," below.) Some recommend purging the system every 30 days, to minimize the company's potential legal exposure. Others suggest waiter a longer period of time between purges—for example, 90 days or more—to make sure that important business information isn't lost accidentally. Select a time period that makes sense for your company, given its rate of email traffic, the capacities of the system, and how quickly employees read (and respond to) their email.

Reality Check: Don't Fight the Urge to Purge Email

There are two very good reasons to purge your company's email system by deleting older messages regularly. First, if employees don't delete messages, the company will eventually have a storage problem on its hands. Many employees simply don't get around to deleting old messages, no matter what the company's policy asks them to do. If your company has a lot of email traffic, the system's capacity to store information will be overwhelmed unless it is cleaned out periodically.

Second, purging emails can reduce your company's legal liability—and its legal obligations if it faces a lawsuit. In many kinds of business lawsuits, including lawsuits brought by employees, customers, or other businesses, email becomes evidence. Realizing this, lawyers who sue businesses routinely ask for months, or even years, of the company's email messages in "discovery," the legal process by which parties to a lawsuit gather documents and information from each other and from third parties. Although courts often put limits on what companies have to hand over (for example, they may require a company to disclose only emails on a certain subject matter or emails for a limited time period), businesses that get hit with one of these requests can spend a lot of time trying to pull together the requested documents. What's worse, they may end up having to turn over an email that hurts their cause.

An email purging policy reduces these risks and obligations. After all, the company can only hand over what it has. If your company regularly deletes older emails, management won't have to wade through—and, perhaps, give an opponent—years' worth of messages.

Alternate Modifications on Personal Use of Email

Your email policy should let employees know the company's position on personal use of email. Many companies allow employees to use the email system for the occasional personal message, as long as things don't get out of hand. If your company wants to follow their lead, use Alternate Modification A. On the other hand, some companies prohibit all personal use of the email system. If this is your company's policy, use Alternate Modification B. Insert the modification you choose after the first paragraph of the sample policy, above.

To Allow Occasional Personal Use of Email

This modification balances employees' desire to send an occasional personal message against the company's interest in preventing a lot of personal use of its equipment. It allows employees to send personal messages, but only outside of work hours and only at the company's discretion. It also leaves the company room to discipline an employee who taxes the system by sending files with gigantic attachments, spending hours sending instant messages, or sending "chain letter" correspondence to dozens of recipients.

Alternate Modification A

Use of the Email System

The email system is intended for official Company business. Although you may use the email system for personal messages, you may do so during nonwork hours only. If you send personal messages through the Company's email system, you must exercise discretion as to the number and type of messages you send. Any employee who abuses this privilege may be subject to discipline.

To Prohibit Personal Use of Email

Some employers don't want employees to use their email systems for personal messages at all. Although this is entirely reasonable, such a policy might pose practical and legal problems. The practical problem is quite straightforward: Most people will send the occasional personal message using their office email system. Some might not have an Internet connection at home; others might have a message that has to be conveyed immediately ("I'll be home late" or "Don't forget to pick the kids up after soccer practice"). Whatever the reason, the truth is that a policy forbidding any personal use of email will probably be violated regularly by everyone from the CEO on down, and if the company doesn't enforce the policy, it isn't worth much (and may undermine the company's credibility).

The legal problem is a bit more complicated. The National Labor Relations Board (NLRB), the federal government agency that issues decisions and makes rules relating to union workplace issues, has said that prohibiting all personal uses of email might illegally prevent workers from talking about forming a union. Although employers can prohibit workers from talking about union issues during work hours in work areas, they cannot prohibit these discussions during nonwork hours in nonwork areas (a locker room or lunch room, for example). The NLRB says that a ban on all personal messages deprives employees of the right to talk about union issues during nonwork hours and might therefore run afoul of the law.

If your company is intent on prohibiting any personal use of its email system, you can insert the following modification after the first paragraph of the policy.

Alternate Modification B

Use of the Email System

The email system is to be used for official Company business only—not for personal reasons.

Alternate Modifications on Email Privacy

Your email policy absolutely must inform employees that their messages are not private and must reserve the company's right to monitor and read messages at any time. However, the language you use in the policy will depend on whether management plans to actually monitor employee email—and what system or procedures it will use to do so.

If the company has monitoring software that it plans to use, or if managers intend to read employee email on a regular basis, you should modify this portion of the policy to let employees know. After all, the purpose of an email policy is not only to allow the company to read those problematic messages after they've been sent, but also to deter employees from sending them in the first place. Telling employees that their messages will be read will almost certainly help accomplish this second goal.

Whether someone at your company should read employee email on a regular basis is a tough issue to sort through. Doing so will force employees to take the email policy seriously and thereby reduce the possibility that they will send messages that are harassing, threatening, or otherwise in violation of your policy. It's just human nature: We are less likely to break rules if we think we will get caught. But there are some serious downsides as well, with employee dissatisfaction topping the list. Employees don't want to feel like the company doesn't trust them or plans to check up on their every keystroke. Monitoring also costs time and money: The company will have to invest in monitoring software and assign someone the task of actually reading the messages. And some employers just find monitoring distasteful. They don't want to be cast in the role of Big Brother.

Ultimately, the company's philosophy, workforce, and needs will determine whether the benefits of monitoring outweigh the disadvantages. If your company has no immediate plans to monitor, use Alternate Modification A. If your company will use a monitoring system that copies every message, use Alternate Modification B. Alternate Modification C is for monitoring systems that flag key words, while Alternate Modification D is for random monitoring. Use the modification that fits your workplace procedures. Insert the modification you choose after the language you insert on personal use of the email system, immediately before the heading "Email Rules."

Alternate Modification A: Reserve the Right to Monitor

Email Is Not Private

Email messages sent using Company communications equipment are the property of the Company. We reserve the right to access, monitor, read, and/or copy email messages at any time, for any reason. You should not expect that any email message you send using Company equipment—including messages you consider to be, or label as, personal—will be private.

Alternate Modification B: Monitoring Systems That Copy Every Draft

Email Is Not Private

Email messages sent using Company communications equipment are the property of the Company. The Company's monitoring software automatically creates a copy of every message you draft—even if you never send it. Company personnel will regularly read these copies to make sure that no employee violates this policy. You should not expect that any email message you draft or send using Company equipment—including messages you consider to be personal—will be private.

Alternate Modification C: Monitoring Systems that Flag Key Words

Email Is Not Private

Email messages sent using Company communications equipment are the property of the Company. The Company's software automatically searches the messages you send for questionable content—including sexual or racial comments, threats, Company trade secrets or competitive information, and inappropriate language. Any message deemed questionable will be forwarded to, and read by, Company management. In addition, the Company reserves the right to read any message, whether or not the software singles it out for review. You should not expect that any email message you send using Company equipment—including messages you consider to be personal—will be private.

Alternate Modification D: Random Monitoring

Email Is Not Private

Email messages sent using Company communications equipment are the property of the Company. We reserve the right to access, monitor, read, and/or copy email messages at any time, for any reason. In addition, the Company will select and read employee messages at random to ensure that employees are in compliance with this policy. You should not expect that any email message you send using Company equipment—including messages you consider to be personal—will be private.

Additional Clause on Email Rules and Style

You can include as much—or as little—in the policy about appropriate use of the email system as you wish. However, you should tell employees that their email messages are subject to the same rules (no harassment, no threats, and so on) that apply to their workplace behavior in general. You can make a general statement to this effect or go into more detail, listing the types of misconduct to which email is particularly susceptible.

Some employers include email-writing guidelines in their policies. Because email is seen as an informal medium, some workers send out even work-related messages sprinkled with icons (smiley faces or other symbols) and exclamation points, written in all lower- or uppercase letters, or filled with acronyms or usages peculiar to the online world. What's worse, some workers send out email without considering its content or style, then later regret having expressed anger too hastily or sent a message that doesn't look professional.

The standard email policy provided includes a general statement about proper email use. If your company is concerned about usage and "netiquette" problems, however, you can include more explicit instructions on the proper use of email.

Additional Clause

Guidelines for Email Writing

1. Always spell-check or proofread. Email is official Company correspondence. Spelling errors in email are all too common—and they look sloppy and unprofessional. Always take the time to check for spelling errors before you send email.

2. Use lowercase and capital letters in the same way that you would in a letter. Using all capital letters is the email equivalent of shouting at someone—and it can be hard on the eyes. Failing to use capital letters at all (to begin a sentence or a formal noun) can confuse your reader and seem overly cute. Unless you are writing poetry, use standard capitalization.

3. Remember your audience. Although email encourages informal communication, that might not be the most appropriate style to use if you are addressing the CEO of an important customer. And remember that your email can be forwarded to unintended recipients—some of whom may not appreciate joking comments or informalities.

4. Don't use email for confidential matters. Again, remember the unintended recipient—your email might be forwarded to someone you didn't anticipate or might be sitting on a printer for all to see. If you need to have a confidential discussion, do it in person or over the phone.

5. Send messages sparingly. There is rarely a need to copy everyone in the Company on an email. Carefully consider who really needs to see the message, and address it accordingly.

6. Always think before you send. Resist the urge to respond in anger, to "flame" your recipient, or to get emotional. Although email gives you the opportunity to respond immediately, you don't have to take it.

15:2 Internet Use

CD File: 15_Computers.rtf

Include This Policy?
☐ Yes
    Choose one: ☐ A ☐ B
☐ No
☐ Use our existing policy
☐ Other _____

Alternate Modifications
None

Additional Clauses
Personal Use of the Internet
    Choose one: ☐ A ☐ B

Related Policies
None

Notes

_____
_____
_____
_____
_____
_____
_____
_____
_____
_____
_____
_____
_____
_____
_____
_____
_____
_____
_____
_____
_____

15:2 Internet Use

If your company offers employees Internet access, you should have a policy telling them what uses of the Internet the company considers appropriate. Without such a policy, an employer runs the practical risk that its employees will spend work time surfing the Web, shopping online, exchanging instant messages with friends both near and far, and perhaps unwittingly downloading viruses that will crash the company's computer system. An employer also runs the legal risk that employees will use its Internet access to engage in illegal behavior—such as pirating software or viewing pornographic images that create a hostile work environment (and therefore a potential sexual harassment problem).

Your Internet policy should describe proper uses of the Internet and tell employees which sites are off limits. If your company uses software that prevents employees from visiting certain sites and/or makes a record of sites an employee visits, you should include that information in your policy as well.

We offer you two different versions of an Internet policy. Policy A is a basic Internet policy, while Policy B is designed for employers who use blocking or screening software to prevent their employees from visiting certain websites.

Alternate Policy A

Using the Internet

We may provide you with computer equipment and capabilities, including Internet access, to help you perform your job. This policy governs your use of that equipment to access the Internet.

Prohibited Uses of the Internet

Employees may not, at any time, access the Internet using Company equipment or links for any of the following purposes:

- To visit websites that feature pornography, gambling, or violent images, or are otherwise inappropriate in the workplace.
- To operate an outside business, solicit money for personal purposes, or to otherwise act for personal financial gain— this includes running online auctions.
- To download software, articles, or other printed materials in violation of copyright laws.
- To download any software program without the express consent of _____ _____ .
- To read, open, or download any file from the Internet without first screening that file for viruses using the Company's virus detection software.

Internet Use Is Not Private

We reserve the right to monitor employee use of the Internet at any time, to ensure compliance with this policy. You should not expect that your use of the Internet—including but not limited to the sites you visit, the amount of time you spend online, and the communications you have—will be private.

Alternate Policy B

Using the Internet

We may provide you with computer equipment and capabilities, including Internet access, to help you perform your job. This policy governs your use of that equipment to access the Internet.

Prohibited Uses of the Internet

Employees may not, at any time, access the Internet using Company equipment or links for any of the following purposes:

- To visit websites that feature pornography, gambling, or violent images, or are otherwise inappropriate in the workplace.
- To operate an outside business, solicit money for personal purposes, or to otherwise act for personal financial gain— this includes running online auctions.
- To download software, articles, or other printed materials in violation of copyright laws.
- To download any software program without the express consent of _____ .
- To read, open, or download any file from the Internet without first screening that file for viruses using the Company's virus detection software.

Internet Use Is Not Private

To assure that employees comply with this policy, we use filtering software, which will block your access to many prohibited sites. However, some inappropriate websites may escape detection by the software—the fact that you can access a particular site does not necessarily mean that site is appropriate for workplace viewing.

We also use monitoring software, which keeps track of the sites an employee visits and how much time is spent at a particular site, among other things. You should not expect that your use of the Internet—including but not limited to the sites you visit, the amount of time you spend online, and the communications you have—will be private.

How to Complete This Policy

Both versions of our policy leave you a space to designate someone authorized to approve software downloads. The purpose of this provision is to keep the company out of trouble for unauthorized use of copyrighted software, otherwise known as software "piracy." If someone in your company has to approve downloads ahead of time, that person will help prevent employees from unwittingly violating someone else's copyright or license.

For companies with computer specialists or dedicated technical help, simply fill in the position of the appropriate person (for example, the systems operator). If yours is a smaller company, don't worry—you don't need to have a highly paid technical army on staff to enforce this provision. If an employee oversees your company's computer system, that person should be able to figure out which software can be downloaded freely (and which can't). If your company uses an outside consultant to provide technical support, you can simply name a company official, who can pass questions on to the consultant then let employees know what to do. In either case, name the person to whom employees should bring their questions.

Alternate Modification on Personal Use of the Internet

No matter which policy you choose, you will have to address the issue of personal use of the Internet. Many employers allow employees to use the Internet outside of work hours—as long as that use is not excessive and does not violate the policy's other prohibitions. The purpose of such a provision is simple: Employees use the Internet for personal purposes (such as holiday gift shopping, keeping up with their investments, or checking the news or weather), and allowing them to do so during nonwork hours will make it more likely that they spend their work hours actually doing what they are paid to do.

However, some employers ban any personal use of the Internet, reasoning that a flat prohibition is clearer for employees and easier for employers to enforce. If your company wishes to allow some personal use of the Internet, use Alternate Modification A. To ban personal use, use Alternate Modification B. In either case, insert the appropriate modification after the first paragraph of the sample policy, before "Prohibited Uses of the Internet."

Alternate Modification A

Personal Use of the Internet

Our network and Internet access are for official Company business only. Employees may access the Internet for personal use only outside of work hours and only in accordance with the other terms of this policy. An employee who engages in excessive Internet use, even during nonwork hours, may be subject to discipline.

Alternate Modification B

Personal Use of the Internet Is Prohibited

Our network and Internet access are for official Company business only. Employees may not access the Internet for personal use at any time. Any employee who uses the Company's Internet access for personal reasons, or who violates any other provision of this policy, may be subject to discipline.

Form D: Email and Internet Policy Acknowledgment Form

If your company adopts an email and/or Internet policy that allows the company to monitor, you should ask employees to sign a form acknowledging that they have read the policy and agree to abide by its terms. (You can find this and all other forms in Appendix C in the back of this book and on the accompanying CD-ROM.)

Currently, at least one state (Delaware) requires employers to get a signed acknowledgment form from their employees before monitoring their employees Internet or email use. (Employers who don't get a signed form must give daily electronic notice that they are monitoring for every day an employee accesses the employer's email or Internet access system.) Other states are considering legislation that would impose a similar requirement. If your company does business in a state with this type of law, you must use this acknowledgment form.

Even if your state doesn't require an employee's signed acknowledgment, however, it's a good idea to use this form. Having to sign a form draws an employee's attention to the policy—which not only makes the employee more likely to comply with the policy but also takes away the employee's ability to argue, later, that he or she was unaware of it.

How to Complete This Form

You will have to modify this form depending on whether you have adopted an email policy, an Internet policy, or both. For example, if you've adopted an email policy but have chosen not to adopt a policy that allows the company to monitor Internet traffic, be sure to modify the form to delete the language referring to Internet monitoring. If, on the other hand, you have adopted a policy to monitor Internet traffic but not email use, you will need to modify the form to delete the language referring to email policies. Appendix C provides a tear-out version of this form that includes acknowledgment of both an email and an Internet policy. The CD-ROM provides three different versions of this form from which you can choose, depending on the your company's policies.

Email and Internet Policy Acknowledgment

My signature on this form indicates that I have read the Company's email and Internet policies and I agree to abide by their terms. I understand that any email messages I send or receive using Company equipment are not private, and that the Company may access, monitor, read, and/or copy those messages at any time, for any reason. I also understand that the Company reserves the right to monitor my Internet use, and that such monitoring may occur at any time, for any reason.

_____ _____

Signature   Date

_____

Print Name

15:3 Software Use

The purpose of a software policy is to prevent employees from using company software in violation of its licensing agreements—and to make sure that employees don't download pirated software from the Internet. If employees violate the terms of a software license agreement that the company is party to, the company will be on the hook. Illegal software copying and use is very common—so much so that many employees don't even know it's illegal. An employee might think it's perfectly fine to make a copy of company software to install on a home computer as long as that computer is used for work, for example. But software licenses typically authorize only a single user, at a single computer. Adopting a software use policy will let employees know the rules.

This policy also tells employees that the company will conduct periodic audits of its computer equipment to monitor compliance with the software policy. This language lets employees know that the company is serious about enforcing the policy—and puts them on notice that the company reserves the right to inspect their computers.

Software Use

It is our Company's policy to use licensed software only in accordance with the terms of its license agreement. Violating a license agreement is not only unethical—it is also illegal and can subject the Company to criminal prosecution and substantial monetary penalties.

To help us adhere to this policy, employees may not do any of the following without permission from _____

_____ :

- Make a copy of any Company software program, for any reason.
- Install a Company software program on a home computer.
- Install a personal software program (that is, software owned by the employee) on any Company computer.
- Download any software program from the Internet to a Company computer.

The Company may audit Company-owned computers at any time to ensure compliance with this policy.

15:3   Software Use

CD File: 15_Computers.rtf

Include This Policy?
- ☐ Yes
- ☐ No
- ☐ Use our existing policy
- ☐ Other _____

Alternate Modifications
None

Additional Clauses
None

Related Policies
None

Notes

_____
_____
_____
_____
_____
_____
_____
_____
_____
_____
_____
_____
_____
_____
_____
_____
_____
_____
_____
_____

How to Complete This Policy

We've left you a space to designate someone authorized to approve any deviations from the policy. Choose the same person that you designated to approve software downloads in your Internet Policy, above.

■

16

Employee Records

If you are like most employers, you keep all of the records pertaining to an employee in one place—usually a manila folder in a file cabinet labeled "personnel files." Typically, these files contain documents such as the employee's job application and resume, letters of reference, offer letter, IRS W-4 Form, records of performance and discipline, emergency contacts, signed handbook acknowledgment form, and so on.

Prudent employers keep these files under lock and key. After all, personnel records contain highly sensitive, personal information. Sometimes, however, it is appropriate for an employee, manager, or supervisor to review some or all of the file's contents.

The records section of your handbook should inform employees that you maintain personnel files, explain that the files are confidential, and indicate whether—and under what circumstances—employees and others can inspect them.

16:1   Your Personnel File

CD File: 16_Records.rtf

Include This Policy?
- ☐ Yes
- ☐ No
- ☐ Use our existing policy
- ☐ Other _____

Alternate Modifications

None

Additional Clauses

None

Related Policies

For a Handbook Acknowledgment form, see Chapter 2.

Notes

_____
_____
_____
_____
_____
_____
_____
_____
_____
_____
_____
_____
_____
_____
_____
_____
_____
_____

16:1 Personnel Records

Your personnel file policy should start with some general information to lay the foundation for the policies to come—in particular, the policy requiring employees to notify you of changes to personal information and the policy alerting employees to their right to inspect personnel records. After all, employees can understand their rights and obligations regarding personnel records only if they know about the records in the first place.

The following policy notifies employees that you maintain personnel files, and it gives employees an idea of what records you do—and do not—keep in the file.

Your Personnel File

This Company maintains a personnel file on each employee. The purpose of this file is to allow us to make decisions and take actions that are personally important to you, including notifying your family in case of an emergency, calculating income tax deductions and withholdings, and paying for appropriate insurance coverage.

Although we cannot list here all of the types of documents that we keep in your personnel file, examples include: _____
_____
_____

[list examples of the documents you keep in the file].

We do not keep medical records or work eligibility forms in your personnel file. Those are kept separately. To find out more about those types of records, see Section _____ and Section _____, respectively, of this Handbook.

Your personnel file is physically kept by _____
_____.

If you have any questions about your personnel file, contact
_____.

16:2 Confidentiality

An employer always should treat employee personnel records as private. To do otherwise is to risk embarrassment for the employee and a lawsuit for the company. Employees need to feel confident that their personal information won't become public knowledge just because it is in a file. Otherwise, employees might be reticent to provide personal information.

The need for confidentiality must sometimes give way to other considerations, however. For example, an employee's supervisor might want to look at the employee's resume when it becomes clear that the employee is not able to do his or her job. Or an office manager might need an employee's emergency contact information if the employee becomes incapacitated at work. You want a confidentiality policy that gives you the flexibility to reveal information in the file to people in the organization who need to know it.

The following policy gives the confidentiality assurance employees need while keeping things flexible.

Confidentiality of Personnel Files

Because the information in your personnel file is by its nature personal, we keep the file as confidential as possible. We allow access to your file only on a need-to-know basis.

16:2   Confidentiality of Personnel Files

CD File: 16_Records.rtf

Include This Policy?
- [ ] Yes
- [ ] No
- [ ] Use our existing policy
- [ ] Other _____

Alternate Modifications
None

Additional Clauses
None

Related Policies
None

Notes

16:3 Changes in Personal Information

Personnel records are only as good as the information that's in them. Take good care to keep the information up to date. Obviously, the employee is the best person to keep the records from becoming stale. As things happen in their personal lives, however, it may not occur to employees to let their employer know of the changes, which could have implications at work.

For example, the boss may not be the first person an employee thinks to tell when the employee's spouse files for divorce. If the employee becomes sick at work, however, and the office manager calls the soon-to-be-ex spouse (who is still listed as an emergency contact) the situation could turn embarrassing at best and medically dangerous at worst.

This policy reminds employees of the importance of keeping your company posted about certain changes in their personal information.

Please Notify Us If Your Information Changes

Because we use the information in your personnel file to take actions on your behalf, it is important that the information in that file be accurate. Please notify _____

_____

whenever any of the following changes:

- your name
- your mailing address
- your phone number
- your dependents
- the number of dependents you are designating for income tax withholding
- your marital status
- the name and phone number of the individual whom we should notify in case of an emergency, or
- restrictions on your driver's license.

16:3 Please Notify Us If Your Information Changes

CD File: 16_Records.rtf

Include This Policy?
- ☐ Yes
- ☐ No
- ☐ Use our existing policy
- ☐ Other _____

Alternate Modifications
None

Additional Clauses
None

Related Policies
None

Notes

_____

_____

_____

_____

_____

_____

_____

_____

_____

_____

_____

_____

_____

_____

_____

_____

_____

_____

_____

_____

16:4 Inspection of Personnel Records

Although many employers would rather not have employees inspecting their own personnel records, many state laws require that employees be granted access. These laws vary greatly in the details. In some states, employees may review their files only at specified hours. In other states, only past employees, not current employees, have the right to inspect their files.

Typically, these laws state who can inspect, when they can inspect, whether they have to give notice, whether they can photocopy their file, and whether they have to pay for the copies. To find out about your state's law, refer to "State Laws on Access to Personnel Records" at the end of this chapter. You can also check with your state labor department. (See Appendix A for contact information.)

Because the laws vary so much, we cannot provide a standard policy for you to use. The following is an example of what your policy might look like.

> ### SAMPLE POLICY LANGUAGE
>
> Current employees who want to inspect their personnel files must make an appointment with the Human Resources Department. Appointments will typically take place Monday through Friday between 1:00 p.m. and 5:00 p.m. Although we will make every effort to give employees an appointment quickly, it may take up to 48 hours. If an employee would like a representative to view his or her file, the employee must make the request in writing.
>
> Former employees who would like to inspect their files must make a written request to do so. Upon receiving the written request, the Human Resources Department will call the former employee to schedule an appointment.
>
> We do not allow current or former employees to photocopy their file. If you would like a copy of a document in the file, the Human Resources Department will copy it for you at a price of $.10 per page.
>
> If you have any questions about this policy, please contact Myrtle Means, the Human Resources Manager.

Drafting Your Own Policy

When drafting your own policy on employee access to personnel records, be sure to check your state's law so that you don't create a policy that is contrary to legal requirements. A typical inspection policy will state:

16:4 Inspecting Your Records

CD File: 16_Records.rtf

Include This Policy?
- ☐ Yes
- ☐ No
- ☐ Use our existing policy
- ☐ Other _____

Alternate Modifications

None

Additional Clauses

None

Related Policies

None

Notes

_____

_____

_____

_____

_____

_____

_____

_____

_____

_____

_____

_____

_____

_____

_____

_____

_____

_____

_____

_____

_____

- who can inspect the file (current employees, former employees, designated representatives, and so on)
- when they can inspect the file
- where they can inspect the file
- whether they need to make a request
- whether their request must be in writing
- whether they can photocopy the file, and
- how much you will charge for photocopying.

16:5 Work Eligibility

Federal law requires employers to check whether their employees can legally work in the United States. As part of this process, the employer has to complete a form issued by the federal Bureau of Citizenship and Immigration Services ("BCIS") called Form I-9. Employers should not keep Form I-9 or other work eligibility forms in employee personnel files. The BCIS is entitled to inspect these forms (and often does). If the forms are kept in a worker's personnel file, the BCIS will be able to see all the other documents in the file as well. Not only does this compromise a worker's privacy, but it could also open the company up to additional questions and investigation.

The following policy reassures employees that their work status records will not be kept in their personnel files.

Work Eligibility Records

In compliance with federal law, all newly hired employees must present proof that they are legally eligible to work in the United States. We must keep records related to that proof, including a copy of the BCIS Form I-9 that each employee completes for us.

Those forms are kept as confidential as possible. We do not keep them in your personnel file.

If you would like more information about your I-9 form, see Section _____ of this Handbook or contact _____ _____ .

16:5 Work Eligibility Records
CD File: 16_Records.rtf

Include This Policy?
☐ Yes
☐ No
☐ Use our existing policy
☐ Other _____

Alternate Modifications
None

Additional Clauses
None

Related Policies
For more information about work eligibility forms, including a policy telling employees that they must complete these forms, see Chapter 4.

Notes

_____
_____
_____
_____
_____
_____
_____
_____
_____
_____
_____
_____
_____
_____
_____
_____
_____

16:6 Medical Records
CD File: 16_Records.rtf
Include This Policy?
☐ Yes
☐ No
☐ Use our existing policy
☐ Other _____
Alternate Modifications
None
Additional Clauses
None
Related Policies
None
Notes

16:6 Medical Records

Employers come into possession of worker medical records for a variety of reasons. Perhaps a worker has requested an accommodation for a disability and has presented your company with a medical evaluation verifying the disability. Or maybe a worker has requested medical leave and has given your company documentation to show the seriousness of the medical condition.

Medical records should not go into a worker's personnel file. The federal Americans With Disabilities Act includes strict rules on how to handle records relating to an employee's disability: Medical information must be kept separate from nonmedical records, and medical files must be stored in a locked cabinet. Your state might have a similar, or perhaps even stricter, law on this topic. Although the confidentiality provisions of these laws apply only to workers who are disabled, it's a good practice to keep all medical records confidential and in a separate, locked file cabinet.

The following standard policy informs employees that their medical records will be kept separate from their personnel files.

Medical Records

We understand the particularly sensitive nature of an employee's medical records, so we do not place any such records in the employee's personnel file. We keep all medical records in a separate and secure place.

If you have any questions about the storage of your medical records or about inspecting your medical records, contact

_____ .

State Laws on Access to Personnel Records

This chart deals with only those states that authorize access to personnel files. Generally, an employee is allowed to see evaluations, performance reviews, and other documents that determine a promotion, bonus, or raise; access usually does not include letters of reference, test results, or records of a criminal or workplace-violation investigation. Under other state laws, employees may have access to their medical records and records of exposure to hazardous substances; these laws are not included in this chart.

Alaska

Alaska Stat. § 23.10.430

Employers affected: All.

Employee access to records: Employee or former employee may view and copy personnel files.

Conditions for viewing records: Employee may view records during regular business hours under reasonable rules.

Copying records: Employee pays (if employer so requests).

California

Cal. Lab. Code §§ 1198.5; 432

Employers affected: All employers subject to wage and hour laws.

Employee access to records: Employee has right to inspect at reasonable intervals any personnel records relating to performance or to a grievance proceeding. Employee also has a right to a copy of any personnel document employee has signed.

Conditions for viewing records: Employee may view records at reasonable times, during break or nonwork hours. If records are kept offsite or employer does not make them available at the workplace, then employee must be allowed to view them at the storage location without loss of pay.

Connecticut

Conn. Gen. Stat. Ann. §§ 31-128a to 31-128h

Employers affected: All.

Employee access to records: Employee has right to inspect personnel files within a reasonable time after making a request, but not more than twice a year. Employer must keep files on former employees for at least one year after termination.

Written request required: Yes.

Conditions for viewing records: Employee may view records during regular business hours in a location at or near worksite. Employer may require that files be viewed on the premises and in the presence of employer's designated official.

Copying records: Employer must provide copies within a reasonable time after receiving employee's written request; request must identify the materials employee wants copied. Employer may charge a fee that is based on the cost of supplying documents.

Employee's right to insert rebuttal: Employee may insert a written statement explaining any disagreement with information in the personnel record. Rebuttal must be maintained as part of the file.

Delaware

Del. Code Ann. tit. 19, §§ 730 to 735

Employers affected: All.

Employee access to records: Current employee, employee who is laid off with reemployment rights, or employee on leave of absence may inspect personnel record; employee's agent is not entitled to have access to records. Unless there is reasonable cause, employer may limit access to once a year.

Written request required: Yes. Employer may require employee to file a form and indicate either the purpose of the review or what parts of the record employee wants to inspect.

Conditions for viewing records: Records may be viewed during employer's regular business hours. Employer may require that employees view files on their own time and may also require that files be viewed on the premises and in the presence of employer's designated official.

Copying records: Employer is not required to permit employee to copy records. Employee may take notes.

Employee's right to insert rebuttal: If employee disagrees with information in personnel file and cannot reach an agreement with employer to remove or correct it, employee may submit a written statement explaining her position. Rebuttal must be maintained as part of the personnel file.

Illinois

820 Ill. Comp. Stat. §§ 40/1 to 40/12

Employers affected: Businesses with 5 or more employees.

Employee access to records: Current employee, or former employee terminated within the past year, is permitted to inspect records twice a year at reasonable

State Laws on Access to Personnel Records (continued)

intervals, unless a collective bargaining agreement provides otherwise. An employee involved in a current grievance may designate a representative of the union or collective bargaining unit, or other agent, to inspect personnel records that may be relevant to resolving the grievance. Employer must make records available within 7 working days after employee makes request (if employer cannot meet deadline, may be allowed an additional 7 days).

Written request required: Yes. Employer may require use of a form.

Conditions for viewing records: Records may be viewed during employer's normal business hours at or near employee's worksite or, at employer's discretion, during nonworking hours at a different location. Employer may require that records be viewed on the premises.

Copying records: After reviewing records, employee may get a copy. Employer may charge only actual cost of duplication. If employee is unable to view files at worksite, employer, upon receipt of a written request, must mail employee a copy.

Employee's right to insert rebuttal: If employee disagrees with any information in the personnel file and cannot reach an agreement with employer to remove or correct it, employee may submit a written statement explaining his position. Rebuttal must remain in file with no additional comment by employer.

Iowa

Iowa Code § 91B.1

Employers affected: All employers with salaried employees or commissioned salespeople.

Employee access to records: Employee may have access to personnel file at time agreed upon by employer and employee.

Conditions for viewing records: Employer's representative may be present.

Copying records: Employer may charge copying fee for each page that is equivalent to a commercial copying service fee.

Maine

Me. Rev. Stat. Ann. tit. 26, § 631

Employers affected: All.

Employee access to records: Within 10 days of submitting request, employee, former employee, or authorized representative may view and copy personnel files.

Written request required: Yes.

Conditions for viewing records: Employee may view records during normal business hours at the location where the files are kept, unless employer, at own discretion, arranges a time and place more convenient for employee. If files are in electronic or any other nonprint format, employer must provide equipment for viewing and copying.

Copying records: Employee entitled to one free copy of personnel file during each calendar year, including any material added to file during that year. Employee must pay for any additional copies.

Massachusetts

Mass. Gen. Laws ch. 149, § 52C

Employers affected: All. (Employers with 20 or more employees must maintain personnel records for 3 years after termination.)

Employee access to records: Employee or former employee must have opportunity to review personnel files within 5 business days of submitting request. (Law does not apply to tenured or tenure-track employees in private colleges and universities.)

Written request required: Yes.

Conditions for viewing records: Employee may view records at workplace during normal business hours.

Copying records: Employee must be given a copy of record within 5 business days of submitting a written request.

Employee's right to insert rebuttal: If employee disagrees with any information in personnel record and cannot reach an agreement with employer to remove or correct it, employee may submit a written statement explaining her position. Rebuttal becomes a part of the personnel file.

Michigan

Mich. Comp. Laws §§ 423.501 to 423.505

Employers affected: Employers with 4 or more employees.

Employee access to records: Current or former employee is entitled to review personnel records at reasonable intervals, generally not more than twice a year, unless a collective bargaining agreement provides otherwise.

Written request required: Yes. Request must describe the record employee wants to review.

Conditions for viewing records: Employee may

State Laws on Access to Personnel Records (continued)

view records during normal office hours either at or reasonably near the worksite. If these hours would require employee to take time off work, employer must provide another time and place that is more convenient for the employee.

Copying records: After reviewing files, employee may get a copy; employer may charge only actual cost of duplication. If employee is unable to view files at the worksite, employer, upon receipt of a written request, must mail employee a copy.

Employee's right to insert rebuttal: If employee disagrees with any information in personnel record and cannot reach an agreement with employer to remove or correct it, employee may submit a written statement explaining his position. Statement may be no longer than five 8½" by 11" pages.

Minnesota

Minn. Stat. Ann. §§ 181.960 to 181.966

Employers affected: All.

Employee access to records: Current employee may review files once per 6-month period; former employee may have access to records once only during the first year after termination. Employer must be given 7 days' advance request (14 days' if personnel records kept out of state). Employer may not retaliate against an employee who asserts rights under these laws.

Written request required: Yes.

Conditions for viewing records: Current employee may view records during employer's normal business hours at worksite or a nearby location; does not have to take place during employee's working hours. Employer or employer's representative may be present.

Copying records: Employer must provide copy free of charge. Current employee must first review record and then submit written request for copies. Former employee must submit written request; providing former employee with a copy fulfills employer's obligation to allow access to records.

Employee's right to insert rebuttal: If employee disputes specific information in the personnel record, and cannot reach an agreement with employer to remove or revise it, employee may submit a written statement identifying the disputed information and explaining her position. Statement may be no longer than 5 pages and must be kept with personnel record as long as it is maintained.

Nevada

Nev. Rev. Stat. Ann. § 613.075

Employers affected: All.

Employee access to records: An employee who has worked at least 60 days and a former employee, within 60 days of termination, must be given a reasonable opportunity to inspect personnel records.

Conditions for viewing records: Employee may view records during employer's normal business hours.

Copying records: Employer may charge only actual cost of providing access and copies.

Employee's right to insert rebuttal: Employee may submit a reasonable written explanation in direct response to any entry in personnel record. Statement must be of moderate length; employer may specify the format.

New Hampshire

N.H. Rev. Stat. Ann. § 275:56

Employers affected: All.

Employee access to records: Employer must provide employees a reasonable opportunity to inspect records.

Copying records: Employer may charge a fee related to actual cost of supplying copies.

Employee's right to insert rebuttal: If employee disagrees with any of the information in personnel record and cannot reach an agreement with the employer to remove or correct it, employee may submit a written statement of her version of the information along with evidence to support her position.

Oregon

Or. Rev. Stat. § 652.750

Employers affected: All.

Employee access to records: Employer must provide employees a reasonable opportunity to inspect personnel records used to determine qualifications for employment, promotion, or additional compensation, termination, or other disciplinary action. Employer must keep records for 60 days after termination of employee.

Conditions for viewing records: Employee may view records at worksite or place of work assignment.

Copying records: Employer must provide a certified copy of requested record to current or former employee (if request made within 60 days of termination). May charge only actual cost of providing copy.

Pennsylvania

43 Pa. Cons. Stat. Ann. §§ 1321 to 1324

State Laws on Access to Personnel Records (continued)

Employers affected: All.

Employee access to records: Employer must allow employee to inspect personnel record at reasonable times. (Employee's agent, or employee who is laid off with reemployment rights or on leave of absence, must also be given access.) Unless there is reasonable cause, employer may limit review to once a year by employee and once a year by employee's agent.

Written request required: At employer's discretion. Employer may require the use of a form as well as a written indication of the parts of the record employee wants to inspect or the purpose of the inspection. For employee's agent: Employee must provide signed authorization designating agent; must be for a specific date and indicate the reason for the inspection or the parts of the record the agent is authorized to inspect.

Conditions for viewing records: Employee may view records during normal business hours at the office where records are maintained, when there is enough time for employee to complete the review. Employer may require that employee or agent view records on their own time and may also require that inspection take place on the premises and in the presence of employer's designated official.

Copying records: Employer not obligated to permit copying. Employee may take notes.

Employee's right to insert rebuttal: The Bureau of Labor Standards, after a petition and hearing, may allow employee to place a counterstatement in the personnel file, if employee claims that the file contains an error.

Rhode Island

R.I. Gen. Laws § 28-6.4-1

Employers affected: All.

Employee access to records: Employer must permit employee to inspect personnel files when given at least 7 days' advance notice (excluding weekends and holidays). Employer may limit access to no more than 3 times a year.

Written request required: Yes.

Conditions for viewing records: Employee may view records at any reasonable time other than employee's work hours. Inspection must take place in presence of employer or employer's representative.

Copying records: Employee may not make copies or remove files from place of inspection. Employer may charge a fee reasonably related to cost of supplying copies.

Washington

Wash. Rev. Code Ann. §§ 49.12.240 to 49.12.260

Employers affected: All.

Employee access to records: Employee may have access to personnel records at least once a year within a reasonable time after making a request.

Employee's right to insert rebuttal: Employee may petition annually that employer review all information in employee's personnel file. If there is any irrelevant or incorrect information in the file, employer must remove it. If employee does not agree with employer's review, employee may request to have a statement of rebuttal or correction placed in file. Former employee has right of rebuttal for two years after termination.

Wisconsin

Wis. Stat. Ann. § 103.13

Employers affected: All employers who maintain personnel records.

Employee access to records: Employee and former employee must be allowed to inspect personnel records within 7 working days of making request. Access is permitted twice per calendar year unless a collective bargaining agreement provides otherwise. Employee involved in a current grievance may designate a representative of the union or collective bargaining unit, or other agent, to inspect records that may be relevant to resolving the grievance.

Written request required: At employer's discretion.

Conditions for viewing records: Employee may view records during normal working hours at a location reasonably near worksite. If this would require employee to take time off work, employer may provide another reasonable time and place for review that is more convenient for the employee.

Copying records: Employee's right of inspection includes the right to make or receive copies. If employer provides copies, may charge only actual cost of reproduction.

Employee's right to insert rebuttal: If employee disagrees with any information in the personnel record and cannot come to an agreement with the employer to remove or correct it, employee may submit a written statement explaining his position. Employer must attach the statement to the disputed portion of the personnel record.

Current as of February 2005

17

Drugs and Alcohol

Employee drug and alcohol problems can take a toll on a workplace in so many ways. Employees who abuse alcohol and drugs (including illegal drugs, prescription drugs, and over-the-counter drugs) pose significant problems for their employers, managers, and coworkers—from diminished job performance and low productivity to excessive absenteeism and tardiness. Out-of-pocket costs include increased workers' compensation claims, increased occupational health claims, and higher health insurance premiums.

As a result, most employers include in their handbook a policy or set of policies designed to combat substance abuse. These policies range from bare-bones statements prohibiting alcohol and drug use to complicated frameworks that include rehabilitation, employee searches, and drug testing.

From a legal standpoint, the bare-bones approach is the easiest, because the law clearly gives employers the right to prohibit illegal drug and alcohol use in the workplace. If you confine your policies to conduct and activities in which you have a legitimate business interest—for example, performance and safety—you should be on safe legal ground.

If you decide to enter the world of employee searches and drug testing, however, you'll have a number of legal obstacles to face. Remember that your employees have a right to privacy. Depending on the state in which you live, the law may be more or less aggressive in protecting this right. We address these legal issues in more detail in the individual policy discussions below.

The set of policies you choose will depend on your company's values and type of business. In this chapter, we help you tailor your company's policies to its business needs by explaining your various options.

This chapter provides information about substance abuse policies that you can include in your handbook. It does not discuss in detail the legal issues involved in actually dealing with an employee who abuses substances. Both state and federal law have a lot to say about what employers can and cannot do when faced with such an employee, and prudent employers familiarize themselves with these laws before taking action. For more information on this issue, see Chapter 1, Section E, of *Dealing With Problem Employees: A Legal Guide*, by Amy DelPo and Lisa Guerin (Nolo).

17:1   Prohibition Against Drug and Alcohol Use at Work

Given the amount of social drinking and drug use in our culture, there's no room for ambiguity in a substance use policy; it must be clear as to when employees can and cannot partake. Although illegal drug use is always unacceptable, there are times when a drink on company time may be appropriate (see modifications, below).

Your drug and alcohol use policy should explain to employees when they can and cannot use alcohol and legal drugs, that your company prohibits substance use for their own safety and well-being, and that your company can discipline or even terminate them for violating the policy.

This policy does not prohibit legal drug use. When crafting any substance abuse policy, it is important to understand the difference between legal drug use and illegal drug use. You can prohibit the latter, but not the former. This is because legal drug use—for example, taking prescription or over-the-counter drugs according to a doctor's orders—is sometimes protected by state and federal disability laws. For more information on this issue, see Chapter 1, Section E, of *Dealing With Problem Employees: A Legal Guide*, by Amy DelPo and Lisa Guerin (Nolo). To learn more about federal disability law, contact the U.S. Equal Employment Opportunity Commission; to learn more about your state's disability law, contact your state labor department. (See Appendix A for contact information.)

Who Needs This Policy

Federal law requires federal contractors to have policies that ensure a drug-free workplace. (See "The Drug-Free Workplace Act of 1988," below.) Some state laws also have this requirement. To find out if your state has such a law, contact your state labor department. (See Appendix A for contact information.) If you are an employer covered by these laws, then you will need some type of antidrug/ antialcohol policy. That policy might look like the one below or, depending on the legal requirements, be even more comprehensive.

All other employers are free to choose whether to have this type of policy. Given the negative impact of drugs and alcohol on morale, performance, and productivity, we cannot imagine a reason for failing to include such a policy in a handbook. As we explained above, there are no murky legal issues involved in such a bare-bones policy, and including one gives employers more leeway in combating any drug and alcohol problems that arise in their workplace.

17:1   Policy Against Alcohol and Illegal Drug Use

CD File: 17_Drugs Alcohol.rtf

Include This Policy?
☐ Yes
☐ No
☐ Use our existing policy
☐ Other _____

Alternate Modifications
None

Additional Clauses
Serving Alcohol at Functions
Insert?:   ☐ Yes   ☐ No

Entertaining Clients
Insert?:   ☐ Yes   ☐ No

Related Policies
None

Notes

_____
_____
_____
_____
_____
_____
_____
_____
_____
_____
_____
_____
_____
_____
_____
_____

Policy Against Alcohol and Illegal Drug Use

This Company is committed to providing a safe, comfortable, and productive work environment for its employees. We recognize that employees who abuse drugs or alcohol at work—or who appear at work under the influence of alcohol or illegal drugs—harm both themselves and the work environment.

As a result, we prohibit employees from doing the following:

- appearing at work under the influence of alcohol or illegal drugs
- conducting Company business while under the influence of alcohol or illegal drugs (whether or not the employee is actually on work premises at the time)
- using alcohol or illegal drugs on the worksite
- using alcohol or illegal drugs while conducting Company business (whether or not the employee is actually on work premises at the time)
- possessing, buying, selling, or distributing alcohol or illegal drugs on the worksite, and
- possessing, buying, selling, or distributing alcohol or illegal drugs while conducting Company business (whether or not the employee is actually on work premises at the time).

Illegal drug use includes more than just outlawed drugs such as marijuana, cocaine, or heroin. It also includes the misuse of otherwise legal prescription and over-the-counter drugs.

This policy covers times when employees are on call but not working and times when employees are driving Company vehicles or using Company equipment.

Employees who violate this policy may face disciplinary action, up to and including termination.

The Drug-Free Workplace Act of 1988

If your company is a federal government contractor or grant recipient, it must abide by the federal Drug-Free Workplace Act of 1988. (41 U.S.C. §§ 701 and following.) This law requires such companies to do a number of things, including publish an antidrug-use statement (perhaps in a handbook) and establish a drug awareness program.

While the specifics of the Drug-Free Workplace Act are beyond the scope of this book, the U.S. Department of Labor (DOL) enforces the Act and can provide you with the information you need to comply with its requirements. (See Appendix A for contact information.) The DOL keeps a lot of this information on its website at www.dol.gov. Click on the search index at the top right-hand portion of the home page; scroll down to "D," and then click on "Drug-free workplace."

If you'd like to read the text of the law, you can do so by researching a statute on Nolo's website, at www.nolo.com/statute/index.cfm. Search for the U.S. Code, Title 41, Section 701.

Be aware that many states have similar drug-free workplace laws. To find out about your state's law, see "State Drug and Alcohol Testing Laws" at the end of this chapter. You can also contact your state department of labor. (See Appendix A for contact details.)

Additional Clause for Serving Alcohol at Functions

Some companies sponsor functions, such as holiday parties or anniversary celebrations, at which the company serves alcohol. Those companies will have to modify the policy above to allow alcohol use sometimes. Otherwise, the company is sending employees contradictory and confusing messages, serving them alcohol while at the same time prohibiting it.

There are certain legal risks involved whenever a company allows employees to consume alcohol—either because the company has served them the alcohol or because the company has sanctioned their drinking while on the job. If the employee consumes the alcohol and then hurts himself or someone else, the company might be liable for those injuries—and the company's workers' compensation policy might not provide coverage. (Check your company's insurance policy before serving alcohol or allowing employees to consume alcohol at a company function.) If your company plans to serve alcohol to employees or sanction employee drinking on the job, consider consulting legal counsel to learn ways to shield your company from liability.

If you think that your company will serve alcohol, either on site or during work hours, consider adding the following paragraph to the policy.

Additional Clause

> We do not prohibit employees from consuming alcohol at social or business functions that we sponsor where alcohol is served. Even at these functions, however, employees may not consume alcohol to the point of intoxication or to the point where they endanger their own safety or the safety of others. In addition, employees involved in security and employees who work with heavy or dangerous machinery or materials may not consume any alcohol at these functions if they will be returning to work that same day.

Additional Clause for Entertaining Clients

Some employees must entertain clients and customers as part of their job. For example, a salesman might take a buyer to dinner to seal a deal, or an attorney might celebrate with a client after winning a big case. Often, entertainment includes sharing a drink or two.

If you'd like your employees to be able to consume alcohol while entertaining clients, consider adding the following paragraph to your policy.

Additional Clause

> This policy does not prohibit employees from consuming alcohol while entertaining clients or prospective clients. However, employees may not consume alcohol to the point of intoxication, nor may they consume alcohol if they are going to drive. In addition, employees must always conduct themselves professionally and appropriately while on Company business.

17:2 Inspections to Enforce Policy Against Drugs and Alcohol

Some employers choose to inspect the workplace and their employees to enforce their policy against alcohol and illegal drug use. Although most state laws allow inspections in some form, these same laws impose strict limits on how and when employers can conduct these inspections. Most often, these laws seek to balance the employer's right to keep the workplace free of drugs and alcohol against the employee's right to privacy. Exactly how to strike this balance varies from state to state.

Because the legal rules regarding inspections are so varied and complicated, we recommend you consult with an attorney before your company conducts an inspection.

The sample policy below reserves your company's right to inspect without going into detail, thereby giving you the flexibility to use procedures that comply with your state's law.

Inspections to Enforce Drug and Alcohol Policy

This Company reserves the right to inspect employees, their possessions, and their workspaces to enforce our policy against alcohol and illegal drug use.

Who Needs This Policy

Not every employer needs to inspect the workplace, but if you would like to have the option of searching employees and their workspaces for drugs and alcohol, then you should probably include this type of policy in your handbook.

Whether you want to have this option depends in large part on your company's needs and values as an employer. One drawback of the policy is that it sends a message of mistrust to employees. If your company is a large employer that has experienced large-scale problems with employees abusing drugs and alcohol, however, you might be willing to live with that drawback in exchange for being able to aggressively address drug and alcohol use in the workplace. On the other hand, if your company is a small employer that has not had many problems with substance-abusing employees, you probably do not need to include this type of policy in the handbook.

17:2   Inspections to Enforce Drug and Alcohol Policy

CD File: 17_Drugs Alcohol.rtf

Include This Policy?
☐ Yes
☐ No
☐ Use our existing policy
☐ Other _____

Alternate Modifications
None

Additional Clauses
None

Related Policies
None

Notes

_____
_____
_____
_____
_____
_____
_____
_____
_____
_____
_____
_____
_____
_____
_____
_____
_____
_____
_____

17:3   Drug Testing

CD File: 17_Drugs Alcohol.rtf

Include This Policy?
☐ Yes
☐ No
☐ Use our existing policy
☐ Other _____

Alternate Modifications
None

Additional Clauses
None

Related Policies
None

Notes

_____

_____

_____

_____

_____

_____

_____

_____

_____

_____

_____

_____

_____

_____

_____

_____

_____

_____

_____

_____

17:3 Drug Testing

In recent years, drug tests have become cheaper and more reliable, spurring more and more employers to use drug testing as a tool for creating a drug-free workplace. Employers test for drugs in a variety of contexts: Some test all prospective hires, others test only when an employee seems to be under the influence, and still others randomly test employees who are in jobs where safety or security is an issue.

Your state's laws will determine whether, when, and how your company can test employees. Many states ban outright any drug testing of employees, while other states only allow it for certain occupations or in certain circumstances. In addition, state privacy laws regulate how and when an employer can conduct the test.

To learn more about your state's rules on drug testing, contact your state labor department. (See Appendix A for contact information.) You can also refer to "State Drug and Alcohol Testing Laws" at the end of this chapter.

Although the varied nature of state laws means that we cannot provide a standard drug testing policy, here is an example of what such a policy might look like.

> **SAMPLE POLICY LANGUAGE**
>
> As part of our efforts to keep this workplace safe and free of illegal drug use, we will conduct random and intermittent drug tests of all employees in positions where the safety or security of the employee or others is an issue.
>
> In addition, we may ask any employee, regardless of job responsibilities, to submit to a drug test in the following circumstances:
> - when we suspect that the employee is under the influence of illegal drugs
> - when we suspect that the employee has been involved in the sale, purchase, use, or distribution of illegal drugs on the work site or while performing job duties
> - when the employee has been involved in a workplace accident or incident
> - when the employee has been involved in an accident or incident off site but while on company business, or
> - when the employee has violated a safety rule.

Who Needs This Policy

The U.S. Department of Transportation (DOT) requires drug testing in certain transportation industries, including aviation, trucking, railway, maritime, and mass transit. Those regulations are beyond the scope of this book. If your business uses trucks or boats or is involved in transporting goods or people, you can find out more by contacting the Department of Transportation. Contact details and other helpful information are available on the DOT's website, at www.dot.gov. (From the home page, click on "Safety" in the left-hand column. Then click on "Drug and Alcohol Safety.")

There are so many legal risks and practical problems involved in drug testing that employers other than those covered by DOT regulations—or similar state regulations—should think twice before taking this step. Nonetheless, if you do want to have the option of drug testing employees, be sure to include this type of policy in the handbook. In addition, we suggest you consult with an attorney when drafting a drug testing policy and before conducting any drug test.

17:4   Leave to Participate in
        Rehabilitation Program

CD File: 17_Drugs Alcohol.rtf

Include This Policy?
☐ Yes
☐ No
☐ Use our existing policy
☐ Other _____

Alternate Modifications
None

Additional Clauses
None

Related Policies
None

Notes

_____

_____

_____

_____

_____

_____

_____

_____

_____

_____

_____

_____

_____

_____

_____

_____

_____

_____

_____

17:4   Leave for Rehabilitation

Although some employers take a zero tolerance approach to employee substance abuse problems, others recognize that they can help employees who have fallen prey to alcohol and drug abuse kick their habits—and become valuable, productive, and loyal workers in the process. For some employers, this means something as small and inexpensive as giving employees paid or unpaid leave to participate in a rehabilitation program.

Your rehabilitation policy should let employees know that their employer cares about them and their well-being and that, as a result, your company may allow them to take leave to deal with their substance abuse problem. It should not, however, promise such leave to anyone who requests it. You policy should also remind employees who have a substance abuse problem that they must meet the same performance, productivity, and conduct standards as everyone else.

Leave to Participate in Rehabilitation Program

We believe that employees who have a substance abuse problem can help themselves by enrolling in a rehabilitation program. Not only will overcoming their problem help these employees in their personal lives, it will help them to be more effective and productive workers.

Although we cannot guarantee that we will grant this leave to all employees who request it, employees who would like to participate in a rehabilitation program may, subject to approval, be able to use up to _____ weeks of _____ [*paid or unpaid*] leave from work to attend the program.

Employees _____ [*will or will not*] be entitled to health and other benefits while on rehabilitation leave.

Employees _____ [*will or will not*] be allowed to accrue vacation and other benefits while on rehabilitation leave.

At the end of the rehabilitation leave, we _____ [*will or will not*] require proof that the employee successfully completed the program.

To learn more about this type of leave, including whether you qualify for it, the circumstances under which we will grant it, and the requirements that you must meet, contact _____ _____ .

We will keep all conversations regarding employee substance abuse problems as confidential as possible.

Please note that even as you might be seeking assistance for your substance abuse problem, we still expect you to meet the same standards of performance, productivity, and conduct that we expect of all employees. We reserve the right to discipline you—up to and including termination—for failing to meet those standards.

Who Needs This Policy

Some states require employers to allow employees to take leave to participate in a rehabilitation program. If you operate in such a state, include this policy (or one similar to it) in your handbook. To find out about your state's law, contact your state department of labor. (See Appendix A for contact information.)

If you don't operate in a state that requires rehabilitation leave, you can still benefit from this type of policy. The expense of the policy is quite small when compared to the potential reward of assisting problem employees in becoming valuable and productive members of the workforce.

How to Complete This Policy

As you can see from reading the standard rehabilitation leave policy, above, you will have to make a number of decisions when drafting your leave policy. You will have to decide:

- Which employees qualify for the leave. For example, will you have a length-of-service requirement—that is, a requirement that employees have been in your employ for a certain amount of time before they qualify? Will only full-time employees be eligible? Will you require employees to provide medical proof of the substance abuse problem?
- The amount of leave you will allow. When making this decision, you might consult with rehabilitation programs in your area to get an estimate of what is reasonable.
- Whether you will require employees to provide proof that they successfully completed the program.
- Whether the leave will be paid or unpaid.
- Whether you will allow employees to accrue benefits while on leave.

In most states, the law does not provide you with much direction on these issues. The way you answer these questions will depend on your company's values and what it can afford.

In the states that require this type of leave, however, the law may also have rules about issues relating to the leave. These rules typically mandate such things as whether employees are entitled to benefits while on leave and whether the leave is paid or unpaid. If your state has such a law, you may have to modify the policy that we provide above.

17:5 Rehabilitation and Your EAP

Most employee assistance plans (EAPs) include drug and alcohol rehabilitation and counseling services. If you offer an EAP as a benefit to your employees, check to see whether your plan includes these things. If it does, inform employees of this fact either through the policy below or through a policy provided by your EAP administrator.

Rehabilitation and Your EAP

Because we care about the health and welfare of our employees, your benefits package includes an Employee Assistance Program (EAP) that provides assistance to employees who suffer from substance abuse problems, personal problems, or emotional problems.

   If you would like assistance in dealing with your substance abuse problem, see _____

_____

for information about our EAP program. Your request for assistance will be kept as confidential as possible.

   [*If you will include in your handbook a policy allowing leave to participate in a rehabilitation program, refer to that policy here.*]

_____

_____

_____

_____

_____

_____

_____

_____

_____

_____

   Please note that even as you might be seeking assistance for your substance abuse problem, we still expect you to meet the same standards of performance, productivity, and conduct that we expect of all employees. We reserve the right to discipline you for failing to meet those standards.

17:5   Rehabilitation and Your EAP
CD File: 17_Drugs Alcohol.rtf

Include This Policy?
☐ Yes
☐ No
☐ Use our existing policy
☐ Other _____

Alternate Modifications
None

Additional Clauses
None

Related Policies
None

Notes

_____

_____

_____

_____

_____

_____

_____

_____

_____

_____

_____

_____

_____

_____

_____

_____

_____

_____

_____

_____

_____

State Drug and Alcohol Testing Laws

Note: The states of Colorado, Delaware, Kansas, Kentucky, Massachusetts, Michigan, Missouri, Nevada, New Hampshire, New Jersey, New Mexico, New York, Pennsylvania, South Dakota, Texas, Washington, West Virginia, Wisconsin, Wyoming, and the District of Columbia are not included in this chart because they do not have specific drug and alcohol testing laws governing private employers. Additional laws may apply. Check with your state department of labor for more information. (See Appendix A for contact list.)

Alabama

Ala. Code §§ 25-5-330 to 25-5-340

Employers affected: Employers who establish a drug-free workplace program to qualify for a workers' compensation rate discount.

Testing applicants: Must test upon conditional offer of employment. Must test all new hires. Job ads must include notice that drug and alcohol testing required.

Testing employees: Random testing permitted. Must test after an accident that results in lost work time. Must also test upon reasonable suspicion; reasons for suspicion must be documented and made available to employee upon request.

Employee rights: Employees have 5 days to contest or explain a positive test result. Employer must have an employee assistance program or maintain a resource file of outside programs.

Notice and policy requirements: All employees must have written notice of drug policy. Must give 60 days' advance notice before implementing testing program. Policy must state consequences of refusing to take test or testing positive.

Drug-free workplace program: Yes.

Alaska

Alaska Stat. §§ 23.10.600 and following

Employers affected: Voluntary for employers with one or more full-time employees. (There is no state-mandated drug and alcohol testing.)

Testing employees: Employer may test:
- for any job-related purpose
- to maintain productivity and safety
- as part of an accident investigation, or
- upon reasonable suspicion.

Employee rights: Employer must provide written test results within 5 working days. Employee has 10 working days to request opportunity to explain positive test results; employer must grant request within 72 hours or

before taking any adverse employment action.

Notice and policy requirements: Before implementing a testing program employer must distribute a written drug policy to all employees and must give 30 days' advance notice. Policy must state consequences of a positive test or refusal to submit to testing.

Arizona

Ariz. Rev. Stat. §§ 23-493 and following

Employers affected: Employers with one or more full-time employees.

Testing applicants: Employer must inform prospective hires that they will undergo drug testing as a condition of employment.

Testing employees: Employees are subject to random and scheduled tests:
- for any job-related purpose
- to maintain productivity and safety, or
- upon reasonable suspicion.

Employee rights: Policy must inform employees of their right to explain positive results.

Notice and policy requirements: Before conducting tests employer must give employees a copy of the written policy. Policy must state the consequences of a positive test or refusal to submit to testing.

Drug-free workplace program: Yes.

Arkansas

Ark. Code Ann. §§ 11-14-105 to 11-14-112

Employers affected: Employers who establish a drug-free workplace program to qualify for a workers' compensation rate discount.

Testing applicants: Must test upon conditional offer of employment. Job ads must include notice that drug and alcohol testing required.

Testing employees: Employer must test any employee:
- on reasonable suspicion of drug use
- as part of a routine fitness-for-duty medical exam
- after an accident that results in injury, or
- as follow-up to a required rehabilitation program.

Employee rights: Employer may not refuse to hire applicant or take adverse personnel action against an employee on the basis of a single positive test that has not been verified by a confirmation test. An applicant or employee has 5 days after receiving test results to contest or explain them.

Notice and policy requirements: Employer must give all employees a written statement of drug policy and

State Drug and Alcohol Testing Laws (continued)

must give 60 days' advance notice before implementing program.

Drug-free workplace program: Yes.

California

Cal. Lab. Code §§ 1025, 1026

Employers affected: No provisions for private employer testing. An employer with 25 or more employees must reasonably accommodate an employee who wants to enter a treatment program. Employer is not, however, required to provide paid leave. Employer may fire or refuse to hire an employee whose drug or alcohol use interferes with job duties or workplace safety.

Employee rights: Employer must safeguard privacy of employee who enters treatment program.

Connecticut

Conn. Gen. Stat. Ann. §§ 31-51t to 31-51bb

Employers affected: All.

Testing applicants: Employer must inform job applicants in writing that drug testing is required as a condition of employment.

Testing employees: Employer may test:
- when there is reasonable suspicion that employee is under the influence of drugs or alcohol and job performance is or could be impaired
- when authorized by federal law
- when employee's position is dangerous or safety-sensitive, or
- as part of a voluntary employee assistance program.

Employee rights: Employer may not take any adverse personnel action on the basis of a single positive test that has not been verified by a confirmation test.

Florida

Fla. Stat. Ann. §§ 440.101 to 440.102

Employers affected: Employers who establish a drug-free workplace program to qualify for a workers' compensation rate discount.

Testing applicants: Must inform job applicants that drug and alcohol testing is required as a condition of employment.

Testing employees: Must test any employee:
- on reasonable suspicion of drug use
- as part of a routine fitness-for-duty medical exam, or
- as part of a required rehabilitation program.

Employee rights: Employees who voluntarily seek treatment for substance abuse cannot be fired, disciplined, or discriminated against, unless they have

tested positive or have been in treatment in the past. All employees have the right to explain positive results within 5 days. Employer may not take any adverse personnel action on the basis of an initial positive result that has not been verified by a confirmation test.

Notice and policy requirements: Prior to implementing testing, employer must give 60 days' advance notice and must give employees written copy of drug policy.

Drug-free workplace program: Yes.

Georgia

Ga. Code Ann. §§ 34-9-410 to 34-9-421

Employers affected: Employers who establish a drug-free workplace program to qualify for a workers' compensation rate discount.

Testing applicants: Applicants are required to submit to a substance abuse test after they have been offered employment.

Testing employees: Must test any employee:
- on reasonable suspicion of drug use
- as part of a routine fitness-for-duty medical exam, or
- as part of a required rehabilitation program.

Employee rights: Employees have 5 days to explain or contest a positive result. Employer must have an employee assistance program or maintain a resource file of outside programs.

Notice and policy requirements: Employer must give applicants and employees notice of testing and must give 60 days' notice before implementing program. All employees must receive a written policy statement; policy must state the consequences of refusing to submit to a drug test or of testing positive.

Drug-free workplace program: Yes.

Hawaii

Haw. Rev. Stat. §§ 329B-1 and following

Employers affected: All.

Testing applicants: Same conditions as current employees.

Testing employees: Employer may test employees only if these conditions are met:
- employer pays all costs including confirming test
- tests are performed by a licensed laboratory
- employee receives a list of the substances being tested for
- there is a form for disclosing medicines and legal drugs, and
- the results are kept confidential.

State Drug and Alcohol Testing Laws (continued)

Idaho

Idaho Code §§ 72-1701 to 72-1714

Employers affected: Voluntary for all private employers.

Testing applicants: Employer may test as a condition of hiring.

Testing employees: May test as a condition of continued employment.

An employer who follows drug-free workplace guidelines may fire employees who refuse to submit to testing or who test positive for drugs or alcohol. Employees will be fired for misconduct and denied unemployment benefits.

Employee rights: An employee or applicant who receives notice of a positive test may request a retest within 7 working days. If the retest results are negative, the employer must pay for the cost; if they are positive, the employee must pay.

Drug-free workplace program: Yes (compliance is optional).

Illinois

775 Ill. Comp. Stat. § 5/2-104(C)(3)

Employers affected: Employers with 15 or more employees.

Testing employees: Statute does not "encourage, prohibit, or authorize" drug testing, but employers may test employees who have been in rehabilitation.

Indiana

Ind. Code Ann. §§ 22-9-5-6(b), 22-9-5-24

Employers affected: Employers with 15 or more employees.

Testing employees: Employer may prohibit all employees from using or being under the influence of alcohol and illegal drugs. Employer may test employees who have been in rehabilitation. Employee may be held to the same standards as other employees, even if the unsatisfactory job performance or behavior is due to drug use or alcoholism.

Iowa

Iowa Code § 730.5

Employers affected: Employers with one or more full-time employees.

Testing applicants: Employer may test as a condition of hiring.

Testing employees: Employer may test employees:
- as a condition of continued employment
- upon reasonable suspicion

- during and after rehabilitation, or
- following an accident that caused a reportable injury or more than $1,000 property damage.

Employee rights: Employee has 7 days to request a retest. Employers with 50 or more employees must provide rehabilitation for any employee who has worked for at least one year and has not previously violated the substance abuse policy; no adverse action may be taken if employee successfully completes rehabilitation. Employer must have an employee assistance program or maintain a resource file of outside programs.

Drug-free workplace program: Yes (compliance is optional).

Louisiana

La. Rev. Stat. Ann. §§ 49:1001 and following

Employers affected: Employers with one or more full-time employees. (Does not apply to oil drilling, exploration, or production.)

Testing applicants: Employer may require all applicants to submit to drug and alcohol test. Employer does not have to confirm a positive result of a preemployment drug screen but must offer the applicant the opportunity to pay for a confirmation test and a review by a medical review officer.

Employee rights: Except for a preemployment test, employer may not take adverse personnel action on the basis of an initial screen. Employees with confirmed positive results have 7 working days to request access to all records relating to the drug test. Employer may allow employee to undergo rehabilitation without termination of employment.

Maine

Me. Rev. Stat. Ann. tit. 26, §§ 681 to 690

Employers affected: Employers with one or more full-time employees. (Law does not require or encourage employers to conduct substance abuse testing.)

Testing applicants: Employer may require applicant to take a drug test only if offered employment or placed on an eligibility list.

Testing employees: Employer may test based upon probable cause but may not base belief on a single accident; must document the facts and give employee a copy. May test when:
- there could be an unreasonable threat to the health and safety of coworkers or the public, or

State Drug and Alcohol Testing Laws (continued)

- an employee returns to work following a positive test.

Employee rights: Employee who tests positive has 3 days to explain or contest results. Employee must be given an opportunity to participate in a rehabilitation program for up to 6 months; an employer with more than 20 full-time employees must pay for half of any out-of-pocket costs. After successfully completing the program, employee is entitled to return to previous job with full pay and benefits.

Notice and policy requirements: All employers must have a written policy approved by the state department of labor. Policy must be distributed to each employee at least 30 days before it takes effect. Any changes to policy require 60 days' advance notice. An employer with more than 20 full-time employees must have an employee assistance program certified by the state office of substance abuse before implementing a testing program.

Maryland

Md. Code Ann., [Health-Gen.] § 17-214

Employers affected: Law applies to all employers.

Testing applicants: May use preliminary screening to test applicant. If initial result is positive, may make job offer conditional on confirmation of test results.

Testing employees: Employer may require substance abuse testing for legitimate business purposes only.

Employee rights: The sample must be tested by a certified laboratory; at the time of testing employee may request laboratory's name and address. An employee who tests positive must be given:

- a copy of the test results
- a copy of the employer's written drug and alcohol policy
- a written notice of any adverse action employer intends to take, and
- a statement of employee's right to an independent confirmation test at own expense.

Minnesota

Minn. Stat. Ann. §§ 181.950 to 181.957

Employers affected: Employers with one or more full-time employees. (Employers are not required to test.)

Testing applicants: Employers may require applicants to submit to a drug or alcohol test only after they have been given a job offer and have seen a written notice of testing policy. May only test if required of all applicants for same position.

Testing employees: Employers may require drug or alcohol testing only according to a written testing policy. Testing may be done if there is a reasonable suspicion that employee:

- is under the influence of drugs or alcohol
- has violated drug and alcohol policy
- has been involved in an accident, or
- has sustained or caused another employee to sustain a personal injury.

Random tests permitted only for employees in safety-sensitive positions. With two weeks' notice, employers may also test as part of an annual routine physical exam.

Employee rights: If test is positive, employee has 3 days to explain the results; employee must notify employer within 5 days of intention to obtain a retest. Employer may not discharge employee for a first-time positive test without offering counseling or rehabilitation; employee who refuses or does not complete program successfully may be discharged.

Notice and policy requirements: Employees must be given a written notice of testing policy which includes consequences of refusing to take test or having a positive test result. Two weeks' notice required before testing as part of an annual routine physical exam.

Mississippi

Miss. Code Ann. §§ 71-7-1 and following, 71-3-205 and following

Employers affected: Employers with one or more full-time employees. Employers who establish a drug-free workplace program to qualify for a workers' compensation rate discount must implement testing procedures.

Testing applicants: May test all applicants as part of employment application process. Employer may request a signed statement that applicant has read and understands the drug and alcohol testing policy or notice. (Must test applicants if drug-free workplace.)

Testing employees: May require drug and alcohol testing of all employees:

- on reasonable suspicion
- as part of a routinely scheduled fitness for duty medical examination
- as a follow-up to a rehabilitation program, or
- if they have tested positive within the previous 12 months.

Employee rights: Employer must inform an employee in writing within 5 working days of receipt of a positive

State Drug and Alcohol Testing Laws (continued)

confirmed test result; employee may request and receive a copy of the test result report. Employee has 10 working days after receiving notice to explain the positive test results. Private employer who elects to establish a drug-free workplace program must have an employee assistance program or maintain a resource file of outside programs.

Notice and policy requirements: 30 days before implementing testing program employer must give employees written notice of drug and alcohol policy which includes consequences:
- of a positive confirmed result
- of refusing to take test, and
- of other violations of the policy.

Drug-free workplace program: Yes.

Montana

Mont. Code Ann. §§ 39-2-205 to 39-2-211

Employers affected: Employers with one or more employees.

Testing applicants: May test as a condition of hire.

Testing employees: Employees may be tested:
- on reasonable suspicion
- after involvement in an accident that causes personal injury or more than $1,500 property damage
- as a follow-up to a previous positive test, or
- as a follow-up to treatment or a rehabilitation program.

Employer may conduct random tests as long as there is an established date and all personnel are subject to testing.

Employer may require an employee who tests positive to undergo treatment as a condition of continued employment.

Employee rights: After a positive result, employee may request additional confirmation by an independent laboratory; if the results are negative, employer must pay the test costs.

Notice and policy requirements: Written policy must be available for review 60 days before testing.

Nebraska

Neb. Rev. Stat. §§ 48-1901 and following

Employers affected: Employers with 6 or more full-time and part-time employees.

Testing employees: Employer may require employees to submit to drug or alcohol testing and may discipline or discharge any employee who refuses.

Employee rights: Employer may not take adverse action on the basis of an initial positive result unless it is confirmed according to state and federal guidelines.

North Carolina

N.C. Gen. Stat. §§ 95-230 to 95-235

Employers affected: Law applies to all employers.

Testing employees: Employer must preserve samples for at least 90 days after confirmed test results are released.

Employee rights: Employee has right to retest a confirmed positive sample at own expense.

North Dakota

N.D. Cent. Code § 34-01-15

Employers affected: Any employer who requires a medical exam as a condition of hire or continued employment may include a drug or alcohol test.

Testing employees: Employer may test following an accident or injury that will result in a workers' compensation claim, if employer has a mandatory policy of testing under these circumstances, or if employer or physician has reasonable grounds to suspect injury was caused by impairment due to alcohol or drug use.

Ohio

Ohio Admin. Code §§ 4123-17-58, 4123-17-58.1

Employers affected: Employers who establish a drug-free workplace program to qualify for a workers' compensation rate discount.

Testing applicants: Must test all applicants and new hires within 90 days of employment.

Testing employees: Must test employees:
- on reasonable suspicion
- following a return to work after a positive test, or
- after an accident which results in an injury requiring offsite medical attention or property damage over limit specified in drug and alcohol policy
- at random to meet requirements for greater discounts.

Employee rights: Employer must have an employee assistance plan. Employer must offer health care coverage which includes chemical dependency counseling and treatment.

Notice and policy requirements: Policy must state consequences for refusing to submit to testing or for violating guidelines. Policy must include a commitment to rehabilitation.

Drug-free workplace program: Yes.

State Drug and Alcohol Testing Laws (continued)

Oklahoma

Okla. Stat. Ann. tit. 40, §§ 551 to 565

Employers affected: Employers with one or more employees. (Drug or alcohol testing not required or encouraged.)

Testing applicants: Employer may test applicants as a condition of employment and may refuse to hire applicant who refuses to undergo test or has a confirmed positive result.

Testing employees: Before requiring testing, employer must provide an employee assistance program. Random testing is allowed. May test employees:
- on reasonable suspicion
- after an accident resulting in injury or property damage over $500
- as part of a routine fitness-for-duty examination, or
- as follow-up to a rehabilitation program.

Employee rights: Employee has right to retest a positive result at own expense; if the confirmation test is negative, employer must reimburse costs.

Notice and policy requirements: Before requiring testing employer must:
- adopt a written policy
- give a copy to each employee and to any applicant offered a job, and
- allow 30 days' notice.

Oregon

Or. Rev. Stat. §§ 659.840, 659A.300, 438.435

Employers affected: Law applies to all employers.

Testing applicants: Unless there is reasonable suspicion that an applicant is under the influence of alcohol, no employer may require a breathalyzer test as a condition of employment. Employer is not prohibited from conducting a test if applicant consents.

Testing employees: Unless there is reasonable suspicion that an employee is under the influence of alcohol, no employer may require a breathalyzer or blood alcohol test as a condition of continuing employment. Employer is not prohibited from conducting a test if employee consents.

Employee rights: No action may be taken based on the results of an on-site drug test without a confirming test performed according to state health division regulations. Upon written request, test results will be reported to the employee.

Rhode Island

R.I. Gen. Laws §§ 28-6.5-1 to 28-6.5-2

Employers affected: Law applies to all employers.

Testing employees: May require employee to submit to a drug test only if there are reasonable grounds, based on specific observations, to believe employee is using controlled substances that are impairing job performance.

Employee rights: Employee who tests positive may have the sample retested at employer's expense and must be given opportunity to explain or refute results. Employee may not be terminated on the basis of a positive result but must be referred to a licensed substance abuse professional. After referral, employer may require additional testing and may terminate employee if test results are positive.

South Carolina

S.C. Code Ann. §§ 41-1-15, 38-73-500

Employers affected: Employers who establish a drug-free workplace program to qualify for a workers' compensation rate discount.

Testing employees: Must conduct random testing among all employees. Must conduct a follow-up test within 30 minutes of the first test.

Employee rights: Employee must receive positive test results in writing within 24 hours.

Notice and policy requirements: Employer must notify all employees of the drug-free workplace program at the time it is established or at the time of hiring, whichever is earlier. Program must include a policy statement that balances respect for individuals with the need to maintain a safe, drug-free environment.

Drug-free workplace program: Yes.

Tennessee

Tenn. Code Ann. §§ 50-9-101 and following

Employers affected: Employers who establish a drug-free workplace program to qualify for a workers' compensation rate discount.

Testing applicants: Must test applicants upon conditional offer of employment. Job ads must include notice that drug and alcohol testing is required.

Testing employees: Employer must test upon reasonable suspicion; must document behavior on which the suspicion is based within 24 hours or before test results are released, whichever is earlier; and must give a copy to the employee upon request. Employer must test employees:
- who are in safety-sensitive positions
- as part of a routine fitness-for-duty medical exam

State Drug and Alcohol Testing Laws (continued)

- after an accident that results in injury, or
- as a follow-up to a required rehabilitation program.

Employee rights: Employee has the right to explain or contest a positive result within 5 days. Employee may not be fired, disciplined, or discriminated against for voluntarily seeking treatment unless employee has previously tested positive or been in a rehabilitation program.

Notice and policy requirements: Before implementing testing program, employer must provide 60 days' notice and must give all employees a written drug and alcohol policy statement.

Drug-free workplace program: Yes.

Utah
Utah Code Ann. §§ 34-38-1 to 34-38-15

Employers affected: Employers with one or more employees.

Testing applicants: Employer may test any applicant for drugs or alcohol as long as management also submits to periodic testing.

Testing employees: Employer may test employee for drugs or alcohol as long as management also submits to periodic testing. Employer may also require testing to:
- investigate an accident or theft
- maintain employee or public safety, or
- ensure productivity, quality, or security.

Employee rights: Employer may suspend, discipline, discharge, or require treatment on the basis of a confirmed positive test result.

Notice and policy requirements: Testing must be conducted according to a written policy that has been distributed to employees and is available for review by prospective employees.

Vermont
Vt. Stat. Ann. tit. 21, §§ 511 and following

Employers affected: Employers with one or more employees.

Testing applicants: Employer may not test applicants for drugs or alcohol unless there is a job offer conditional on a negative test result and applicant is given written notice of the testing procedure and a list of the drugs to be tested for.

Testing employees: Random testing not permitted unless required by federal law. Employer may not require testing unless:
- there is probable cause to believe an employee is using or is under the influence
- employer has an employee assistance program which provides rehabilitation, and
- employee who tests positive and agrees to enter employee assistance program is not terminated.

Employee rights: Employer must contract with a medical review officer who will review all test results and keep them confidential. Medical review officer is to contact employee or applicant to explain a positive test result. Employee or applicant has right to an independent retest at own expense. Employee who successfully completes employee assistance program may not be terminated, although employee may be suspended for up to 3 months to complete program. Employee who tests positive after completing treatment may be fired.

Virginia
Va. Code Ann. § 65.2-813.2

Employers affected: Employers who establish drug-free workplace programs to qualify for workers' compensation insurance discount.

Drug-free workplace program: State law gives insurers the authority to establish guidelines and criteria for testing.

Current as of February 2005

18

Trade Secrets and Conflicts of Interest

Often, what gives a company a competitive advantage is the specialized knowledge that it has gained through the ingenuity, innovation, or just plain hard work of its owners and employees. This specialized knowledge could be something as mundane as a list of customers who have a specific need for your company's services or as glamorous as the top-secret formula for your company's product. The law of trade secrets protects this specialized knowledge from disclosure to, and use by, your competitors.

Employees pose a thorny dilemma for businesses with valuable trade secrets. After all, a business has to let some workers in on its trade secrets—either because they need the information to do their jobs or because they helped develop the information in the first place. Yet these same people may harm the business—either accidentally or through bad intentions—by revealing trade secrets to competitors.

Most states impose on employees a duty of loyalty that includes keeping trade secrets confidential. Nonetheless, it doesn't hurt to specifically inform employees in the handbook that they must keep mum.

A similar issue arises with regard to conflicts of interest. Most employers do not want their current employees also working for competitors. Such work inherently divides an employee's loyalties and creates a risk that the employee will reveal trade secrets to the competitor. By the same token, such work creates the risk that the employee will reveal the competitor's trade secrets to someone in your company. Although having a double agent on your team might not sound so bad at first, it's illegal—and a competitor could drag your company into court.

One of the first steps in protecting your company is to put employees on notice about what is expected of them in this area, which the policies included in this chapter will do. If your company has valuable information to protect, however, it will need more than a few handbook policies to do the job. It will need policies and procedures in place to identify confidential information and limit access to it, among other things.

18:1   Confidentiality and Trade
Secrets

CD File: 18_Trade Secrets.rtf

Include This Policy?
☐ Yes
☐ No
☐ Use our existing policy
☐ Other _____

Alternate Modifications
None

Additional Clauses
Companies With Confidentiality
Procedures in Place
Insert?:   ☐ Yes   ☐ No

Related Policies
None

Notes
_____
_____
_____
_____
_____
_____
_____
_____
_____
_____
_____
_____
_____
_____
_____
_____

18:1   Confidentiality and Trade Secrets

Often, ensuring that employees don't disclose sensitive information is as simple as cluing them in to the importance of keeping quiet and alerting them to the consequences of failing to do so. The sample policy in this section serves these purposes.

Reality Check: Use Confidentiality Agreements and Designate Confidential Information

As you read the policy, below, notice that it raises more questions than it answers. What information qualifies as "sensitive information, confidential information, proprietary information, or trade secret information"? What does it mean to "improperly disclose" such information? Unfortunately, the handbook cannot answer these questions for employees; only your company can—through training, procedures, and practices. If your business depends on trade secret information to keep a competitive advantage, it behooves you to develop confidentiality procedures to protect valuable information from disclosure. These procedures typically include fairly simple means—such as labeling certain documents as "confidential"—of informing employees about what information is confidential and what information isn't.

In addition, it's important to remember that a handbook is not a contract. It does not bind you, and it does not bind employees. This means that your company cannot go to court to enforce the provisions in the handbook. If your company has employees who will learn or develop sensitive information while working there, consider having them sign a confidentiality agreement (also called a "nondisclosure agreement"). Although the duty of loyalty that we mentioned above should be technically sufficient to protect your company's trade secrets, nondisclosure agreements underscore the importance of confidentiality and clear up any ambiguity about what information your company considers a trade secret. They can also be helpful if your company ever has to haul an employee into court for revealing a trade secret, whether the employee is still working for your company or not.

Confidentiality and Trade Secrets

Information is part of what makes this Company competitive. During your employment here, you will periodically learn sensitive information, either because you help to develop that information or because you need that information to do your job. It is important for the health of this business—and for the well-being of employees who depend on this business for their livelihood—that you keep information you learn through your employment confidential. Employees who improperly disclose sensitive information, confidential information, proprietary information, or trade secret information to anyone outside the Company will face disciplinary action, up to and including termination. Therefore, we encourage you to contact _____

_____

if you would like to learn more about this policy or if you have any questions.

After you leave this Company, you are still legally prohibited from disclosing sensitive, proprietary, trade secret, or confidential information. If you disclose such information, we will seek legal remedies.

Additional Clause for Companies With Confidentiality Procedures in Place

If you have procedures in place to protect your confidential information, pat yourself on the back. Then modify the standard policy above to inform employees of this fact. You don't need to give exhaustive detail about the procedures. It is sufficient to alert employees to their existence and tell employees where they can go for more information. Consider adding the following paragraph to the standard policy above.

Additional Clause

Because of the grave importance of keeping certain information confidential, this Company follows practices designed to alert employees to sensitive and confidential information, to limit access to that information, and to inform employees about what disclosures are and are not acceptable. We expect employees to follow these procedures. Employees who fail to do so face discipline, up to and including termination. To find out more about these procedures, refer to

_____ .

If you have any questions about these procedures, contact

_____ .

18:2 Conflicts of Interest

Your company wants and expects its employees to be loyal to the company—and not to its competitors. After all, a company and its employees work together as a team to compete in the marketplace and create a healthy, thriving business.

In most instances, the fact that an employee has a little job on the side isn't going to do much—if any—damage to your company. If that job is with a competitor, however, there is a risk that the side job will divide the employee's loyalties.

Similarly, employee investments will pose little harm to your company, unless those investments make the employees act in a way that is contrary to your company's interests.

Although your company has a legal right to protect itself from conflicts of interest, your employees also have legal rights to invest as they see fit and to work for whomever they want. The law balances your company's rights and against those of its employees. If you need to discipline an employee or terminate someone for violating this policy, consult with an attorney first to make sure that your actions don't violate a law designed to protect employees.

This policy tells employees that loyalty is part of their job description—and it informs them that they will face consequences if they act in ways that could harm the company.

This policy applies to current employees only. It does not prohibit former employees from working for competitors. No handbook policy can do that. Instead, you'll need a contract called a noncompete agreement. To learn how to create such an agreement, see *How to Create a Noncompete Agreement*, by Shannon Miehe (Nolo).

18:2   Conflicts of Interest

CD File: 18_Trade Secrets.rtf

Include This Policy?
- ☐ Yes
- ☐ No
- ☐ Use our existing policy
- ☐ Other _____

Alternate Modifications
None

Additional Clauses
None

Related Policies
None

Notes

Conflicts of Interest

Our Company's success depends on the hard work, dedication, and integrity of everyone who works here. In turn, our employees' livelihood depends on the success of our Company.

Because we depend so much on our employees, and because they depend so much on us, we expect all employees to devote their energies and loyalties to our Company. We do not allow employees to engage in any activities or relationships that create either an actual conflict of interest or the potential for a conflict of interest.

Although we cannot list every activity or relationship that would create either an actual or potential conflict of interest, examples of activities that violate this policy include the following:

- working for a competitor or customer or vendor as a part-time employee, full-time employee, consultant, or independent contractor, or in any other capacity
- owning an interest in a competitor, customer, vendor, or anyone else who seeks to do business with this Company
- using the resources of this Company for personal gain, and
- using your position in this Company for personal gain.

Employees who violate this policy face disciplinary action, up to and including termination.

If you are unsure about whether an activity might violate this policy, or if you have any questions at all about this policy, please talk to _____

_____ .

19

Discrimination and Harassment

Most employers are required to follow federal antidiscrimination laws, including laws prohibiting sexual harassment. Depending on where your company does business, it may also have to follow state and even local laws banning discrimination. An employer's obligation to comply with these laws has nothing to do with its personnel policies—whether a company has an antidiscrimination policy or not, it must follow the law.

So why include policies prohibiting discrimination and harassment in an employee handbook? First, these policies educate employees and managers about what constitutes discrimination or harassment, what types of conduct are prohibited, and what the company will do to stop it. Armed with this information, employees and managers will know what to do if they are victims of, or witnesses to, illegal behavior. They will also know that the company believes in equal employment opportunity for everyone, a philosophy that can help a business build solid relations with its workers.

Second, stated policies against discrimination and harassment will encourage workers to bring misconduct to the company's attention immediately. Unless your company is very small, this could be the only way that management finds out that a potentially troublesome situation is brewing. If employees complain quickly, the company has a chance to deal with the problems right away, before they poison the workplace environment.

Finally, a well-crafted policy against harassment buys the company some legal protection, should it ever be sued by an employee. If your company has a clear written policy prohibiting harassment and spelling out a complaint procedure, employees must follow these procedures to make complaints. If they fail to alert the company to a problem, courts might not let them sue the company for failing to deal with it.

19:1 Our Commitment to Equal
Employment Opportunity

CD File: 19_Discrimination.rtf

Include This Policy?
☐ Yes
☐ No
☐ Use our existing policy
☐ Other _____

Alternate Modifications
None

Additional Clauses
Emphasize Company's
Commitment
Insert?: ☐ Yes ☐ No

Related Policies
Chapter 20 covers policies for
making a discrimination or
harassment complaint.

Notes
_____
_____
_____
_____
_____
_____
_____
_____
_____
_____
_____
_____
_____
_____
_____
_____

19:1 Antidiscrimination Policy

Your antidiscrimination policy should explain the company's commitment to equal opportunity. It should describe what is prohibited, let employees know what to do if they witness or suffer discrimination, and tell employees how the company will deal with discrimination in the workplace.

Our Commitment to Equal Employment Opportunity

[*Company name*] is strongly committed to providing equal employment opportunity for all employees and all applicants for employment. For us, this is the only acceptable way to do business.

All employment decisions at our Company—including those relating to hiring, promotion, transfers, benefits, compensation, placement, and termination—will be made without regard to

_____
_____
_____
_____
_____

[*list prohibited bases for discrimination*].

Any employee or applicant who believes that he or she has been discriminated against in violation of this policy should immediately file a complaint with _____

_____,
as explained in our Complaint Policy. We encourage you to come forward if you have suffered or witnessed what you believe to be discrimination—we cannot solve the problem until you let us know about it. The Company will not retaliate, or allow retaliation, against any employee or applicant who complains of discrimination, assists in an investigation of possible discrimination, or files an administrative charge or lawsuit alleging discrimination.

Managers are required to report any discriminatory conduct or incidents, as described in our Complaint Policy.

Our Company will not tolerate discrimination against any employee or applicant. We will take immediate and appropriate disciplinary action against any employee who violates this policy.

Who Needs This Policy

No law requires an employer to include an antidiscrimination policy in its handbook. Because of the benefits such a policy can provide, however, all employers who are subject to antidiscrimination laws should have one. For details on which employers have a legal obligation not to discriminate, see "Which Federal Antidiscrimination Laws Apply to Your Company," below.

How to Complete This Policy

Before you can complete our sample policy, you will need to know what antidiscrimination laws your company is required to follow under both federal and state law. This will tell you what to put in the blank in our sample policy, above, where you list prohibited bases for discrimination at your company.

Federal laws require many employers not to discriminate on the basis of race, color, national origin, religion, sex, age, disability, or citizenship status. However, these laws don't apply to every employer—only to employers who have a specified minimum number of employees. To find out which federal laws your company has to follow—and, therefore, which characteristics to list in your policy—refer to "Which Federal Antidiscrimination Laws Apply to Your Company," below.

In addition, most states and some municipalities have their own antidiscrimination laws. Some of these laws duplicate the federal protections, while others apply to smaller employers or prohibit discrimination based on additional characteristics that federal law does not include—such as marital status or sexual orientation. To find out whether your state imposes any additional obligations, consult "State Laws Prohibiting Discrimination in Employment" at the end of this chapter. You can find out whether any local laws apply by getting in touch with your state fair employment department (see Appendix A for contact information) or your local Chamber of Commerce.

Which Federal Antidiscrimination Laws Apply to Your Company

Not every antidiscrimination law applies to every employer. For the most part, whether your company has to follow these laws depends on its size and location. Federal antidiscrimination laws apply only to employers with more than a minimum number of employees—and this minimum number is different for each law.

Name of Law:	Discrimination Prohibited on the Basis of:	Applies to:
Title VII	Race, national origin, religion, sex	Employers with 15 or more employees
Age Discrimination in Employment Act	Age (over 40 only)	Employers with 20 or more employees
Americans With Disabilities Act	Physical or mental disability	Employers with 15 or more employees
Equal Pay Act	Sex (applies only to wage discrimination)	All employers
Civil Rights Act of 1866	Race	All employers
Immigration Reform and Control Act	Citizenship status, national origin	Employers with 4 or more employees

Your handbook should refer only to those types of discrimination that are prohibited for your company. For example, if your company does business in a state that outlaws discrimination based on sexual orientation, you should include sexual orientation in the list of prohibited bases for discrimination. Similarly, if your company has only 15 employees, it does not have to comply with the federal Age Discrimination in Employment Act—so, unless a separate state law prohibits age discrimination in companies of your size, you should not include age in your list.

You will also have to decide who in your company will receive complaints of discrimination. In this blank in the sample policy, designate the person or persons named in your complaint policy. (See Chapter 20 for complaint policies and related discussions.) If you have a human resources department, you can refer employees there.

Additional Clause to Emphasize Company's Commitment

You may want to include additional language to further explain and emphasize your company's commitment to equal employment opportunity. Some employers take special pride in their efforts to combat discrimination, to provide goods or services to traditionally underserved communities, or to honor cultural diversity. Consider the following examples of additions based on the purpose each company serves.

SAMPLE POLICY LANGUAGE

Our Company was founded to help women achieve equal opportunity in the field of sports. This commitment to equal opportunity for everyone extends to our workplace and the way we treat each other. Discrimination of any kind is contrary to the principles for which our Company stands.

SAMPLE POLICY LANGUAGE

Our mission is to bring fresh, high-quality food products from around the world to customers in the United States. We take pride in the great diversity of our customers and our employees. We treat our employees, and expect our employees to treat each other, with respect and dignity. Discrimination of any kind is against our Company philosophy and policies and will not be tolerated.

19:2   Harassment Will Not Be
          Tolerated

CD File: 19_Discrimination.rtf

Include This Policy?
☐ Yes
☐ No
☐ Use our existing policy
☐ Other

Alternate Modifications
None

Additional Clauses
None

Related Policies
Chapter 20 covers policies for
making a discrimination or
harassment complaint.

Notes

_____
_____
_____
_____
_____
_____
_____
_____
_____
_____
_____
_____
_____
_____
_____
_____
_____
_____

19:2 Harassment

Legally, harassment is a form of discrimination. The same laws that prohibit discrimination also require employers to stop harassment. Therefore, every employer who is subject to the antidiscrimination laws discussed above should also have a policy against harassment.

No law requires an employer to have a policy prohibiting harassment. However, in addition to the practical benefits such a policy can provide, a harassment policy creates one very substantial legal benefit: protection against certain harassment lawsuits. If your company has a policy prohibiting harassment that includes the essential elements we discuss below (and include in our sample policy), and the company fully and fairly investigates complaints of harassment, a court may decide that an employee who failed to complain of harassment cannot sue the company.

This protection applies only to certain types of harassment cases, however. If management was aware of the harassment even though the employee did not complain (for example, there were lewd posters and X-rated graffiti displayed prominently throughout the workplace), the employee's failure to complain won't get the company off the hook. And if the harassment was committed by a manager or supervisor and resulted in a serious, negative job action against the employee (for example, the employee was fired or denied a promotion because she refused to have a sexual relationship with a supervisor), the company will be responsible whether or not the employee complained. However, if no negative job action was taken against the employee (for example, an employee was repeatedly teased or subjected to lewd jokes and stories but was not demoted or fired), she can sue the company for harassment by a manager or supervisor only if she first complained, using the company's harassment and complaint policies.

Your harassment policy should explain what harassment is, let workers know that harassment will not be tolerated, tell workers and managers what to do if they witness or suffer harassment, and assure everyone that retaliation against those who complain of harassment or participate in a harassment investigation is strictly prohibited.

Harassment Will Not Be Tolerated

It is our policy and our responsibility to provide our employees with a workplace free from harassment. Harassment on the basis of _____

_____

_____

_____

_____

_____

_____

_____

_____

_____

_____

_____

_____

[list prohibited bases for discrimination] undermines our workplace morale and our commitment to treat each other with dignity and respect. Accordingly, harassment will not be tolerated at our Company.

Harassment can take many forms, including but not limited to touching or other unwanted physical contact, posting offensive cartoons or pictures, using slurs or other derogatory terms, telling offensive or lewd jokes and stories, and sending email messages with offensive content. Unwanted sexual advances, requests for sexual favors and sexually suggestive gestures, jokes, propositions, email messages, or other communications all constitute harassment.

If you experience or witness any form of harassment in the workplace, please immediately notify the company by following the steps outlined in our Complaint Policy (see Section _____ of this Handbook). We encourage you to come forward with complaints—the sooner we learn about the problem, the sooner we can take steps to resolve it. The Company will not retaliate, or allow retaliation, against anyone who complains of harassment, assists in a harassment investigation, or files an administrative charge or lawsuit alleging harassment. All managers are required to immediately report any incidents of harassment, as set forth in our Complaint Policy.

Complaints will be investigated quickly. Those who are found to have violated this policy will be subject to appropriate disciplinary action, up to and including termination.

How to Complete This Policy

Because harassment is legally considered to be a type of discrimination, a company's obligation to prevent and remedy harassment tracks its obligation not to discriminate—for example, if the law protects employees from discrimination on the basis of race, they are also protected from racial harassment. In the blank space, fill in the same prohibited bases for harassment that you included in your antidiscrimination policy.

For more information on federal antidiscrimination laws, see *Federal Employment Laws: A Desk Reference,* by Amy DelPo and Lisa Guerin (Nolo). This helpful resource devotes an entire chapter to each of the major federal employment laws, including the antidiscrimination laws listed above. You can also find helpful factsheets, posters, compliance assistance, and more on the website of the Equal Employment Opportunity Commission—the federal agency that interprets and enforces federal antidiscrimination laws—at www.eeoc.gov.

State Laws Prohibiting Discrimination in Employment

Private employers may not make employment decisions based on

State	Law applies to employers with	Age (protected ages, if specified)	Ancestry or national origin	Disability	AIDS/HIV	Gender	Marital status	Pregnancy, childbirth, and related medical conditions	Race or color	Religion or creed	Sexual orientation	Genetic testing information	Additional protected categories
Alabama Ala. Code §§ 21-7-1, 25-1-20	20 or more employees	✓ (40 and older)											
Alaska Alaska Stat. §§ 18.80.220, 47.30.865	One or more employees	✓ (40 and older)	✓	Physical and mental	✓	✓	✓ (Includes changes in status)	✓ Parent-hood	✓	✓			• Mental illness
Arizona Ariz. Rev. Stat. § 41-1461	15 or more employees	✓ (40 and older)	✓	Physical	✓	✓			✓	✓		✓	
Arkansas Ark. Code Ann. §§ 16-12-101, 11-4-601, 11-5-403	9 or more employees		✓	Physical and mental		✓		✓	✓	✓		✓[1]	
California Cal. Gov't. Code §§ 12920, 12941; Cal. Lab. Code § 1101	5 or more employees	✓ (40 and older)	✓	Physical and mental	✓	✓	✓	✓	✓	✓	✓	✓	• Gender identity • Medical condition • Political activities or affiliations
Colorado Colo. Rev. Stat. §§ 24-34-301, 24-34-401, 27-10-115	One or more employees	✓ (40 to 70)	✓	Physical, mental, and learning	✓	✓		✓	✓	✓			• Lawful conduct outside of work • Mental illness
Connecticut Conn. Gen. Stat. Ann. §§ 46a-51, 46a-60	3 or more employees	✓ (40 and older)	✓	Present or past physical, mental, or learning	✓	✓	✓	✓	✓	✓	✓	✓	• Mental retardation
Delaware Del. Code Ann. tit. 19, § 710	4 or more employees	✓ (40 to 70)	✓	Physical or mental	✓	✓	✓	✓	✓	✓		✓	
District of Columbia D.C. Code Ann. §§ 2-1401.01, 7-1703.03	One or more employees	✓ (18 and older)	✓	Physical or mental	✓	✓	✓	✓ Parent-hood	✓	✓	✓		• Enrollment in vocational, professional, or college education • Family duties • Perceived race • Personal appearance • Political affiliation • Smoker
Florida Fla. Stat. Ann. §§ 760.01, 760.50, 448.075	15 or more employees	✓	✓	"Handicap"	✓	✓	✓		✓	✓			• Family status • Sickle cell trait • Breastfeeding at work

[1] Employees covered by FLSA

State Laws Prohibiting Discrimination in Employment (continued)

Private employers may not make employment decisions based on

State	Law applies to employers with	Age (protected ages, if specified)	Ancestry or national origin	Disability	AIDS/HIV	Gender	Marital status	Pregnancy, childbirth, and related medical conditions	Race or color	Religion or creed	Sexual orientation	Genetic testing information	Additional protected categories
Georgia Ga. Code Ann. §§ 34-6A-1, 34-1-23, 34-5-1	15 or more employees (disability) 10 or more employees (gender)	✓ (40 to 70)		Physical or mental		✓²							
Hawaii Haw. Rev. Stat. § 378-1	One or more employees	✓	✓	Physical or mental	✓	✓	✓	✓ Breastfeeding	✓	✓	✓	✓	• Arrest and court record (unless there is a conviction directly related to job)
Idaho Idaho Code § 67-5909	5 or more employees	✓ (40 and older)	✓	Physical or mental		✓		✓	✓	✓			
Illinois 775 Ill. Comp. Stat. §§ 5/1-101, 5/2-101; Ill. Admin. Code tit. 56, § 5210.110	15 or more employees	✓ (40 and older)	✓	Physical or mental	✓	✓	✓	✓	✓	✓			• Arrest record • Expunged juvenile record • Citizen status • Military status • Unfavorable military discharge • Victim of domestic violence or sexual assault
Indiana Ind. Code Ann. §§ 22-9-1-1, 22-9-2-1	6 or more employees	✓ (40 to 70)	✓	Physical or mental (15 or more employees)		✓			✓	✓			
Iowa Iowa Code § 216.1	4 or more employees	✓ (18 or older)	✓	Physical or mental	✓	✓		✓	✓	✓		✓	
Kansas Kan. Stat. Ann. §§ 44-1001, 44-1111, 44-1125, 65-6002(e)	4 or more employees	✓ (18 or older)	✓	Physical or mental	✓	✓			✓	✓		✓	• Military status
Kentucky Ky. Rev. Stat. Ann. §§ 344.040, 207.130, 342.197	8 or more employees	✓ (40 or older)	✓	Physical	✓	✓			✓	✓			• Smoker or nonsmoker
Louisiana La. Rev. Stat. Ann. §§ 23:301 to 23:352	20 or more employees	✓ (40 or older)	✓	Physical or mental		✓		✓ (Applies to employers with 25 or more employees)	✓	✓		✓	• Sickle cell trait
Maine Me. Rev. Stat. Ann. tit. 5, §§ 4551, 4571	One or more employees	✓	✓	Physical or mental		✓		✓	✓	✓	✓	✓	• Past workers' compensation claim • Past whistleblowing

² Wage discrimination only

DISCRIMINATION AND HARASSMENT **19/11**

State Laws Prohibiting Discrimination in Employment (continued)

Private employers may not make employment decisions based on

State	Law applies to employers with	Age (protected ages, if specified)	Ancestry or national origin	Disability	AIDS/HIV	Gender	Marital status	Pregnancy, childbirth, and related medical conditions	Race or color	Religion or creed	Sexual orientation	Genetic testing information	Additional protected categories
Maryland Md. Code 1957 Art. 49B, § 15	15 or more employees	✓	✓	Physical or mental		✓	✓	✓	✓	✓	✓	✓	
Massachusetts Mass. Gen. Laws ch. 151B, § 1	6 or more employees	✓ (40 or older)	✓	Physical or mental	✓	✓	✓		✓	✓	✓	✓	• Military service • Arrests
Michigan Mich. Comp. Laws §§ 37.1201, 37.2201, 37.1103	One or more employees	✓	✓	Physical or mental	✓	✓	✓	✓	✓	✓		✓	• Height or weight • Arrest record
Minnesota Minn. Stat. Ann. §§ 363A.03, 363A.08, 181.974	One or more employees	✓ (18 or older)	✓	Physical or mental	✓	✓	✓	✓	✓	✓	✓	✓	• Gender identity • Member of local commission • Perceived sexual orientation • Receiving public assistance
Mississippi Miss. Code Ann. §§ 33-1-15													• Military status (all employers) • No other protected categories unless employer receives public funding
Missouri Mo. Rev. Stat. §§ 213.010, 191.665, 375.1306	6 or more employees	✓ (40 to 70)	✓	Physical or mental	✓	✓		✓	✓	✓		✓	
Montana Mont. Code Ann. §§ 49-2-101, 49-2-303	One or more employees	✓	✓	Physical or mental		✓	✓	✓	✓	✓			
Nebraska Neb. Rev. Stat. §§ 48-1101, 48-1001, 20-168	15 or more employees	✓ (40 to 70) (Applies to employers with 25 or more employees)	✓	Physical or mental	✓	✓	✓	✓	✓	✓		✓	
Nevada Nev. Rev. Stat. Ann. §§ 613.310 and following	15 or more employees	✓ (40 or older)	✓	Physical or mental		✓		✓	✓	✓	✓	✓	• Lawful use of any product when not at work • Use of service animal
New Hampshire N.H. Rev. Stat. Ann. §§ 354-A2 and following, 141-H:3	6 or more employees	✓	✓	Physical or mental		✓	✓	✓	✓	✓	✓	✓	
New Jersey N.J. Stat. Ann. §§ 10:5-1 to 10:5-12; 34:6B-1	One or more employees	✓ (18 to 70)	✓	Past or present physical or mental	✓	✓	✓ (Includes domestic partner)	✓	✓	✓	✓	✓	• Hereditary cellular or blood trait • Military service or status • Smoker or nonsmoker

State Laws Prohibiting Discrimination in Employment (continued)

Private employers may not make employment decisions based on

State	Law applies to employers with	Age (protected ages, if specified)	Ancestry or national origin	Disability	AIDS/HIV	Gender	Marital status	Pregnancy, childbirth, and related medical conditions	Race or color	Religion or creed	Sexual orientation	Genetic testing information	Additional protected categories
New Mexico N.M. Stat. Ann. § 28-1-7	4 or more employees	✓ (40 or older) (applies to employers with 20 or more employees)	✓	Physical or mental		✓	✓ (Applies to employers with 50 or more employees)	✓	✓	✓	✓[3]		• Gender identity (employers with 15 or more employees) • Serious medical condition
New York N.Y. Exec. Law § 296; N.Y. Lab. Law § 201-d	4 or more employees	✓ (18 and over)	✓	Physical or mental	✓	✓	✓	✓	✓	✓	✓	✓	• Lawful use of any product when not at work • Military status • Observance of Sabbath • Political activities
North Carolina N.C. Gen. Stat. §§ 143-422.2, 168A-1, 95-28.1, 130A-148	15 or more employees	✓	✓	Physical or mental	✓	✓			✓	✓		✓	• Lawful use of any product when not at work • Military service • Sickle cell trait
North Dakota N.D. Cent. Code §§ 14-02.4-01, 34-01-17	One or more employees	✓ (40 or older)	✓	Physical or mental		✓	✓	✓	✓	✓			• Lawful conduct outside of work • Receiving public assistance
Ohio Ohio Rev. Code Ann. §§ 4111.17, 4112.01	4 or more employees	✓ (40 or older)	✓	Physical, mental, or learning		✓		✓	✓	✓			
Oklahoma Okla. Stat. Ann. tit. 25, § 1301; tit. 36, § 3614.2; tit. 40, § 500; tit. 44, § 208	15 or more employees	✓ (40 or older)	✓	Physical or mental		✓			✓	✓		✓	• Military service • Smoker or nonsmoker
Oregon Or. Rev. Stat. §§ 659A.100 and following, 659A.303	One or more employees	✓ (18 or older)	✓	Physical or mental (Applies to employers with 6 or more employees)	✓	✓	✓	✓	✓	✓		✓	
Pennsylvania 43 Pa. Cons. Stat. Ann. § 953	4 or more employees	✓ (40 to 70)	✓	Physical or mental		✓		✓	✓	✓			• Familial status • GED rather than high school diploma
Rhode Island R.I. Gen. Laws §§ 28-6-17, 28-5-11, 2-28-10, 23-6-22, 23-20.7.1-1	4 or more employees	✓ (40 or older)	✓	Physical or mental	✓	✓		✓	✓	✓	✓	✓	• Domestic abuse victim • Gender identity or expression
South Carolina S.C. Code Ann. §§ 1-13-20 and following	15 or more employees	✓ (40 or older)	✓	Physical or mental		✓		✓	✓	✓			

[3] Employers with 15 or more employees

State Laws Prohibiting Discrimination in Employment (continued)

State	Law applies to employers with	Age (protected ages, if specified)	Ancestry or national origin	Disability	AIDS/HIV	Gender	Marital status	Pregnancy, childbirth, and related medical conditions	Race or color	Religion or creed	Sexual orientation	Genetic testing information	Additional protected categories
South Dakota S.D. Codified Laws Ann. §§ 20-13-10, 60-12-15, 60-2-20, 62-1-17	One or more employees		✓	Physical, mental, and learning		✓			✓	✓		✓	• Preexisting injury
Tennessee Tenn. Code Ann. §§ 4-21-102, 4-21-401 and following, 8-50-103, 50-2-202	8 or more employees	✓ (40 or older)	✓	Physical or mental		✓			✓	✓			• Refer to chart on Family and Medical Leave
Texas Tex. Lab. Code Ann. §§ 21.002, 21.101, 21.401	15 or more employees	✓ (40 or older)	✓	Physical or mental		✓		✓	✓	✓		✓	
Utah Utah Code Ann. § 34A-5-106	15 or more employees	✓ (40 or older)	✓	Follows federal law	✓	✓		✓	✓	✓			
Vermont Vt. Stat. Ann. tit. 21, § 495; tit. 18, § 9333	One or more employees	✓ (18 or older)	✓	Physical, mental, or learning	✓	✓			✓	✓	✓	✓	• Place of birth
Virginia Va. Code Ann. §§ 2.2-3900, 40.1-28.6, 51.5-3	Law applies to all employers	✓	✓	Physical or mental		✓	✓	✓	✓	✓		✓	
Washington Wash. Rev. Code Ann. §§ 49.60.040, 49.60.172 and following, 49.12.175, 49.44.090; Wash. Admin. Code 162-30-020	8 or more employees	✓ (40 or older)	✓	Physical, mental, or sensory; use of a service animal	✓	✓	✓		✓	✓		✓	• Hepatitis C infection • Member of state militia
West Virginia W.Va. Code §§ 5-11-3, 5-11-9, 21-5B-1	12 or more employees	✓ (40 or older)	✓	Physical or mental	✓	✓⁴			✓	✓			• Smoking away from work
Wisconsin Wis. Stat. Ann. §§ 111.32 and following	One or more employees	✓ (40 or older)	✓	Physical or mental	✓	✓	✓		✓	✓	✓	✓	• Arrest or conviction • Lawful use of any product when not at work • Military service or status
Wyoming Wyo. Stat. §§ 27-9-105, 19-11-104	2 or more employees	✓ (40 or older)	✓			✓			✓	✓			• Military service or status • Smoking off duty

⁴ Equal pay laws apply to employers with one or more employees

Current as of February 2005

20

Complaint Policies

The purpose of a complaint policy is simple: to encourage employees to come forward with concerns and problems. If employees let managers know when trouble is brewing, the company will have an opportunity to resolve workplace difficulties right away, before morale suffers or workers start siding with or against each other. And a complaint policy helps managers and supervisors, by letting them know what their responsibilities are if they observe misconduct or receive a complaint.

As mentioned in Chapter 19 (on antidiscrimination and harassment policies), a complaint policy also offers companies an important legal bonus: some protection against harassment lawsuits brought by current or former employees. If your company has a clear complaint policy, and an employee who did not complain according to this policy later sues the company for harassment, the company can use the employee's failure to make a complaint as a legal defense in the harassment lawsuit—possibly resulting in a court deciding that the employee cannot proceed with the lawsuit. The idea behind this is that an employee who fails to complain when a company has a clear complaint policy deprives the company of the chance to fix the problem.

However, these legal protections kick in only if your policy is user-friendly and genuinely encourages employees to make problems known and make a complaint. In this chapter, we'll show you how to put together policies that do just that.

20:1 Complaint Procedures

CD File: 20_Complaints.rtf

Include This Policy?
☐ Yes
☐ No
☐ Use our existing policy
☐ Other _____

Alternate Modifications
None

Additional Clauses
None

Related Policies
Chapter 19 includes policies against discrimination and harassment (often the subject of complaints).

Notes
_____
_____
_____
_____
_____
_____
_____
_____
_____
_____
_____
_____
_____
_____
_____
_____

20:1 Complaint Procedures

Your complaint policy should describe the conduct about which employees can complain, explain how to make a complaint, and let workers know what will happen once a complaint is filed.

Complaint Procedures

[*Company Name*] is committed to providing a safe and productive work environment, free of threats to the health, safety, and well-being of our workers. These threats include, but are not limited to, harassment, discrimination, violations of health and safety rules, and violence.

Any employee who witnesses or is subject to inappropriate conduct in the workplace may complain to _____

or to any Company officer. Any supervisor, manager, or Company officer who receives a complaint about, hears of, or witnesses any inappropriate conduct is required to immediately notify

_____.

Inappropriate conduct includes any conduct prohibited by our policies about harassment, discrimination, discipline, workplace violence, health and safety, and drug and alcohol use. In addition, we encourage employees to come forward with any workplace complaint, even if the subject of the complaint is not explicitly covered by our written policies.

We encourage you to come forward with complaints immediately, so we can take whatever action is needed to handle the problem. Once a complaint has been made, _____

will determine how to handle it. For serious complaints alleging harassment, discrimination, and other illegal conduct, we will immediately conduct a complete and impartial investigation. All complaints will be handled as confidentially as possible. When the investigation is complete, the Company will take corrective action, if appropriate.

We will not engage in or allow retaliation against any employee who makes a good faith complaint or participates in an investigation. If you believe that you are being subjected to any kind of negative treatment because you made or were questioned about a complaint, report the conduct immediately to _____.

Who Needs This Policy

There are really no drawbacks to having a complaint policy—and plenty of good reasons to adopt one. From a legal standpoint, a complaint policy provides a possible legal defense against claims of harassment, as explained above. There are also many practical advantages of encouraging employees to make workplace problems known: The policy will give the company an opportunity to correct problems before they get out of hand, will promote communication and teamwork, and will let employees know that management cares about their concerns. Because of these benefits, we recommend that every employer adopt a complaint policy.

How to Complete This Policy

Our sample policy leaves you a space to designate the person or department that will be available to receive complaints. If your company has a human resource function, you can simply fill in all these blanks with "the human resources department."

If, like many smaller companies, your company doesn't have a dedicated human resources department, you will need to modify this policy to let employees know where to direct their complaints—and who will deal with them. If you ask workers to complain to their direct supervisor or manager, make sure that employees can also complain to someone outside their chain of command, such as another supervisor or officer or even the head of the company. If an employee is being harassed or mistreated by his or her own supervisor, this allows the worker to bypass that person and complain to someone who isn't part of the problem. Even if the employee's direct supervisor is not the source of the complaint, some employees feel more comfortable talking to someone who won't be responsible for evaluating their performance and making decisions on promotions, raises, and assignments.

Because complaints—particularly complaints of harassment, discrimination, violence, or safety concerns—are a serious matter, many companies prefer to designate someone at the top of the company ladder, such as the president or CEO.

Make sure that the people whom you designate to take complaints are accessible to employees. For example, if the human resources department is located in a distant office or the company president spends most work days traveling to promote the company, you should choose alternate people to accept complaints who are local and available.

20:2 Our Doors Are Open to You

CD File: 20_Complaints.rtf

Include This Policy?
☐ Yes
☐ No
☐ Use our existing policy
☐ Other _____

Alternate Modifications
None

Additional Clauses
None

Related Policies
None

Notes
_____
_____
_____
_____
_____
_____
_____
_____
_____
_____
_____
_____
_____
_____
_____
_____
_____
_____

20:2 Open-Door Promise

Many employers choose to adopt an open-door policy in addition to a more formal complaint policy. While your complaint policy will encourage employees to come forward with big problems, such as serious misconduct and violations of company rules, an open-door policy serves a slightly different purpose. It encourages employees to keep in touch with their supervisors about day-to-day work issues. An employee who has, for example, a personality conflict with a client, a creative idea to boost profits, or a concern that his or her work group isn't coming together as a team, probably wouldn't think of filing a formal complaint. But an open-door policy will encourage employees to bring these issues to the attention of management, thereby giving the company a chance to make improvements—for example, by changing work assignments, adopting that good idea, or offering training to the team.

Our Doors Are Open to You

We want to maintain a positive and pleasant environment for all of our employees. To help us meet this goal, _____

[*Company name*] has an open-door policy, by which employees are encouraged to report work-related concerns.

If something about your job is bothering you, or if you have a question, concern, idea, or problem related to your work, please discuss it with your immediate supervisor as soon as possible. If for any reason you don't feel comfortable bringing the matter to your supervisor, feel free to raise the issue with any company officer.

We encourage you to come forward and make your concerns known to the Company. We can't solve the problem if we don't know about it.

Who Needs This Policy

An open-door policy doesn't offer the legal benefit of a complaint policy, but its practical advantages are similar: It helps managers learn what's going on in the workplace, encourages communication, and promotes good will.

The potential disadvantage of an open-door policy is wasted time. If workers feel compelled to keep management apprised of their every thought and feeling, managers might soon be tempted to close their doors—and lock them. However, this problem can usually be handled effectively through individual counseling—telling the one or two employees who might abuse the policy that their enthusiasm is appreciated, but they need to use more discretion in deciding which matters are important enough to bring to a manager's attention.

In our opinion, the benefits of having an open-door policy outweigh this potential downside. However, this is a decision each company will have to make for itself, based on the character of its workforce and the amount of time managers can afford to spend listening to whoever comes through their open doors.

For more information on investigating complaints and problems, see *Workplace Investigations*, by Lisa Guerin (Nolo), a step-by-step guide to investigating common workplace situations.

CHAPTER

21

Ending Employment

Ending the employment relationship can be difficult for employer and employee alike. An employer's goal is to keep operations running smoothly as employees come and go—and to make sure that any employees who have to be fired or laid off don't decide to respond with a lawsuit.

If your company has adopted an at-will policy, discussed in Chapter 2, it has already gone a long way toward accomplishing this second goal. The company has warned workers that their employment can be terminated at any time and for any reason. And, for those workers who didn't hear it the first time, other policies throughout the handbook we're helping you create will give them fair warning that they can expect to be disciplined or fired for taking part in certain types of prohibited conduct.

Policies about ending employment serve a slightly different purpose: to tell employees how the company will handle the practical concerns that may arise when an employee leaves, such as their severance packages, references, and insurance coverage. Explaining these matters up front will help smooth the transition when employees leave: They'll know exactly what to expect and be able to plan accordingly. End-of-employment policies can also help you make sure that the company has met its legal obligations—to offer health insurance continuation and cut final paychecks on time, for example. By adopting uniform policies and applying them even-handedly when employees leave, employers can also avoid claims of unfairness—and the lawsuits that these feelings sometimes fuel.

21:1   Final Paychecks

CD File: 21_Ending Employment.rtf

Include This Policy?
☐ Yes
☐ No
☐ Use our existing policy
☐ Other _____

Alternate Modifications
None

Additional Clauses
Specify Compensation Included in Final Paycheck

Insert?:   ☐ Yes   ☐ No

Related Policies
Chapter 7 provides information and policies on pay.

Notes

_____
_____
_____
_____
_____
_____
_____
_____
_____
_____
_____
_____
_____
_____
_____
_____
_____

21:1   Final Paychecks

Although no federal law requires employers to pay terminated employees by a particular date, the laws of most states impose fairly tight deadlines for final paychecks. Often, these deadlines vary depending on whether the employee quits or is fired. In some states (including California, Colorado, and Nevada), employers must pay a fired employee immediately. Other states allow employers to wait until the next payday.

Adopting a final paycheck policy that includes these deadlines will help ensure that your company complies with these laws. And employees will know when they can expect that check—a matter of pressing importance to those who don't have another job lined up right away.

Final Paychecks

Employees who quit will receive their final paycheck _____ _____ . Employees who are terminated involuntarily will receive their final paycheck _____ .

Final paychecks will include all compensation earned but not paid through the date of termination.

How to Complete This Policy

This policy includes two blanks for you to complete based on your state's law. The chart at the end of this chapter, "State Laws That Control Final Paychecks," lists employer requirements for final paychecks by state. In the first blank, insert the time limit for paying an employee who is fired (for example, within two weeks after termination). In the second blank, insert the time limit for paying an employee who quits.

Additional Clause to Specify Compensation Included in Final Paycheck

As you'll see from the chart at the end of this chapter, some states require employers to include unused vacation pay in an employee's final check. However, these laws apply only to vacation pay that has already been earned or accrued. For example, if employees accrue one day of vacation leave per month, and the company fires someone who has worked for a year without taking any vacation, that employee would be entitled to 12 additional days of pay in his or her final paycheck. But an employee who is fired after only two months gets only two days of vacation pay, assuming those days haven't been used.

In addition to vacation pay, some employers choose to pay out unused sick leave or personal leave, some portion of a discretionary bonus, or other forms of compensation. No law requires this. Employers who follow this route generally do so to maintain a good relationship with the departing employee and the workers who remain, and to create incentives for solid performance. By paying out unused sick time, for example, employers encourage their employees not to take sick leave unless it's absolutely necessary. And paying out a portion of a discretionary bonus encourages employees to do their best right up until their last day of work.

If your state requires employers to pay out unused vacation time, or if your company wants to pay this or other types of compensation even though it's not legally required, add the sentence below to the end of our sample policy. In the blank space, insert the type of additional compensation employees will receive (for example, all unused vacation time that the employee has earned as of the date of termination, or a pro rata share of any discretionary bonus for which the employee is eligible, based on the length of the employee's employment during the bonus period and the employee's performance).

Additional Clause

Final paychecks will also include _____ .

Seek Legal Advice for Layoffs and Layoff Policies

In a layoff, an employer generally terminates the employment of a group of employees for reasons related to business productivity—for example, because of economic problems or shifts in the company's direction. When an employer lays workers off, it is legally required to provide them with a certain amount of notice and, in a few states, severance pay. If you wish to adopt a layoff policy, you'll have to consider a number of factors, such as how employees will be chosen for layoff, what benefits (if any) laid-off workers will receive, whether laid-off workers are eligible for rehire if circumstances turn around, and how employees will be informed of the layoff. Because these issues can get fairly complicated, we advise you to consult with a lawyer if you plan to adopt a layoff policy.

21:2   Severance Pay

CD File: 21_Ending Employment.rtf

Include This Policy?
☐ Yes
    Choose one: ☐ A   ☐ B   ☐ C
☐ No
☐ Use our existing policy
☐ Other _____

Alternate Modifications
None

Additional Clauses
None

Related Policies
None

Notes

_____
_____
_____
_____
_____
_____
_____
_____
_____
_____
_____
_____
_____
_____
_____
_____
_____
_____
_____
_____

21:2 Severance Pay

Except for the few states that require severance pay when laying workers off, no law says that employers must give their employers severance pay. Unless the company promises severance pay or leads employees to believe they will receive it—for example, by saying so in a written contract or policy—there is no obligation to pay severance to terminated employees.

For many employers, that's all they need to know: If it isn't required, they aren't going to pay it. But before your company decides to join their ranks, consider the benefits of paying severance. For starters, it helps a fired worker get by until another job comes along—which means paying severance sends the message that the company cares about its workers and wants to help out. This can go a long way not only toward building employee morale, but also toward nipping potential lawsuits in the bud. Studies have shown that the way in which employment terminations are handled plays a big role in determining whether a fired employee will sue the employer. Thus, a company will have to weigh these very tangible benefits against the eminently sensible desire not to pay out money unnecessarily.

Your severance policy should let employees know whether and under what circumstances the company offers severance pay. If your company will offer severance, the policy should tell employees who is eligible and how severance pay will be calculated.

We offer you several alternative sample policies below. Policy A is a simple no-severance policy. Policy B provides that a company will pay severance at its own discretion. Policy C is a severance policy with eligibility requirements and a formula for determining severance pay.

⚠ Severance plans can be tricky. If your company plans to adopt a policy to pay severance, whether according to a formula or other criteria, ask a lawyer to review it for you—and to let you know whether your company has to follow the requirements of the federal law known as "ERISA" (the Employees Retirement Income Savings Act, 29 U.S.C. §§ 1001 and following). This highly technical law imposes a number of requirements on employers who provide certain types of benefit plans to their employees. Severance plans may or may not be subject to these requirements, depending on the plan's features and the way courts in your state have interpreted the law.

Alternate Policy A

No Severance Pay

Our Company does not pay severance to terminated employees, whether they quit, are laid off, or are fired for any reason.

Alternate Policy B

Severance Pay Is Discretionary

Generally, _____

[*Company name*] does not pay severance to terminated employees, whether they quit, are laid off, or are fired for any reason. However, we reserve the right to pay severance to a terminated employee. Decisions about severance pay will be made on a case-by-case basis and are entirely within the discretion of the Company. No employee has a right to severance pay, and you should not expect to receive it.

Alternate Policy C

Severance Pay

Employees may be eligible for severance pay upon the termination of their employment. Employees must meet <u>all</u> of the following criteria to be eligible:

- you must have worked for the Company for at least one year prior to your termination
- you must not have quit or resigned, and
- your employment must have been terminated for reasons other than misconduct or violation of company rules.

Eligible employees will receive _____ of severance pay for every full year of employment with _____ _____ [*Company name*].

How to Complete This Policy

If you adopt Sample Policy C, simply fill in the blank with the amount of severance the company plans to offer. Most employers offer one or two weeks of pay, at the employee's current rate, for every year of work. You can do the same by inserting "one week" or "two weeks" in the blank.

21:3 Continuing Your Health
Insurance Coverage

CD File: 21_Ending Employment.rtf

Include This Policy?
☐ Yes
☐ No
☐ Use our existing policy
☐ Other _____

Alternate Modifications
None

Additional Clauses
Include Eligibility Requirements
Insert?: ☐ Yes ☐ No

Related Policies
None

Notes

_____
_____
_____
_____
_____
_____
_____
_____
_____
_____
_____
_____
_____
_____
_____
_____
_____
_____
_____
_____

21:3 Continuing Your Health Insurance Coverage

If your company offers employees health insurance coverage under a group health plan, it may be required to offer them continued coverage under the circumstances outlined in the sample policy below. A federal law known as "COBRA" (the Consolidated Omnibus Budget Reconciliation Act) mandates that employees who quit, suffer a reduction in hours, or are fired for reasons other than serious misconduct are entitled to choose to continue on the employer's group health care plan for up to 18 months. However, the employee (not the employer) must pay the full health care insurance premiums. COBRA applies only to employers with 20 or more employees.

Many states also have their own health insurance continuation laws. These laws generally apply to smaller employers. Some echo most of COBRA's provisions; others provide for shorter periods of insurance continuation and/or place limits on the types of benefits that must be provided. A chart of these state laws, entitled "State Health Insurance Continuation Laws," is included at the end of this chapter.

Your insurance continuation policy should tell employees:
- whether, and under what circumstances, they will be able to continue their insurance coverage after termination
- how long the continued coverage will last, and
- who will pay for the coverage.

Continuing Your Health Insurance Coverage

[*Company name*] offers employees group health insurance coverage as a benefit of employment. If you are no longer eligible for insurance coverage because of a reduction in hours, because you quit, or because you are terminated for reasons other than serious misconduct, you have the right to continue your health insurance coverage for up to _____ . You will have to pay the cost of this coverage.

Others covered by your insurance (your spouse and children, for example) also have the right to continue coverage if they are no longer eligible for certain reasons. If you and your spouse divorce or legally separate, or if you die while in our employ, your spouse may continue coverage under our group health plan. And once your children lose their dependent status, they may continue their health care as well. In any of these situations, your family members are entitled to up to _____ of continued health care. They must pay the cost of this coverage.

You will receive an initial notice of your right to continued health insurance coverage when you first become eligible for health insurance under the Company's group plan. You will receive an additional notice when your hours are reduced, you quit, or you are terminated. This second notice will tell you how to choose continuation coverage, what your obligations will be, and how much the insurance will cost. You must notify us if any of your family members becomes eligible for continued coverage due to divorce, separation, or reaching the age of majority.

How to Complete This Policy

In the blanks in this policy, insert the length of time for which employees and their dependents can continue their health insurance coverage. If your company is covered by COBRA, employees are entitled to continue their coverage for 18 months (insert this in the first blank), and dependents for 36 months (insert this in the second blank).

Smaller employers that are not covered by COBRA may nevertheless have to comply with a state insurance continuation law. Some of these laws also provide for 18 and 36 months of coverage; others provide for shorter periods of coverage. Consult "State Health Insurance Continuation Laws", at the end of this chapter to find out what your state requires.

Who Needs This Policy

If your company is covered by COBRA or a state health insurance continuation law, including this policy can alleviate a lot of anxiety for workers. One of the first questions a newly terminated employee is likely to ask is, "What about my health insurance?" As the costs of medical care skyrocket, many employees cannot afford to go without health insurance until they find another job—and even if they line up new work quickly, their new employer might not offer insurance coverage or there may be a waiting period before coverage begins. By adopting a health insurance continuation policy, your company can let employees know, right up front, that they won't have to worry about insurance coverage, as long as they are able to pay for it.

If your company is not covered by COBRA or a similar state law or doesn't offer health insurance coverage to your employees (see Chapter 8 for information on benefits policies), leave this policy out of the handbook.

Additional Clause to Include Eligibility Requirements

Some states require employers to offer continued coverage only to certain employees. Most commonly, employees are eligible only if they have worked for the employer, and been covered by the employer's health insurance plan, for at least three months. If your company is not covered by COBRA (which protects all employees who are covered by the employer's plan) but is covered by a state health insurance continuation law that protects only certain employees, modify our policy by adding the following language after the first sentence. In the blank, insert your state's eligibility requirements (for example, "have been covered continuously under our insurance policy for at least three months" or "work at least 25 hours a week.")

Additional Clause

Only employees who _____

_____
are entitled to continue their health insurance coverage under this policy.

21:4 Exit Interviews

Exit interviews are a great way to learn valuable information about your company—and to diffuse the tension of an involuntary termination. Former employees can provide the lowdown on dozens of issues, from workplace morale and teamwork to how well (or poorly) managers and supervisors are doing their jobs. An employee on the way out the door is more likely to be candid in offering opinions—maybe brutally so. Although employers should certainly take these parting comments with a healthy dose of salt, they may get some helpful information about how the company is perceived by its workers and where it has room to improve.

The person who interviews employees who quit should try to find out why that employee is moving on: Did your company fail to offer opportunities to advance? Are the company's pay scales in line with those of other businesses in your industry? Are there problems in the company that management doesn't know about?

It can be equally valuable to interview employees you fire, although for a slightly different reason. These employees are probably somewhat upset about losing their jobs—and they may have a long list of negative comments about the company as a result. But they will have a chance to air these complaints during the interview, which allows the company to demonstrate that it cares about their concerns. If a fired employee feels that the company "gets it," that employee is less likely to seek a courtroom forum for his or her grievances. Adopting an exit interview policy tells these employees that there will be a time and a place when their voices can be heard.

Some employers hold exit interviews with every departing employee, while others schedule interviews only if the departing employee wants one. Adopting an optional interview policy has the benefit of drastically reducing the time spent conducting these interviews—very few employees, other than those with a large ax to grind, will bother to take the time to share their opinions on the way out the door. The corresponding drawback is that a company that holds voluntary interviews won't be able to gather as much valuable information, because the interviewer will probably be hearing only from those whose employment experience was negative.

We offer two alternate policies below: Policy A requires an exit interview for all departing employees, while Policy B makes exit interviews optional. If you adopt Policy B, you'll have to make other arrangements to collect company property from employees who opt out of the interview.

21:4 Exit Interviews

CD File: 21_Ending Employment.rtf

Include This Policy?
☐ Yes
　　Choose one:　☐ A　☐ B
☐ No
☐ Use our existing policy
☐ Other _____

Alternate Modifications
None

Additional Clauses
None

Related Policies
None

Notes

_____

_____

_____

_____

_____

_____

_____

_____

_____

_____

_____

_____

_____

_____

_____

_____

_____

Alternate Policy A

Exit Interviews

We will hold an exit interview with every employee who leaves the Company, for any reason. During the interview, you will have the opportunity to tell us about your employment experience here—what you liked, what you didn't like, and where you think we can improve. We greatly value these comments.

The exit interview also gives us a chance to handle some practical matters relating to the end of your employment. You will be expected to return all Company property at the interview. You will also have an opportunity to ask any questions you might have about insurance, benefits, final paychecks, references, or any other matter relating to your employment.

Alternate Policy B

Exit Interviews

We will hold an exit interview with every departing employee who requests one. We strongly encourage employees to schedule exit interviews. During the interview, you will have the opportunity to tell us about your employment experience here—what you liked, what you didn't like, and where you think we can improve. We greatly value these comments.

The exit interview also gives us a chance to handle some practical matters relating to the end of your employment. You will be expected to return all Company property at the interview. You will also have an opportunity to ask any questions you might have about insurance, benefits, final paychecks, references, or any other matter relating to your employment.

21:5 References

Reference requests are fraught with legal and practical dangers for employers. If an employer criticizes a former employee unduly, or unfairly prevents that employee from getting a job, it could face a lawsuit for defamation or blacklisting. If an employer gives a reference that is too positive for an employee it knows to be dangerous or grossly unqualified, it risks legal trouble from the new employer if the truth comes out.

Given these risks, many employers choose to take a "name, rank, and serial number" approach, giving prospective new employers only the dates of employment, title, and salary of a former employee. If your company decides to go this route, our sample Policy A, below—a minimal reference policy to confirm dates of employment, salary, and positions held—will work for you.

But before deciding to adopt this type of policy, consider the purpose of a reference. Former employees count on them to find new work—and the sooner a fired employee finds new work, the less likely you are to face a wrongful termination claim. Prospective employers use references to figure out whom to hire and to read between the lines of carefully prepared resumes and interview responses. Both of these tasks are made a lot tougher by employers who adopt a minimal reference approach.

Employers can give an informative reference without undue risk of legal trouble if they insist on a written release from the employee, giving them permission to talk to a prospective employer. And your company can protect itself further by insisting on written reference requests and responding to them only in writing. This gives the company a clear record of exactly what was said if a company representative is later accused of making a false statement. This approach also gives the person providing the reference time to craft a careful response. If your company decides to go this route, you can use our sample Policy B, below.

Alternate Policy A

> ### References
>
> When we are contacted by prospective employers seeking information about former employees, we will release the following data only: the position(s) the employee held, the dates the employee worked for our Company, and the employee's salary or rate of pay.

21:5 References

CD File: 21_Ending Employment.rtf

Include This Policy?

☐ Yes

　　Choose one: ☐ A ☐ B

☐ No

☐ Use our existing policy

☐ Other _____

Alternate Modifications

None

Additional Clauses

None

Related Policies

None

Notes

_____
_____
_____
_____
_____
_____
_____
_____
_____
_____
_____
_____
_____
_____
_____
_____
_____

Alternate Policy B

References

When we are contacted by prospective employers seeking information about former employees, we will release the following data only: the position(s) the employee held, the dates the employee worked for our Company, and the employee's salary or rate of pay.

If you would like us to give a more detailed reference, you will have to provide us with a written release—a consent form giving us your permission to respond to a reference request. We will respond only to written reference requests, and we will respond only in writing. Please direct all reference requests to

_____ .

 For information on providing references, see *Dealing With Problem Employees*, by Amy DelPo and Lisa Guerin (Nolo).

State Laws That Control Final Paychecks

Note: The states of Alabama, Florida, Georgia, and Mississippi are not included in this chart because they do not have laws specifically controlling final paychecks. Contact your state department of labor for more information. (See Appendix A for contact list.)

State	Paycheck due when employee is fired	Paycheck due when employee quits	Unused vacation pay due	Special employment situations
Alaska *Alaska Stat. § 23.05.140(b)*	Within 3 working days	Next regular payday at least 3 days after employee gives notice	Yes	
Arizona *Ariz. Rev. Stat. § 23-353*	Next payday or within 3 working days, whichever is sooner	Next payday	Yes	
Arkansas *Ark. Code Ann. § 11-4-405(b)*	Within 7 days from discharge date	No provision	No provision	Railroad or railroad construction: day of discharge
California *Cal. Lab. Code §§ 201 to 202, 227.3*	Immediately	Immediately if employee has given 72 hours' notice; otherwise, within 72 hours	Yes	Motion picture business: if fired, within 24 hours (excluding weekends and holidays); if laid off, next payday. Oil drilling industry: within 24 hours (excluding weekends and holidays) of termination. Seasonal agricultural workers: within 72 hours of termination
Colorado *Colo. Rev. Stat. § 8-4-109*	Immediately (within 6 hours of start of next workday, if payroll unit is closed; 24 hours if unit is offsite) employer decides check delivery	Next payday	Yes	
Connecticut *Conn. Gen. Stat. Ann. § 31-71c*	Next business day after discharge	Next payday	Only if policy or collective bargaining agreement requires payment on termination.	
Delaware *Del. Code Ann. tit. 19, § 1103*	Next payday	Next payday	No provision	
District of Columbia *D.C. Code Ann. § 32-1303*	Next business day	Next payday or 7 days after quitting, whichever is sooner	Yes, unless there is express contrary policy	
Hawaii *Haw. Rev. Stat. § 388-3*	Immediately or next day, if timing or conditions prevent immediate payment	Next payday or immediately, if employee gives one pay period's notice	No provision	
Idaho *Idaho Code §§ 45-606, 45-617*	Next payday or within 10 days (excluding weekends and holidays), whichever is sooner; if employee makes written request for earlier payment, within 48 hours of receipt of request (excluding weekends and holidays)	Next payday or within 10 days (excluding weekends and holidays), whichever is sooner; if employee makes written request for earlier payment, within 48 hours of receipt of request (excluding weekends and holidays)	No provision	
Illinois *820 Ill. Comp. Stat. § 115/5*	At time of separation if possible, but no later than next payday	At time of separation if possible, but no later than next payday	Yes	

State Laws That Control Final Paychecks (continued)

State	Paycheck due when employee is fired	Paycheck due when employee quits	Unused vacation pay due	Special employment situations
Indiana *Ind. Code Ann.* *§§ 22-2-5-1, 22-2-9-2*	Next payday	Next payday; if employee has not left address, then 10 days after employee demands wages or when employee provides address where check may be mailed	Yes	
Iowa *Iowa Code §§ 91A.4,* *91A.2(7)(b)*	Next payday	Next payday	Only if required by employer's policies	If employee is owed commission, employer has 30 days to pay
Kansas *Kan. Stat. Ann.* *§ 44-315*	Next payday	Next payday	Only if required by employer's policies	
Kentucky *Ky. Rev. Stat. Ann.* *§§ 337.010(c),* *337.055*	Next payday or 14 days, whichever is later	Next payday or 14 days, whichever is later	Yes	
Louisiana *La. Rev. Stat. Ann.* *§ 23:631*	Next payday or within 15 days, whichever is earlier	Next payday or within 15 days, whichever is earlier	Yes	
Maine *Me. Rev. Stat. Ann.* *tit. 26, § 626*	Next payday or within 2 weeks of requesting final pay, whichever is sooner	Next payday or within 2 weeks of requesting final pay, whichever is sooner	Yes	
Maryland *Md. Code Ann.,* *[Lab. & Empl.]* *§ 3-505*	Next scheduled payday	Next scheduled payday.	Yes, unless employer has contrary policy	
Massachusetts *Mass. Gen. Laws ch.* *149, § 148*	Day of discharge	Next payday; if no scheduled payday, then following Saturday	Yes	
Michigan *Mich. Comp.* *Laws §§ 408.474* *to 408.475; Mich.* *Admin. Code R.* *408.9007*	Next payday	Next payday	Only if required by written policy or contract	Hand-harvesters of crops: within 1 working day of termination
Minnesota *Minn. Stat. Ann.* *§§ 181.13 to 181.14*	Immediately	Next payday; if payday is less than 5 days from last day of work, then following payday or 20 days from last day of work, whichever is earlier	Yes	Migrant agricultural workers who resign: within 5 days
Missouri *Mo. Rev. Stat.* *§ 290.110*	Day of discharge	No provision	No provision	
Montana *Mont. Code Ann.* *§ 39-3-205*	Immediately if fired for cause or laid off (unless there is a written policy extending time to earlier of next payday or 15 days)	Next payday or within 15 days, whichever comes first	No provision	
Nebraska *Neb. Rev. Stat.* *§§ 48-1229 to 48-1230*	Next payday or within 2 weeks, whichever is earlier	No provision	Yes	

State	Paycheck due when employee is fired	Paycheck due when employee quits	Unused vacation pay due	Special employment situations
State Laws That Control Final Paychecks (continued)				
Nevada *Nev. Rev. Stat. Ann. §§ 608.020 to 608.030*	Immediately	Next payday or 7 days, whichever is earlier	No provision	
New Hampshire *N.H. Rev. Stat. Ann. §§ 275:43(III), 275:44*	Within 72 hours; if laid off, next payday	Next payday, or within 72 hours if employee gives one pay period's notice	Yes	
New Jersey *N.J. Stat. Ann. § 34:11-4.3*	Next payday	Next payday	No provision	
New Mexico *N.M. Stat. Ann. §§ 50-4-4 to 50-4-5*	Within 5 days	Next payday	No provision	If paid by task or commission, 10 days after discharge
New York *N.Y. Lab. Law §§ 191(3), 198-c(2)*	Next payday	Next payday	Yes	
North Carolina *N.C. Gen. Stat. §§ 95-25.7, 95-25.12*	Next payday	Next payday	Yes, unless employer has a contrary policy	If paid by commission or bonus, on next payday after amount calculated
North Dakota *N.D. Cent. Code § 34-14-03; N.D. Admin. Code R. 46-02-07-02(12)*	Next payday or 15 days, whichever is earlier	Next payday	Yes	
Ohio *Ohio Rev. Code Ann. § 4113.15*	First of month for wages earned in first half of prior month; fifteenth of month for wages earned in second half of prior month		Yes	
Oklahoma *Okla. Stat. Ann. tit. 40, §§ 165.1(4), 165.3*	Next payday	Next payday	Yes	
Oregon *Or. Rev. Stat. §§ 652.140, 652.145*	End of first business day after termination	Immediately, with 48 hours notice (excluding weekends and holidays). Without notice, within 5 days (excluding weekends and holidays) or next payday, whichever comes first	Only if required by policy or contract	Seasonal farm workers: fired or quitting with 48 hours notice, immediately; quitting without notice, within 48 hours or next payday, whichever comes first
Pennsylvania *43 Pa. Cons. Stat. Ann. § 260.5*	Next payday	Next payday	Yes	
Rhode Island *R.I. Gen. Laws § 28-14-4*	Next payday	Next payday	Yes, if employee has worked for 1 full year	
South Carolina *S.C. Code Ann. §§ 41-10-10(2), 41-10-50*	Within 48 hours or next payday, but not more than 30 days	No provision	Only if required by policy or contract	
South Dakota *S.D. Codified Laws Ann. §§ 60-11-10 to 60-11-14*	Next payday (or until employee returns employer's property)	Next payday (or until employee returns employer's property)	No	

	State Laws That Control Final Paychecks (continued)			
State	**Paycheck due when employee is fired**	**Paycheck due when employee quits**	**Unused vacation pay due**	**Special employment situations**
Tennessee *Tenn. Code Ann. § 50-2-103*	Next payday or 21 days, whichever is later	Next payday or 21 days, whichever is later	Yes	Applies to employers with 5 or more employees
Texas *Tex. Lab. Code Ann. §§ 61.001, 61.014*	Within 6 days	Next payday	Only if required by policy or contract	
Utah *Utah Code Ann. §§ 34-28-2, 34-28-5*	Within 24 hours	Next payday	Only if required by policy or contract	
Vermont *Vt. Stat. Ann. tit. 21, § 342(c)*	Within 72 hours	Next regular payday or next Friday, if there is no regular payday	No provision	
Virginia *Va. Code Ann. § 40.1-29(A.1)*	Next payday	Next payday	No provision	
Washington *Wash. Rev. Code Ann. § 49.48.010*	End of pay period	End of pay period	No provision	
West Virginia *W.Va. Code §§ 21-5-1, 21-5-4*	Within 72 hours	Immediately if employee has given one pay period's notice; otherwise, next payday	Yes	
Wisconsin *Wis. Stat. Ann. §§ 109.01(3), 109.03*	Next payday or 1 month, whichever is earlier; if termination is due to merger, relocation, or liquidation of business, within 24 hours	Next payday	No provision	Does not apply to managers, executives, or sales agents working on commission basis
Wyoming *Wyo. Stat. Ann. §§ 27-4-104, 27-4-507(c)*	5 working days	5 working days	Yes	

Current as of February 2005

State Health Insurance Continuation Laws

Alabama

Ala. Code § 27-55-3(4)

Coverage: 18 months for subjects of domestic abuse who have lost coverage they had under abuser's insurance and who do not qualify for COBRA.

Arizona

Ariz. Rev. Stat. §§ 20-1377, 20-1408

Employers affected: All employers who offer group disability insurance.

Length of coverage for dependents: Insurer must either continue coverage for dependents or convert to individual policy upon death of covered employee or divorce or legal separation. Coverage must be the same unless the insured chooses a lesser plan.

Time employer has to notify employee of continuation rights: No provisions for employer. Insurance policy must include notice of conversion privilege. Clerk of court must provide notice to anyone filing for divorce that dependent spouse entitled to convert health insurance coverage.

Time employee has to apply: 31 days after termination of existing coverage.

Arkansas

Ark. Code Ann. §§ 23-86-114 to 23-86-116

Employers affected: All employers who offer group health insurance.

Eligible employees: Continuously insured for previous 3 months.

Length of coverage for employee: 120 days.

Length of coverage for dependents: 120 days.

Time employee has to apply: 10 days.

California

Cal. Health & Safety Code §§ 1373.6, 1373.621; Cal. Ins. Code §§ 10128.50 to 10128.59

Employers affected: Employers who offer group health insurance and have 2 to 19 employees.

Eligible employees: Continuously insured for previous 3 months.

Qualifying event: Termination of employment ; reduction in hours.

Length of coverage for employee: 36 months.

Length of coverage for dependents: 36 months.

Time employer has to notify employee of continuation rights: 15 days.

Time employee has to apply: 31 days after group plan ends; 30 days after COBRA or Cal-COBRA ends (63 days if converting to an individual plan).

Special situations: Employee who is at least 60 years old and has worked for employer for previous 5 years may continue benefits for self and spouse beyond COBRA or Cal-COBRA limits (also applies to COBRA employers). Employee who began receiving COBRA coverage on or after 1/1/03 and whose COBRA coverage is for less than 36 months may use Cal-COBRA to bring total coverage up to 36 months.

Colorado

Colo. Rev. Stat. § 10-16-108

Employers affected: All employers who offer group health insurance.

Eligible employees: Employees continuously insured for previous 6 months.

Length of coverage for employee: 18 months.

Length of coverage for dependents: 18 months.

Time employer has to notify employee of continuation rights: Within 10 days of termination.

Time employee has to apply: 31 days after termination; 60 days if employers fails to give notice.

Connecticut

Conn. Gen. Stat. Ann. §§ 38a-538, 38a-554, 31-51o

Employers affected: All employers who offer group health insurance.

Eligible employees: Continuously insured for previous 3 months.

Length of coverage for employee: 18 months, or until eligible for Social Security benefits.

Length of coverage for dependents: 18 months, or until eligible for Social Security benefits; 36 months in case of employee's death or divorce.

Time employer has to notify employee of continuation rights: 14 days.

Time employee has to apply: 60 days.

Special situations: When facility closes or relocates, employer must pay for insurance for employee and dependents for 120 days or until employee is eligible for other group coverage, whichever comes first. (Does not affect employee's right to conventional continuation coverage, which begins when 120-day period ends.)

State Health Insurance Continuation Laws (continued)

District of Columbia

D.C. Code Ann. §§ 32-731 to 32-732

Employers affected: Employers with fewer than 20 employees.

Eligible employees: All covered employees are eligible.

Length of coverage for employee: 3 months.

Length of coverage for dependents: 3 months.

Time employer has to notify employee of continuation rights: Within 15 days of termination of coverage.

Time employee has to apply: 45 days after termination of coverage.

Florida

Fla. Stat. Ann. § 627.6692

Employers affected: Employers with fewer than 20 employees.

Eligible employees: Full-time (25 or more hours per week) employees covered by employer's health insurance plan.

Length of coverage for employee: 18 months.

Length of coverage for dependents: 18 months.

Time employer has to notify employee of continuation rights: Carrier notifies within 14 days of learning of qualifying event (employer is responsible for notifying carrier).

Time employee has to apply: 30 days from receipt of carrier's notice.

Georgia

Ga. Code Ann. §§ 33-24-21.1 to 33-24-21.2

Employers affected: All employers who offer group health insurance.

Eligible employees: Employees continuously insured for previous 6 months.

Length of coverage for employee: 3 months plus any part of the month remaining at termination.

Length of coverage for dependents: 3 months plus any part of the month remaining at termination.

Special situations: Employee, spouse, or former spouse who is 60 years old and who has been covered for previous 6 months may continue coverage until eligible for Medicare. (Applies to companies with more than 20 employees; does not apply when employee quits for reasons other than health.)

Hawaii

Haw. Rev. Stat. §§ 393-11, 393-15

Employers affected: All employers required to offer health insurance (those paying a regular employee a monthly wage at least 86.67 times state hourly minimum—about $542).

Length of coverage for employee: If employee is hospitalized or prevented from working by sickness, employer must pay insurance premiums for 3 months or for as long employer continues to pay wages, whichever is longer.

Illinois

215 Ill. Comp. Stat. §§ 5/367e, 5/367.2, 5/367.2-5

Employers affected: All employers who offer group health insurance.

Eligible employees: Employees continuously insured for previous 3 months.

Length of coverage for employee: 9 months.

Length of coverage for dependents: 9 months (but see below).

Time employee has to apply: 10 days after termination or reduction in hours or receiving notice from employer, whichever is later, but not more than 60 days from termination or reduction in hours.

Special situations: Upon death or divorce, 2 years, coverage for spouse under 55 and eligible dependents who were on employee's plan; until eligible for Medicare or other group coverage for spouse over 55 and eligible dependents who were on employee's plan. As of 7/1/2004, dependent child who has reached plan age limit or who was not already covered by plan also entitled to 2 years' continuation coverage.

Indiana

Ind. Code Ann. § 27-8-15-31.1

Employers affected: Employers with at least 3 employees.

Eligible employees: Employed by same employer for at least one year and continuously insured for previous 90 days.

Length of coverage for employee: 12 months.

Length of coverage for dependents: 12 months.

Time employer has to notify employee of continuation rights: 10 days after employee becomes eligible for continuation coverage.

Time employee has to apply: Must apply directly to insurer within 30 days after becoming eligible for continuation coverage.

State Health Insurance Continuation Laws (continued)

Iowa

Iowa Code §§ 509B.3 to 509B.5

Employers affected: All employers who offer group health insurance.

Eligible employees: Employees continuously insured for previous 3 months.

Length of coverage for employee: 9 months.

Length of coverage for dependents: 9 months.

Time employer has to notify employee of continuation rights: 10 days after termination of coverage.

Time employee has to apply: 10 days after termination of coverage or receiving notice from employer, whichever is later, but no more than 31 days from termination of coverage.

Kansas

Kan. Stat. Ann. § 40-2209(i)

Employers affected: All employers who offer group health insurance.

Eligible employees: Employees continuously insured for previous 3 months.

Length of coverage for employee: 6 months.

Length of coverage for dependents: 6 months.

Time employee has to apply: 31 days from termination of coverage.

Kentucky

Ky. Rev. Stat. Ann. § 304.18-110

Employers affected: All employers who offer group health insurance.

Eligible employees: Employees continuously insured for previous 3 months.

Length of coverage for employee: 18 months.

Length of coverage for dependents: 18 months.

Time employer has to notify employee of continuation rights: Employer must notify insurer as soon as employee's coverage ends; insurer then notifies employee.

Time employee has to apply: 31 days from receipt of insurer's notice, but no more than 90 days after termination of group coverage.

Louisiana

La. Rev. Stat. Ann. §§ 22:215.7, 22:215.13

Employers affected: All employers who offer group health insurance and have fewer than 20 employees.

Eligible employees: Employees continuously insured for previous 3 months.

Length of coverage for employee: 12 months.

Length of coverage for dependents: 12 months.

Time employee has to apply: Must apply and submit payment before group coverage ends.

Special situations: Surviving spouse who is 50 or older may have coverage until remarriage or eligibility for Medicare or other insurance.

Maine

Me. Rev. Stat. Ann. tit. 24-A, § 2809-A

Employers affected: All employers who offer group health insurance.

Eligible employees: Employees continuously insured for previous 3 months.

Length of coverage for employee: One year (either group or individual coverage at discretion of insurer).

Length of coverage for dependents: One year (either group or individual coverage at discretion of insurer). Upon death of insured, continuation only if original plan provided for coverage.

Time employee has to apply: 90 days from termination of group coverage.

Special situations: Temporary layoff or work-related injury or disease: Employee and employee's dependents entitled to one year group or individual continuation coverage. (Must have been continuously insured for previous 6 months; must apply within 31 days from termination of coverage.)

Maryland

Md. Code Ann., [Ins.] §§ 15-407 to 15-410

Employers affected: All employers who offer group health insurance.

Eligible employees: Employees continuously insured for previous 3 months.

Length of coverage for employee: 18 months.

Length of coverage for dependents: 18 months upon death of employee; upon change in marital status, 18 months or until spouse remarries or becomes eligible for other coverage.

Time employer has to notify employee of continuation rights: Must notify insurer within 14 days of receiving employee's continuation request.

Time employee has to apply: 45 days from termination of coverage. Employee begins application process by requesting an election of continuation notification form from employer.

State Health Insurance Continuation Laws (continued)

Massachusetts

Mass. Gen. Laws ch. 175, §§ 110G, 110I; ch. 176J, § 9

Employers affected: All employers who offer group health insurance and have fewer than 20 employees.

Eligible employees: All covered employees are eligible.

Length of coverage for employee: 18 months; 29 months if disabled.

Length of coverage for dependents: 18 months upon termination or reduction in hours; 29 months if disabled; 36 months on divorce, death of employee, employee's eligibility for Medicare, or employer's bankruptcy.

Time employer has to notify employee of continuation rights: When employee becomes eligible for continuation benefits.

Time employee has to apply: 60 days.

Special situations: Termination due to plant closing: 90 days' coverage for employee and dependents, at the same payment terms as before closing.

Minnesota

Minn. Stat. Ann. § 62A.17

Employers affected: All employers who offer group health insurance and have 2 or more employees.

Eligible employees: All covered employees are eligible.

Length of coverage for employee: 18 months; indefinitely if employee becomes totally disabled while employed.

Length of coverage for dependents: 18 months for current spouse; divorced or widowed spouse can continue until eligible for Medicare or other group health insurance. Upon divorce, dependent children can continue until they no longer qualify as dependents under plan. Upon death of employee, dependent children can continue for 36 months.

Time employer has to notify employee of continuation rights: Within 10 days of termination of coverage.

Time employee has to apply: 60 days from termination of coverage or receipt of employer's notice, whichever is later.

Mississippi

Miss. Code Ann. § 83-9-51

Employers affected: All employers who offer group health insurance and have fewer than 20 employees.

Eligible employees: Employees continuously insured for previous 3 months.

Length of coverage for employee: 12 months.

Length of coverage for dependents: 12 months.

Time employer has to notify employee of continuation rights: Insurer must notify former or deceased employee's dependent child or divorced spouse of option to continue insurance within 14 days of their becoming ineligible for coverage on employee's policy.

Time employee has to apply: Employee must apply and submit payment before group coverage ends; dependents or former spouse must elect continuation coverage within 30 days of receiving insurer's notice.

Missouri

Mo. Rev. Stat. § 376.428

Employers affected: All employers who offer group health insurance.

Eligible employees: Employees continuously insured for previous 3 months.

Length of coverage for employee: 9 months.

Length of coverage for dependents: 9 months.

Time employer has to notify employee of continuation rights: No later than date group coverage would end.

Time employee has to apply: 31 days from date group coverage would end.

Montana

Mont. Code Ann. §§ 33-22-506 to 33-22-510

Employers affected: All employers who offer group disability insurance.

Eligible employees: All employees.

Length of coverage for employee: One year (with employer's consent).

Time employee has to apply: 31 days from date group coverage would end.

Special situations: Insurer may not discontinue benefits to child with disabilities after child exceeds age limit for dependent status.

Nebraska

Neb. Rev. Stat. §§ 44-1640 and following, 44-7406

Employers affected: Employers not subject to federal COBRA laws.

Eligible employees: All covered employees.

Length of coverage for employee: 6 months.

Length of coverage for dependents: One year upon death of insured employee. Subjects of domestic abuse who have lost coverage under abuser's plan and who do not qualify for COBRA may have 18 months' coverage (applies to all employers).

State Health Insurance Continuation Laws (continued)

Time employer has to notify employee of continuation rights: Within 10 days of termination of employment must send notice by certified mail.

Time employee has to apply: 10 days from receipt of employer's notice.

Nevada

Nev. Rev. Stat. Ann. §§ 689B.245 and following, 689B.0345

Employers affected: Employers with less than 20 employees.

Eligible employees: Employees continuously insured for previous 12 months.

Length of coverage for employee: 18 months.

Length of coverage for dependents: 36 months; insurer cannot terminate coverage for disabled, dependent child who is too old to qualify as a dependent under the plan.

Time employer has to notify employee of continuation rights: 14 days after receiving notice of employee's eligibility.

Time employee has to apply: Must notify employer within 60 days of becoming eligible for continuation coverage; must apply within 60 days after receiving employer's notice.

Special situations: While employee is on leave without pay due to disability, 12 months for employee and dependents (applies to all employers).

New Hampshire

N.H. Rev. Stat. Ann. §§ 415:18(VIIg), (VII-a)

Employers affected: Employers with 2 to 19 employees.

Eligible employees: All insured employees are eligible.

Length of coverage for employee: 18 months; 29 months if disabled at termination or during first 60 days of continuation coverage.

Length of coverage for dependents: 18 months; 29 months if disabled at termination or during first 60 days of continuation coverage; 36 months upon death of employee, divorce or legal separation, loss of dependent status, or employee's eligibility for Medicare.

Time employer has to notify employee of continuation rights: Within 15 days of termination of coverage.

Time employee has to apply: Within 31 days of termination of coverage.

Special situations: Layoff or termination due to strike: 6 months' coverage with option to extend for an additional 12 months. Surviving, divorced, or legally separated spouse who is 55 or older may continue

benefits available until eligible for Medicare or other employer-based group insurance.

New Jersey

N.J. Stat. Ann. §§ 17B:27-30, 17B:27-51.12, 17B:27A-27

Employers affected: Employers with 2 to 50 employees.

Eligible employees: Employed full time (25 or more hours).

Length of coverage for employee: 18 months; 29 months if disabled at termination or during first 60 days of continuation coverage.

Length of coverage for dependents: 18 months; 29 months if disabled at termination or during first 60 days of continuation coverage; 36 months upon death of employee, divorce or legal separation, loss of dependent status, or employee's eligibility for Medicare.

Time employer has to notify employee of continuation rights: At time of qualifying event employer or carrier notifies employee.

Time employee has to apply: Within 30 days of qualifying event.

Special benefits: Coverage must be identical to that offered to current employees.

Special situations: Total disability: Employee who has been insured for previous 3 months and employee's dependents entitled to continuation coverage that includes all benefits offered by group policy (applies to all employers).

New Mexico

N.M. Stat. Ann. § 59A-18-16

Employers affected: All employers who offer group health insurance.

Eligible employees: All insured employees are eligible.

Length of coverage for employee: 6 months.

Length of coverage for dependents: May continue group coverage or convert to individual policies upon death of covered employee or divorce or legal separation.

Time employer has to notify employee of continuation rights: Insurer or employer gives written notice at time of termination.

Time employee has to apply: 30 days after receiving notice.

New York

N.Y. Ins. Law §§ 3221(f), 3221(m)

Employers affected: All employers who offer group

State Health Insurance Continuation Laws (continued)

health insurance and have fewer than 20 employees.

Eligible employees: All covered employees are eligible.

Length of coverage for employee: 18 months; 29 months if disabled at termination or during first 60 days of continuation coverage.

Length of coverage for dependents: 18 months; 29 months if disabled at termination or during first 60 days of continuation; 36 months upon death of employee, divorce or legal separation, loss of dependent status, or employee's eligibility for Medicare.

Time employee has to apply: 60 days after termination or receipt of notice, whichever is later.

North Carolina

N.C. Gen. Stat. §§ 58-53-5 to 58-53-40

Employers affected: All employers who offer group health insurance.

Eligible employees: Employees continuously insured for previous 3 months.

Length of coverage for employee: 18 months.

Length of coverage for dependents: 18 months.

Time employer has to notify employee of continuation rights: Employer has option of notifying employee as part of the exit process.

Time employee has to apply: 60 days.

North Dakota

N.D. Cent. Code §§ 26.1-36-23, 26.1-36-23.1

Employers affected: All employers who offer group health insurance.

Eligible employees: Employees continuously insured for previous 3 months.

Length of coverage for employee: 39 weeks.

Length of coverage for dependents: 39 weeks; 36 months if required by divorce or annulment decree.

Time employee has to apply: Within 10 days of termination or of receiving notice of continuation rights, whichever is later, but no more than 31 days from termination.

Ohio

Ohio Rev. Code Ann. §§ 3923.38, 1751.53

Employers affected: All employers who offer group health insurance.

Eligible employees: Employees continuously insured for previous 3 months who are entitled to unemployment benefits.

Length of coverage for employee: 6 months.

Length of coverage for dependents: 6 months.

Time employer has to notify employee of continuation rights: At termination of employment.

Time employee has to apply: Whichever is earlier: 31 days after coverage terminates; 10 days after coverage terminates if employer notified employee of continuation rights prior to termination; 10 days after employer notified employee of continuation rights, if notice was given after coverage terminated.

Oklahoma

Okla. Stat. Ann. tit. 36, § 4509

Employers affected: All employers who offer group health insurance.

Eligible employees: Employees insured for at least 6 months. (All other employees and their dependents entitled to 30 days' continuation coverage.)

Length of coverage for employee: Only for losses or conditions that began while group policy was in effect: 3 months for basic coverage; 6 months for major medical at the same premium rate prior to termination of coverage.

Length of coverage for dependents: Only for losses or conditions that began while group policy was in effect: 3 months for basic coverage; 6 months for major medical at the same premium rate prior to termination of coverage.

Special benefits: Includes maternity care for pregnancy begun while group policy was in effect.

Oregon

Or. Rev. Stat. §§ 743.600 to 743.610

Employers affected: Employers not subject to federal COBRA laws.

Eligible employees: Employees continuously insured for previous 3 months.

Length of coverage for employee: 6 months.

Length of coverage for dependents: 6 months.

Time employee has to apply: 10 days after termination or after receiving notice of continuation rights, whichever is later, but not more than 31 days.

Special situations: Surviving, divorced, or legally separated spouse who is 55 or older and dependent children entitled to continuation coverage until spouse remarries or is eligible for other coverage. Must include dental, vision, or prescription drug benefits if they were offered in original plan (applies to employers with 20 or more employees).

State Health Insurance Continuation Laws (continued)

Rhode Island

R.I. Gen. Laws §§ 27-19.1-1, 27-20.4-1 to 27-20-4.2

Employers affected: All employers who offer group health insurance.

Eligible employees: All insured employees are eligible.

Length of coverage for employee: 18 months (but not longer than continuous employment). Cannot be required to pay more than one month premium at a time.

Length of coverage for dependents: 18 months (but not longer than continuous employment). Cannot be required to pay more than one month premium at a time.

Time employer has to notify employee of continuation rights: Employers must post a conspicuous notice of employee continuation rights.

Time employee has to apply: 30 days from termination of coverage.

Special situations: If right to receiving continuing health insurance is stated in the divorce judgment, divorced spouse has right to continue coverage as long as employee remains covered or until divorced spouse remarries or becomes eligible for other group insurance. If covered employee remarries, divorced spouse must be given right to purchase an individual policy from same insurer.

South Carolina

S.C. Code Ann. § 38-71-770

Employers affected: All employers who offer group health insurance.

Eligible employees: Employees continuously insured for previous 6 months.

Length of coverage for employee: 6 months (in addition to part of month remaining at termination).

Length of coverage for dependents: 6 months (in addition to part of month remaining at termination).

Time employer has to notify employee of continuation rights: At time of termination must clearly and meaningfully advise employee of continuation rights.

South Dakota

S.D. Codified Laws Ann. §§ 58-18-7.5, 58-18-7.12, 58-18C-1

Employers affected: All employers who offer group health insurance.

Eligible employees: All covered employees.

Length of coverage for employee: 18 months; 29 months if disabled at termination or during first 60 days of continuation coverage.

Length of coverage for dependents: 18 months; 29 months if disabled at termination or during first 60 days of continuation coverage; 36 months upon death of employee, divorce or legal separation, loss of dependent status, employee's eligibility for Medicare.

Special situations: When employer goes out of business: 12 months' continuation coverage available to all employees. Employer must notify employees within 10 days of termination of benefits; employees must apply within 60 days of receipt of employer's notice or within 90 days of termination of benefits if no notice given.

Tennessee

Tenn. Code Ann. § 56-7-2312

Employers affected: All employers who offer group health insurance.

Eligible employees: Employees continuously insured for previous 3 months.

Length of coverage for employee: 3 months (in addition to part of month remaining at termination).

Length of coverage for dependents: 3 months (in addition to part of month remaining at termination); 15 months upon death of employee or divorce.

Special situations: Employee or dependent who is pregnant at time of termination entitled to continuation benefits for 6 months following the end of pregnancy.

Texas

Tex. Ins. Code Ann. Art 3.51-6(d)(3), 3.51-8

Employers affected: All employers who offer group health insurance.

Eligible employees: Employees continuously insured for previous 3 months.

Length of coverage for employee: 6 months.

Length of coverage for dependents: 6 months.

Time employee has to apply: 31 days from termination of coverage or receiving notice of continuation rights from employer or insurer, whichever is later.

Special situations: Layoff due to a labor dispute: Employee entitled to continuation benefits for duration of dispute, but no longer than 6 months.

Utah

Utah Code Ann. §§ 31A-22-722

Employers affected: All employers who offer group health insurance.

State Health Insurance Continuation Laws (continued)

Eligible employees: Employees continuously insured for previous 6 months.

Length of coverage for employee: 6 months.

Length of coverage for dependents: 6 months.

Time employer has to notify employee of continuation rights: In writing within 30 days of termination of coverage.

Time employee has to apply: Within 30 days of receiving employer's notice of continuation rights.

Vermont
Vt. Stat. Ann. tit. 8, §§ 4090a to 4090c

Employers affected: All employers who offer group health insurance and have fewer than 20 employees.

Eligible employees: Employees continuously insured for previous 3 months.

Length of coverage for employee: 6 months.

Length of coverage for dependents: 6 months.

Time employee has to apply: Within 60 days (upon death of employee or group member); within 30 days (upon termination, change of marital status, or loss of dependent status) of the date that group coverage terminates, or the date of being notified of continuation rights, whichever is sooner.

Virginia
Va. Code Ann. §§ 38.2-3541 to 38.2-3452, 38.2-3416

Employers affected: All employers who offer group health insurance.

Eligible employees: Employees continuously insured for previous 3 months.

Length of coverage for employee: 90 days.

Length of coverage for dependents: 90 days.

Time employer has to notify employee of continuation rights: 15 days from termination of coverage.

Time employee has to apply: Must apply for continuation and pay entire 90-day premium before termination of coverage.

Special situations: Employee may convert to an individual policy instead of applying for continuation coverage (must apply within 31 days of termination of coverage).

Washington
Wash. Rev. Code Ann. § 48.21.075

Employers affected: All employers who offer and pay for group health insurance.

Eligible employees: Insured employees on strike.

Length of coverage for employee: 6 months if employee goes on strike.

Length of coverage for dependents: 6 months if employee goes on strike.

West Virginia
W. Va. Code §§ 33-16-2, 33-16-3(e)

Employers affected: Employers providing insurance for at least 10 employees.

Eligible employees: All covered employees are eligible.

Length of coverage for employee: 18 months in case of involuntary layoff.

Wisconsin
Wis. Stat. Ann. § 632.897

Employers affected: All employers who offer group health insurance.

Eligible employees: Employees continuously insured for previous 3 months.

Length of coverage for employee: 18 months (or longer at insurer's option).

Length of coverage for dependents: 18 months (or longer at insurer's option).

Time employer has to notify employee of continuation rights: 5 days from termination of coverage.

Time employee has to apply: 30 days after receiving employer's notice.

Wyoming
Wyo. Stat. § 26-19-113

Employers affected: Employers not subject to federal COBRA laws.

Eligible employees: Employees continuously insured for previous 3 months.

Length of coverage for employee: 12 months.

Length of coverage for dependents: 12 months.

Time employee has to apply: 31 days from termination of coverage.

Current as of February 2005

CHAPTER

Where to Go for Further Information

Departments of Labor

U.S. Department of Labor

Washington, DC 20210
202-693-4650
www.dol.gov

You can find a list of regional offices of the Wage and Hour Division at the Department of Labor's website at:
www.dol.gov/esa/contacts/whd/america2.htm

and a comprehensive list of state labor resources at:
www.dol.gov/dol/location.htm

State Labor Departments

Note: Phone numbers are for department headquarters. Check websites for regional office locations and numbers.

Alabama
Department of Industrial Relations
Montgomery, AL
334-242-8990
www.dir.state.al.us

Alaska
Department of Labor and Workforce Development
Juneau, AK
907-465-2700
www.labor.state.ak.us

Arizona
Industrial Commission
Phoenix, AZ
602-542-4411
www.ica.state.az.us

Arkansas
Department of Labor
Little Rock, AR
501-682-4541
www.state.ar.us/labor

California
Department of Industrial Relations
San Francisco, CA
415-703-5050
www.dir.ca.gov

Colorado
Department of Labor and Employment
Denver, CO
303-318-8000
www.coworkforce.com

Connecticut
Labor Department
Wethersfield, CT
860-263-6505
www.ctdol.state.ct.us

Delaware
Department of Labor
Wilmington, DE
302-761-8000
www.delawareworks.com

District of Columbia
Department of Employment Services
Washington, DC
202-671-1900
http://does.ci.washington.dc.us

Florida
Agency for Workforce Innovation
Tallahassee, FL
850-245-7105
www.floridajobs.org *or* www.MyFlorida.com

Georgia
Department of Labor
Atlanta, GA
404-656-3011
877-709-8185
www.dol.state.ga.us

Hawaii
Department of Labor and Industrial Relations
Honolulu, HI
808-586-8865/8844
http://dlir.state.hi.us

Idaho
Department of Labor
Boise, ID
208-334-6112
www.labor.state.id.us

Illinois
Department of Labor
Chicago, IL
312-793-2800
www.state.il.us/agency/idol

Indiana
Department of Labor
Indianapolis, IN
317-232-2655
www.in.gov/labor

Departments of Labor (continued)

Iowa
Iowa Workforce Development
Des Moines, IA
515-281-5387
800-JOB-IOWA
www.iowaworkforce.org/labor

Kansas
Department of Human Resources
Office of Employment Standards
Topeka, KS
785-296-4062
www.dol.ks.gov

Kentucky
Department of Labor
Frankfort, KY
502-564-3070
www.kylabor.net

Louisiana
Department of Labor
Baton Rouge, LA
225-342-3111
www.ldol.state.la.us

Maine
Department of Labor
Augusta, ME
207-287-3787
www.state.me.us/labor

Maryland
Department of Labor, Licensing, and Regulation
Division of Labor and Industry
Baltimore, MD
410-767-2236
www.dllr.state.md.us/labor

Massachusetts
Department of Labor and Workforce Development
Boston, MA
617-727-6573
www.state.ma.us/dlwd or www.mass.gov/dlwd

Michigan
Department of Labor and Economic Growth
Lansing, MI
517-373-3034
www.cis.state.mi.us or www.michigan.gov/cis

Minnesota
Department of Labor and Industry
St. Paul, MN
651-284-5005
800-342-5354
www.doli.state.mn.us

Mississippi
Department of Employment Security
Jackson, MS
601-321-6100
www.mesc.state.ms.us

Missouri
Department of Labor and Industrial Relations
Jefferson City, MO
573-751-4091
573-751-9691
www.dolir.state.mo.us or www.dolir.mo.gov

Montana
Department of Labor and Industry
Helena, MT
406-444-2840
http://dli.state.mt.us

Nebraska
Department of Labor
Labor and Safety Standards
Lincoln, NE
402-471-2239

Omaha, NE
402-595-3095
www.dol.state.ne.us

Nevada
Division of Industrial Relations
Carson City, NV
775-684-7260
http://dirweb.state.nv.us

New Hampshire
Department of Labor
Concord, NH
603-271-3176
www.labor.state.nh.us

New Jersey
Department of Labor
Labor Standards and Safety Enforcement
Trenton, NJ
609-292-2313/2323
www.state.nj.us/labor

Departments of Labor (continued)

New Mexico
Labor and Industrial Division
Department of Labor
Santa Fe, NM
505-827-6875

Albuquerque, NM
505-841-8993
www.dol.state.nm.us

New York
Department of Labor
Albany, NY
518-457-9000
www.labor.state.ny.us

North Carolina
Department of Labor
Raleigh, NC
919-807-2796
800-625-2267
www.dol.state.nc.us or www.nclabor.com

North Dakota
Department of Labor
Bismarck, ND
701-328-2660
800-582-8032
www.state.nd.us/labor

Ohio
Division of Labor and Worker Safety
Department of Commerce
Columbus, OH
614-644-2239
www.com.state.oh.us/ODOC/laws/default.htm

Oklahoma
Department of Labor
Oklahoma City, OK
405-528-1500, ext. 200
888-269-5353
www.okdol.state.ok.us or www.ok.gov

Oregon
Bureau of Labor and Industries
Portland, OR
503-731-4200
www.boli.state.or.us

Pennsylvania
Department of Labor and Industry
Harrisburg, PA
717-787-5279
www.dli.state.pa.us

Rhode Island
Department of Labor and Training
Cranston, RI
401-462-8000
www.dlt.state.ri.us or www.det.state.ri.us

South Carolina
Department of Labor, Licensing, and Regulation
Columbia, SC
803-896-4300
www.llr.state.sc.us

South Dakota
Division of Labor and Management
Pierre, SD
605-773-3681
www.state.sd.us/dol/dlm/dlm-home.htm

Tennessee
Department of Labor and Workforce Development
Nashville, TN
615-741-6642
www.state.tn.us/labor-wfd

Texas
Texas Workforce Commission
Austin, TX
512-463-2222
www.twc.state.tx.us

Utah
Labor Commission
Salt Lake City, UT
801-530-6801
800-222-1238
www.labor.state.ut.us

Vermont
Department of Labor and Industry
Montpelier, VT
808-828-2288
www.state.vt.us/labind

Virginia
Department of Labor and Industry
Richmond, VA
804-371-2327
www.dli.state.va.us

Washington
Department of Labor and Industries
Olympia, WA
360-902-5800
800-547-8367
www.lni.wa.gov

Departments of Labor (continued)

West Virginia
Division of Labor
Charleston, WV
877-558-5134
304-558-7890
www.labor.state.wv.us

Wisconsin
Department of Workforce Development
Madison, WI
608-266-3131
www.dwd.state.wi.us

Wyoming
Department of Employment
Cheyenne, WY
307-777-6763
http://wydoe.state.wy.us

Current as of February 2005

Agencies That Enforce Laws Prohibiting Discrimination in Employment

United States Agencies

Equal Employment Opportunity Commission (EEOC)
Washington, DC
202-663-4900
800-669-4000
www.eeoc.gov
Field Office locations and phone numbers: www.eeoc.gov/offices.html

State Agencies

Alabama
EEOC District Office
Birmingham, AL
205-212-2100
205-212-2112
http://eeoc.gov/birmingham/index.html

Alaska
Commission for Human Rights
Anchorage, AK
907-274-4692
800-478-4692
www.gov.state.ak.us/aschr/aschr.htm

Arizona
Civil Rights Division
Phoenix, AZ
602-542-5263
www.attorneygeneral.state.az.us/civil_rights/index.html

Arkansas
Equal Employment Opportunity Commission
Little Rock, AR
501-324-5060
www.eeoc.gov/littlerock/index.html

California
Department of Fair Employment and Housing
Sacramento District Office
Sacramento, CA
916-445-5523
800-884-1684
www.dfeh.ca.gov

Colorado
Civil Rights Division
Denver, CO
303-894-2997
800-262-4845
www.dora.state.co.us/Civil-Rights

Connecticut
Commission on Human Rights and Opportunities
Hartford, CT
860-541-3400
800-477-5737
www.state.ct.us/chro

Delaware
Office of Labor Law Enforcement
Division of Industrial Affairs
Wilmington, DE
302-761-8200
www.delawareworks.com/industrialaffairs/welcome.shtml

District of Columbia
Office of Human Rights
Washington, DC
202-727-4559
http://ohr.dc.gov/ohr/site/default.asp

Florida
Commission on Human Relations
Tallahassee, FL
850-488-7082
800-342-8170
http://fchr.state.fl.us

Georgia
Atlanta District Office
U.S. Equal Employment Opportunity Commission
Atlanta, GA
404-562-6800
800-669-4000
www.eeoc.gov/atlanta/index.html

Hawaii
Hawai'i Civil Rights Commission
Honolulu, HI
808-586-8636 (Oahu only)
800-468-4644 x68636 (other islands)
http://dlir.state.hi.us/divisions/hcrc

Idaho
Idaho Commission on Human Rights
Boise, ID
208-334-2873
www2.state.id.us/ihrc

Illinois
Department of Human Rights
Chicago, IL
312-814-6200
www.state.il.us/dhr

Agencies That Enforce Laws Prohibit Discrimination in Employment (continued)

Indiana
Civil Rights Commission
Indianapolis, IN
317-232-2600
800-628-2909
www.in.gov/icrc

Iowa
Iowa Civil Rights Commission
Des Moines, IA
515-281-4121
800-457-4416
www.state.ia.us/government/crc

Kansas
Human Rights Commission
Topeka, KS
785-296-3206
www.ink.org/public/khrc

Kentucky
Human Rights Commission
Louisville, KY
502-595-4024
800-292-5566
www.state.ky.us/agencies2/kchr

Louisiana
Commission on Human Rights
Baton Rouge, LA
225-342-6969

Maine
Human Rights Commission
Augusta, ME
207-624-6050
www.state.me.us/mhrc/index.shtml

Maryland
Commission on Human Relations
Baltimore, MD
410-767-8600
800-637-6247
www.mchr.state.md.us

Massachusetts
Commission Against Discrimination
Boston, MA
617-994-6000
www.state.ma.us/mcad

Michigan
Department of Civil Rights
Detroit, MI
313-456-3700
800-482-3604

www.michigan.gov/mdcr

Minnesota
Department of Human Rights
St. Paul, MN
651-296-5663
800-657-3704
www.humanrights.state.mn.us

Mississippi
Equal Opportunity Department
Employment Security Commission
Jackson, MS
601-961-7420
www.mesc.state.ms.us

Missouri
Commission on Human Rights
Jefferson City, MO
573-751-3325
www.dolir.state.mo.us/hr

Montana
Human Rights Bureau
Employment Relations Division
Department of Labor and Industry
Helena, MT
406-444-2884
800-542-0807
http://erd.dli.state.mt.us/HumanRight/HRhome.asp

Nebraska
Equal Opportunity Commission
Lincoln, NE
402-471-2024
800-642-6112
www.nol.org/home/NEOC

Nevada
Equal Rights Commission
Reno, NV
775-688-1288
http://detr.state.nv.us/nerc/NERC-index.htm

New Hampshire
Commission for Human Rights
Concord, NH
603-271-2767
http://webster.state.nh.us/hrc

New Jersey
Division on Civil Rights
Newark, NJ
973-648-2700
www.state.nj.us/lps/dcr

Agencies That Enforce Laws Prohibiting Discrimination in Employment (continued)

New Mexico
Human Rights Division
Santa Fe, NM
505-827-6838
800-566-9471
www.dol.state.nm.us/dol_hrd.html

New York
Division of Human Rights
Bronx, NY
718-741-8400
www.nysdhr.com

North Carolina
Employment Discrimination Bureau
Department of Labor
Raleigh, NC
919-807-2796
800-NCLABOR (625-2267)
www.dol.state.nc.us/edb/edb.htm

North Dakota
Human Rights Division
Department of Labor
Bismarck, ND
701-328-2660
800-582-8032
www.state.nd.us/labor/services/human-rights

Ohio
Civil Rights Commission
Columbus, OH
614-466-5928
888-278-7101
www.state.oh.us/crc

Oklahoma
Human Rights Commission
Oklahoma City, OK
405-521-2360
www.youroklahoma.com/ohrc

Oregon
Civil Rights Division
Bureau of Labor and Industries
Portland, OR
503-731-4874
www.boli.state.or.us/BOLI/CRD/index.shtml

Pennsylvania
Human Relations Commission
Philadelphia, PA
215-560-2496
www.phrc.state.pa.us

Rhode Island
Commission for Human Rights
Providence, RI
401-222-2661
www.state.ri.us/manual/data/queries/stdept_.idc?id=16

South Carolina
Human Affairs Commission
Columbia, SC
803-737-7800
800-521-0725
www.state.sc.us/schac

South Dakota
Division of Human Rights
Pierre, SD
605-773-4493
www.state.sd.us/dcr/hr/HR_HOM.htm

Tennessee
Human Rights Commission
Knoxville, TN
865-594-6500
800-251-3589
www.state.tn.us/humanrights

Texas
Commission on Human Rights
Austin, TX
512-437-3450
888-452-4778
http://tchr.state.tx.us

Utah
Anti-Discrimination and Labor Division
Labor Commission
Salt Lake City, UT
801-530-6801
800-222-1238
http://laborcommission.utah.gov/Utah_Antidiscrimination
   ___Labo/utah_antidiscrimination___labo.htm

Vermont
Attorney General's Office
Civil Rights Division
Montpelier, VT
802-828-3171
888-745-9195
www.state.vt.us/atg/civil rights.htm

Virginia
Council on Human Rights
Richmond, VA
804-225-2292
www.chr.state.va.us

Agencies That Enforce Laws Prohibit Discrimination in Employment (continued)

Washington
Human Rights Commission
Seattle, WA
206-464-6500
www.wa.gov/hrc

West Virginia
Human Rights Commission
Charleston, WV
304-558-2616
888-676-5546
www.wvf.state.wv.us/wvhrc

Wisconsin
Department of Workforce Development
Madison, WI
608-266-6860
www.dwd.state.wi.us/er

Wyoming
Department of Employment
Cheyenne, WY
307-777-7261
http://wydoe.state.wy.us/doe.asp?ID=3

Current as of February 2005

How to Use the CD-ROM

The employee handbook sections discussed in this book are included on a CD-ROM in the back of the book. This CD-ROM, which can be used with Windows computers, installs files that can be opened, printed, and edited using a word processor or other software. It is *not* a standalone software program. Please read this appendix and the README.TXT file included on the CD-ROM for instructions on using the Forms CD.

Note to Mac users: This CD-ROM and its files should also work on Macintosh computers. Please note, however, that Nolo cannot provide technical support for non-Windows users.

How to View the README File

If you do not know how to view the file README. TXT, insert the Forms CD-ROM into your computer's CD-ROM drive and follow these instructions:

- Windows 9x, 2000, Me, and XP: (1) On your PC's desktop, double click the My Computer icon; (2) double click the icon for the CD-ROM drive into which the Forms CD-ROM was inserted; (3) double click the file README.TXT.
- Macintosh: (1) On your Mac desktop, double click the icon for the CD-ROM that you inserted; (2) double click on the file README.TXT.

While the README file is open, print it out by using the Print command in the File menu.

A. Installing the Handbook Section Files Onto Your Computer

Handbook section files that you can open, complete, print, and save with your word processing program (see Section B, below) are contained on the CD-ROM. Before you can do anything with the files on the CD-ROM, you need to install them onto your hard disk. In accordance with U.S. copyright laws, remember that copies of the CD-ROM and its files are for your personal use only.

Insert the Forms CD and do the following.

1. Windows 9x, 2000, Me, and XP Users

Follow the instructions that appear on the screen. (If nothing happens when you insert the Forms CD-ROM, then (1) double click the My Computer icon; (2) double click the icon for the CD-ROM drive into which the Forms CD-ROM was inserted; (3) double click the file WELCOME.EXE.)

By default, all the files are installed to the \Employee Handbook Sections folder in the \Program Files folder of your computer. A folder called "Employee Handbook Sections" is added to the "Programs" folder of the Start menu.

2. Macintosh Users

Step 1: If the "Employee Handbook CD" window is not open, open it by double clicking the "Employee Handbook CD" icon.

Step 2: Select the "Employee Handbook Sections" folder icon.

Step 3: Drag and drop the folder icon onto the icon of your hard disk.

B. Using the Handbook Section Files to Create an Employee Handbook

This discussion concerns the files for handbook sections that can be opened and edited with your word processing program.

All word processing handbook section files come in rich text format. These files have the extension ".RTF." For example, the handbook section for The Employment Relationship discussed in Chapter 2 is on the file 02_Employment.rtf. All forms and their filenames are listed in Section C, below.

RTF files can be read by most recent word processing programs including all versions of MS Word for Windows and Macintosh, WordPad for Windows, and recent versions of WordPerfect for Windows and Macintosh.

To use the handbook section files from the CD to create your employee handbook you must: (1) open a file in your word processor or text editor; (2) edit the handbook section by filling in the required information; (3) rename and save your revised handbook section file; (4) assemble your employee handbook by pasting your completed handbook sections into the Employee Handbook Outline; and 5) print it out.

The following are general instructions. However, each word processor uses different commands to open, format, save, and print documents. Please read your word processor's manual for specific instructions on performing these tasks.

Do not call Nolo's technical support if you have questions on how to use your word processor.

Step 1: Opening a File

There are three ways to open the word processing files included on the CD-ROM after you have installed them onto your computer:

- Windows users can open a file by selecting its "shortcut" as follows: (1) Click the Windows "Start" button; (2) open the "Programs" folder; (3) open the "Employee Handbook Sections" subfolder; and (4) click on the shortcut to the handbook section you want to work with.

- Both Windows and Macintosh users can open a file directly by double clicking on it. Use My Computer or Windows Explorer (Windows 9x, 2000, Me, or XP) or the Finder (Macintosh) to go to the folder you installed or copied the CD-ROM's files to. Then, double click on the specific file you want to open.

- You can also open a file from within your word processor. To do this, you must first start your word processor. Then, go to the File menu and choose the Open command. This opens a dialog box where you will tell the program (1) the type of file you want to open (*.RTF);

and (2) the location and name of the file (you will need to navigate through the directory tree to get to the folder on your hard disk where the CD's files have been installed). If these directions are unclear, you will need to look through the manual for your word processing program—Nolo's technical support department will *not* be able to help you with the use of your word processing program.

Where Are the Files Installed?

Windows Users
- RTF files are installed by default to a folder named \Employee Handbook Sections in the \Program Files folder of your computer.

Macintosh Users
- RTF files are located in the "Employee Handbook Sections" folder.

Step 2: Editing Your Employee Handbook Sections

Fill in the appropriate information according to the instructions and sample agreements in the book. Underlines are used to indicate where you need to enter your information, frequently with bracketed instructions embedded within them. *Be sure to delete the underlines and instructions from your edited document.* If you do not know how to use your word processor to edit a document, you will need to look through the manual for your word processing program—Nolo's technical support department will *not* be able to help you with the use of your word processing program.

Editing Handbook Sections That Have Optional or Alternative Text

Some of the forms have optional or alternate text:

- With optional text, you choose whether to include or exclude the given text.
- With alternative text, you select one alternative to include and exclude the other alternatives.

When editing these forms, we suggest you do the following.

Optional text

If you **don't want** to include optional text, just delete it from your document.

If you **do want** to include optional text, just leave it in your document.

In either case, delete the italicized instructions.

Note: If you choose not to include an optional numbered policy, be sure to renumber all the subsequent clauses after you delete it.

Alternative text

First delete all the alternatives that you do not want to include, then delete the italicized instructions.

Step 3: Saving Your Handbook Section Files

After filling in a particular handbook section, use the "Save As" command to save and rename the file. (This is an intermediate step; later we'll help you combine the handbook section files into a single document.) Because all the files are "read-only," you will not be able to use the "Save" command. This is for your protection. *If you save the file without renaming it, the underlines that indicate where you need to enter your information will be lost and you will not be able to create a new document with this file without recopying the original file from the CD-ROM.*

If you do not know how to use your word processor to save a file, you will need to look through the manual for your word processing program—Nolo's technical support department will *not* be able to help you with the use of your word processing program.

 Tips for saving your completed files. As you edit and save your handbook section files, bear in mind that:

- You won't be able to access your saved files using shortcuts that opened the unedited, blank section files (Step 1, above).
- You'll need to access these saved files later to put together your employee handbook (Step 5, below).

So, to make the task of putting together your handbook as easy as possible, remember these tips:

- As you rename the files, use names that you will recognize.
- Save all your handbook section files to the same location (or folder) on your computer.
- Note the location to which you saved the files.

Step 4: Assembling Your Employee Handbook

When you've edited the handbook sections to your satisfaction and are ready to begin assembling your employee handbook, open the Employee Handbook Outline following the instructions in Step 1, above. You can then start opening, copying, and pasting from your completed handbook section files into the Employee Handbook Outline. *Be sure to delete the bracketed instructions from the Employee Handbook Outline as you paste in your handbook sections.* If you do not know how to use your word processor to copy and paste to and from a file, you will need to look through the manual for your word processing program—Nolo's technical support department will *not* be able to help you with the use of your word processing program.

After you've finished pasting in your handbook sections, save your final document following the instructions in Step 3, above.

Step 5: Printing Out the Employee Handbook

Use your word processor's or text editor's "Print" command to print out your final document. If you do not know how to use your word processor to print a document, you will need to look through the manual for your word processing program—Nolo's technical support department will *not* be able to help you with the use of your word processing program.

C. Files Included on the Employee Handbook CD

File Name	Section Name
00_Outline.rtf	Employee Handbook Outline
01_Introduction.rtf	1 Introduction
02_Employment.rtf	2 The Employment Relationship
03_Hiring.rtf	3 Hiring
04_New Employee Info.rtf	4 New Employee Information
05_Employee Class.rtf	5 Employee Classifications
06_Hours.rtf	6 Hours
07_Pay Policies.rtf	7 Pay Policies
08_Employee Benefits.rtf	8 Employee Benefits
09_Company Property.rtf	9 Use of Company Property
10_Time Off.rtf	10 Leave and Time Off
11_Performance.rtf	11 Performance
12_Work Behavior.rtf	12 Workplace Behavior
13_Health Safety.rtf	13 Health and Safety
14_Privacy.rtf	14 Employee Privacy
15_Computers.rtf	15 Computers, Email, and the Internet
16_Records.rtf	16 Employee Records
17_Drugs Alcohol.rtf	17 Drugs and Alcohol
18_Trade Secrets.rtf	18 Trade Secrets and Conflicts of Interest
19_Discrimination.rtf	19 Discrimination and Harassment
20_Complaints.rtf	20 Complaint Policies
21_Ending Employment.rtf	21 Ending Employment
Acknowledgment.rtf	Handbook Acknowledgment Form
Payroll Deduction.rtf	Payroll Deduction Authorization Form
Policy.rtf	Email and Internet Policy Acknowledgment Forms
Reimbursement.rtf	Expense Reimbursement Form

Forms

Handbook Acknowledgment Form

By signing this form, I acknowledge that I have received a copy of the Company's Employee Handbook. I understand that it contains important information about the Company's policies, that I am expected to read the Handbook and familiarize myself with its contents, and that the policies in the Handbook apply to me. I understand that nothing in the Handbook constitutes a contract or promise of continued employment and that the Company may change the policies in the Handbook at any time.

By signing this form, I acknowledge that my employment is at will. I understand that I have the right to end the employment relationship at any time and for any reason, with or without notice, with or without cause, and that the Company has the same right. I acknowledge that neither the Company nor I has entered into an employment agreement for a specified period of time, that only _____ _____ may make any agreement contrary to the at-will policy, and that any such agreement must be in writing, signed by myself and _____ .

_____   _____
Employee's Signature   Date

_____
Employee's Name (Print)

Payroll Deduction Authorization Form

I have requested an advance from the Company. This advance is a loan, which I am fully obligated to repay. In consideration of the Company's decision to grant this request, I agree to repay the Company through payroll deductions. I hereby authorize the Company to withhold _____ from my paycheck in _____ equal installments to repay the advance. The total amount deducted from my pay shall be equal to the amount of the advance.

If my employment is terminated or I quit before this advance is repaid, I hereby authorize the Company to deduct the full amount I still owe the Company from my final paycheck, if allowed by law.

_____ _____
Employee's Signature   Date

_____
Employee's Name (Print)

Expense Reimbursement Form

Date of Expense	Item or Service Purchased	Reason for Expense	Cost	Receipt Attached
_____	_____	_____	_____	☐ Yes ☐ No
_____	_____	_____	_____	☐ Yes ☐ No
_____	_____	_____	_____	☐ Yes ☐ No
_____	_____	_____	_____	☐ Yes ☐ No
_____	_____	_____	_____	☐ Yes ☐ No
_____	_____	_____	_____	☐ Yes ☐ No
_____	_____	_____	_____	☐ Yes ☐ No
_____	_____	_____	_____	☐ Yes ☐ No
_____	_____	_____	_____	☐ Yes ☐ No
_____	_____	_____	_____	☐ Yes ☐ No
_____	_____	_____	_____	☐ Yes ☐ No
_____	_____	_____	_____	☐ Yes ☐ No
_____	_____	_____	_____	☐ Yes ☐ No
_____	_____	_____	_____	☐ Yes ☐ No
_____	_____	_____	_____	☐ Yes ☐ No
_____	_____	_____	_____	☐ Yes ☐ No
_____	_____	_____	_____	☐ Yes ☐ No
_____	_____	_____	_____	☐ Yes ☐ No
_____	_____	_____	_____	☐ Yes ☐ No
_____	_____	_____	_____	☐ Yes ☐ No

Employee's Signature _____   Date Submitted _____

Employee's Name (Print) _____

Supervisor's Signature _____   Date Approved _____

Supervisor's Name (Print) _____

Email and Internet Policy Acknowledgment

My signature on this form indicates that I have read the Company's email and Internet policies and I agree to abide by their terms. I understand that any email messages I send or receive using Company equipment are not private, and that the Company may access, monitor, read, and/or copy those messages at any time, for any reason. I also understand that the Company reserves the right to monitor my Internet use, and that such monitoring may occur at any time, for any reason.

_____   _____
Signature   Date

_____
Print Name

Index

CATALOG
...more from Nolo

	PRICE	CODE

BUSINESS

	PRICE	CODE
Becoming a Mediator: Your Guide to Career Opportunites	$29.99	BECM
Business Buyout Agreements (Book w/CD-ROM)	$49.99	BSAG
The CA Nonprofit Corporation Kit (Binder w/CD-ROM)	$59.99	CNP
Consultant & Independent Contractor Agreements (Book w/CD-ROM)	$29.99	CICA
The Corporate Minutes Book (Book w/CD-ROM)	$69.99	CORMI
Create Your Own Employee Handbook (Book w/CD-ROM)	$49.99	EMHA
Dealing With Problem Employees	$44.99	PROBM
Deduct It! Lower Your Small Business Taxes	$34.99	DEDU
The Employer's Legal Handbook	$39.99	EMPL
Everyday Employment Law	$29.99	ELBA
Federal Employment Laws	$49.99	FELW
Form Your Own Limited Liability Company (Book w/CD-ROM)	$44.99	LIAB
Hiring Independent Contractors: The Employer's Legal Guide (Book w/CD-ROM)	$34.99	HICI
Home Business Tax Deductions: Keep What You Earn	$34.99	DEHB
How to Create a Noncompete Agreement (Book w/CD-ROM)	$44.95	NOCMP
How to Form a California Professional Corporation (Book w/CD-ROM)	$59.99	PROF
How to Form a Nonprofit Corporation (Book w/CD-ROM)—National Edition	$44.99	NNP
How to Form a Nonprofit Corporation in California (Book w/CD-ROM)	$44.99	NON
How to Form Your Own California Corporation (Binder w/CD-ROM)	$59.99	CACI
How to Form Your Own California Corporation (Book w/CD-ROM)	$34.99	CCOR
How to Get Your Business on the Web	$29.99	WEBS
How to Run a Thriving Business: Strategies for Sucess & Satisfaction	$19.99	THRV
How to Write a Business Plan	$34.99	SBS
Incorporate Your Business	$49.95	NIBS
The Independent Paralegal's Handbook	$34.99	PARA
Leasing Space for Your Small Business	$34.95	LESP
Legal Guide for Starting & Running a Small Business	$34.99	RUNS
Legal Forms for Starting & Running a Small Business (Book w/CD-ROM)	$29.99	RUNSF
Marketing Without Advertising	$24.00	MWAD
Mediate, Don't Litigate	$24.99	MEDL
Music Law (Book w/CD-ROM)	$39.99	ML
Nolo's Guide to Social Security Disability	$29.99	QSS

Prices subject to change.

	PRICE	CODE
The Guardianship Book for California	$39.99	GB
A Legal Guide for Lesbian and Gay Couples	$29.99	LG
Living Together: A Legal Guide (Book w/CD-ROM)	$34.99	LTK
Medical Directives and Powers of Attorney in California (Book w/CD-ROM)	$21.99	CPOA
Prenuptial Agreements: How to Write a Fair & Lasting Contract (Book w/CD-ROM)	$34.99	PNUP
Using Divorce Mediation: Save Your Money & Your Sanity	$29.99	UDMD

GOING TO COURT

	PRICE	CODE
Beat Your Ticket: Go To Court & Win! (National Edition)	$21.99	BEYT
The Criminal Law Handbook: Know Your Rights, Survive the System	$34.99	KYR
Everybody's Guide to Small Claims Court (National Edition)	$26.99	NSCC
Everybody's Guide to Small Claims Court in California	$29.99	CSCC
Fight Your Ticket & Win in California	$29.99	FYT
How to Change Your Name in California	$34.99	NAME
How to Collect When You Win a Lawsuit (California Edition)	$29.99	JUDG
How to Seal Your Juvenile & Criminal Records (California Edition)	$34.95	CRIM
The Lawsuit Survival Guide	$29.99	UNCL
Nolo's Deposition Handbook	$29.99	DEP
Represent Yourself in Court: How to Prepare & Try a Winning Case	$34.99	RYC
Sue in California Without a Lawyer	$34.99	SLWY

HOMEOWNERS, LANDLORDS & TENANTS

	PRICE	CODE
California Tenants' Rights	$27.99	CTEN
Deeds for California Real Estate	$24.99	DEED
Dog Law	$21.95	DOG
Every Landlord's Legal Guide (National Edition, Book w/CD-ROM)	$44.99	ELLI
Every Tenant's Legal Guide	$29.99	EVTEN
For Sale by Owner in California	$29.99	FSBO
How to Buy a House in California	$34.99	BHCA
The California Landlord's Law Book: Rights & Responsibilities (Book w/CD-ROM)	$44.99	LBRT
The California Landlord's Law Book: Evictions (Book w/CD-ROM)	$44.99	LBEV
Leases & Rental Agreements	$29.99	LEAR
Neighbor Law: Fences, Trees, Boundaries & Noise	$26.99	NEI
The New York Landlord's Law Book (Book w/CD-ROM)	$39.99	NYLL
New York Tenants' Rights	$27.99	NYTEN
Renters' Rights (National Edition)	$24.99	RENT

HUMOR

	PRICE	CODE
Poetic Justice	$9.95	PJ

	PRICE	CODE

IMMIGRATION

Becoming A U.S. Citizen: A Guide to the Law, Exam and Interview	$24.99	USCIT
Fiancé & Marriage Visas (Book w/CD-ROM)	$44.99	IMAR
How to Get a Green Card	$29.99	GRN
Student & Tourist Visas	$29.99	ISTU
U.S. Immigration Made Easy	$44.99	IMEZ

MONEY MATTERS

101 Law Forms for Personal Use (Book w/CD-ROM)	$29.99	SPOT
Bankruptcy: Is It the Right Solution to Your Debt Problems?	$21.99	BRS
Chapter 13 Bankruptcy: Repay Your Debts	$36.99	CHB
Creating Your Own Retirement Plan	$29.99	YROP
Credit Repair (Book w/CD-ROM)	$24.99	CREP
Getting Paid: How to Collect form Bankrupt Debtors	$29.99	CRBNK
How to File for Chapter 7 Bankruptcy	$34.99	HFB
IRAs, 401(k)s & Other Retirement Plans: Taking Your Money Out	$34.99	RET
Money Troubles: Legal Strategies to Cope With Your Debts	$29.99	MT
Stand Up to the IRS	$24.99	SIRS
Surviving an IRS Tax Audit	$24.95	SAUD
Take Control of Your Student Loan Debt	$26.95	SLOAN

PATENTS AND COPYRIGHTS

The Copyright Handbook: How to Protect and Use Written Works (Book w/CD-ROM)	$39.99	COHA
Copyright Your Software	$34.95	CYS
Domain Names	$26.95	DOM
Getting Permission: How to License and Clear Copyrighted Materials Online and Off (Book w/CD-ROM)	$34.99	RIPER
How to Make Patent Drawings Yourself	$29.99	DRAW
Inventor's Guide to Law, Business and Taxes (Book w/CD-ROM)	$34.99	ILAX
The Inventor's Notebook	$24.99	INOT
Nolo's Patents for Beginners	$29.99	QPAT
License Your Invention (Book w/CD-ROM)	$39.99	LICE
Patent, Copyright & Trademark	$39.99	PCTM
Patent It Yourself	$49.99	PAT
Patent Pending in 24 Hours	$29.99	PEND
Patent Searching Made Easy	$29.95	PATSE
Patenting Art & Entertainment: New Stategies for Protecting Creative Ideas	$39.99	PATAE
The Public Domain	$34.99	PUBL
Trademark: Legal Care for Your Business and Product Name	$39.99	TRD
Web and Software Development: A Legal Guide (Book w/ CD-ROM)	$44.99	SFT

	PRICE	CODE

RESEARCH & REFERENCE

Legal Research: How to Find & Understand the Law .... $39.99   LRES

SENIORS

Long-Term Care: How to Plan & Pay For It .... $21.99   ELD

The Conservatorship Book for California .... $44.99   CNSV

Social Security, Medicare & Goverment Pensions .... $29.99   SOA

SOFTWARE
Call or check our website at www.nolo.com
for special discounts on Software!

LLC Maker—Windows $89.95   LLP1

PatentEase—Windows .... $349.00   PEAS

Personal RecordKeeper 5.0 CD—Windows $59.95   RKD5

Quicken Legal Business Pro 2005—Windows $109.99   SBQB5

Quicken WillMaker Plus 2005—Windows $79.99   WQP5

Order Form

Name _____

Address _____

City _____

State, Zip _____

Daytime Phone _____

E-mail _____

Our "No-Hassle" Guarantee

Return anything you buy directly from Nolo for any reason and we'll cheerfully refund your purchase price. No ifs, ands or buts.

☐ Check here if you do not wish to receive mailings from other companies

Item Code	Quantity	Item	Unit Price	Total Price

Method of payment

☐ Check ☐ VISA ☐ MasterCard
☐ Discover Card ☐ American Express

Subtotal	
Add your local sales tax (California only)	
Shipping: RUSH $9, Basic $5 (See below)	
"I bought 3, ship it to me FREE!"(Ground shipping only)	
TOTAL	

Account Number _____

Expiration Date _____

Signature _____

Shipping and Handling

Rush Delivery—Only $9

We'll ship any order to any street address in the U.S. by UPS 2nd Day Air* for only $9!

* Order by noon Pacific Time and get your order in 2 business days. Orders placed after noon Pacific Time will arrive in 3 business days. P.O. boxes and S.F. Bay Area use basic shipping. Alaska and Hawaii use 2nd Day Air or Priority Mail.

Basic Shipping—$5

Use for P.O. Boxes, Northern California and Ground Service.

Allow 1-2 weeks for delivery. U.S. addresses only.

For faster service, use your credit card and our toll-free numbers

**Call our customer service group
Monday thru Friday 7am to 7pm PST**

Phone   1-800-728-3555
Fax   1-800-645-0895
Mail   Nolo
           950 Parker St.
           Berkeley, CA 94710

Order 24 hours a day @ **www.nolo.com**

Remember:

Little publishers have big ears.
We really listen to you.

Take 2 Minutes
& Give Us
Your 2 cents

Your comments make a big difference in the development and revision of Nolo books and software. Please take a few minutes and register your Nolo product—and your comments—with us. Not only will your input make a difference, you'll receive special offers available only to registered owners of Nolo products on our newest books and software. Register now by:

PHONE
1-800-728-3555

FAX
1-800-645-0895

EMAIL
cs@nolo.com

or **MAIL** us
this registration card

fold here

Registration Card

NAME _____ DATE _____

ADDRESS _____

_____

CITY _____ STATE _____ ZIP _____

PHONE _____ E-MAIL _____

WHERE DID YOU HEAR ABOUT THIS PRODUCT? _____

WHERE DID YOU PURCHASE THIS PRODUCT? _____

DID YOU CONSULT A LAWYER? (PLEASE CIRCLE ONE)   YES   NO   NOT APPLICABLE

DID YOU FIND THIS BOOK HELPFUL?   (VERY)   5   4   3   2   1   (NOT AT ALL)

COMMENTS _____

_____

_____

WAS IT EASY TO USE?   (VERY EASY)   5   4   3   2   1   (VERY DIFFICULT)

We occasionally make our mailing list available to carefully selected companies whose products may be of interest to you.

❏ If you do not wish to receive mailings from these companies, please check this box.

❏ You can quote me in future Nolo promotional materials.
    Daytime phone number _____.

EMHA 2.0

- - - - - - - - - - - fold here -

Place
stamp here

Nolo
950 Parker Street
Berkeley, CA 94710-9867

Attn: EMHA 2.0